Robert Douglas

Somewhere to Lay My Head

HODDER

Copyright © 2006 by Robert Douglas

First published in Great Britain in 2006 by Hodder & Stoughton
A division of Hodder Headline

This paperback edition published in 2007

The right of Robert Douglas to be identified as the Author
of the Work has been asserted by him in accordance with
the Copyright, Designs and Patents Act 1988.

A Hodder paperback

8

A CIP catalogue record for this title is available from the British Library.

ISBN 978-0-340-89844-4

Typeset in Sabon by Hewer Text UK Ltd, Edinburgh
Printed and bound by CPI Group (UK) Ltd, Croydon, CR0 4YY

Hodder Headline's policy is to use papers that are natural, renewable
and recyclable products and made from wood grown in sustainable forests.
The logging and manufacturing processes are expected to conform to
the environmental regulations of the country of origin.

Hodder & Stoughton Ltd
A division of Hodder Headline
338 Euston Road
London NW1 3BH

In remembrance of Nancy

Acknowledgements

I'd like to express my gratitude to Nick Sayers, Bob McDevitt, Kerry Hood and Anne Clarke at Hodder, who always keep me right, as well as Mark Read in the Art Department. Thanks also to Amber Burlinson for copyediting.

Special thanks to
Maureen Ellis up in Glasgow for all her support

and

the faithful stalwarts of our Writing Group: Gellie Draper; Christine Lowes; and David Wedderburn.

Last of all – but really *first* of all – my darling wife
Patricia

Illustrations from the author's private collection.
Additional sources:
© Herald and Evening Times, Glasgow: pages 163, 175;
© Getty Images: pages 75, 161, 201, 251

Contents

Working My Ticket

It was 1955 – the year I turned sixteen – when I first experienced that Proustian thing when the smell of something instantly evokes a memory. Puts pictures in your mind. Of course, in those days I'd never heard of Marcel Proust. During that same year I found there was something else just as effective at stirring up memories – music; old records. Proust had maybe got the 'smell thing' all to himself, but it was Noel Coward who pointed out that hearing a few bars from a once favourite song could do the same. 'The potency of cheap music' he called it. By 'cheap' he meant popular.

During my first fifteen years I'd had no experience of this phenomenon. I'd had no need of it. I was too busy living my young life – and storing away the memories; good and bad. It was from sixteen onwards, after I'd lost my ma, then was taken away from everything I'd known, that, unbidden, sounds and smells began to regularly flash pictures from my childhood into my head. They were nearly always welcome. Perhaps I'd catch a few bars of the Glenn Miller Orchestra playing 'American Patrol' . . . immediately I'm four years old and Ma's dancing me round our tenement single-end. If it's not a song, it's a smell. Just a whiff of carbolic soap . . . I'm up at the Steamie (public wash house) sitting on the draining board reading the *Beano* as Ma does her weekly wash. The merest hint of Jeyes Fluid . . . I'm standing in the small toilet in the Blythswood Cinema, short trousers pulled to the side as I have a wee-wee.

*　　　*　　　*

Even now, aged sixty-seven, the stimulus of some song, smell – or sometimes a taste – is enough to open a little door and bring forth a memory so fresh you'd think it was new-minted. Three cheers for Marcel and Noel!

The Tannoy in the hut blares into life. It's always tuned to the Light Programme. Eddie Fisher's singing 'I Need You Now'. At the same instant the lights are snapped on. I screw my eyes tight shut. Ma's always doing that. For a delicious second I'm in my bed-chair in our house in Maryhill and she's starting her morning routine for getting me up. Then Corporal Graham goes and spoils it. 'HANDS OFF COCKS AND ON WITH SOCKS! C'mon, let's be 'aving you, rise and shine!' It was funny when I first heard it two weeks ago. Not now. It just reminds me where I am – and how I got here. Ma's dead and my father's unloaded me into the RAF Boys Service so he's free to go off with his fancy woman. Everything's gone. Ma, our house, my pals, Glasgow. I've just turned sixteen and the life I've known has been taken away. All I have is Ma's wedding ring and a few photos. And my memories. Lots of them. All locked up in my head. I'm NEVER going to let them go.

Ahead of me is twelve years in the RAF. I don't want to be here. Each new morning is a repeat of the one before; the lights go on and I always think I'm back in Glasgow. Then I realise where I am and I'm instantly depressed.

The covers are snatched off me. My willy is 'piss proud' so I scrabble to tuck it into my pyjamas. At least part of me is standing to attention.

'UP! NOW!'

Some of the lads laugh as they hurry by, anxious to get into the washroom before the hot water runs out. It's the end of February 1955. I've been at RAF Cosford since the 16th. How can I get out of here? If I get out, where can I go? I won't go and live with my father's fancy bit. I hate the mornings most of all. I grab soap, towel and razor and head for 'the bogs'.

Boys are standing two and three deep at the inadequate number of basins. There are just twenty to serve two huts – over fifty lads. I'm shaving three times a week now. Today is a shaving day. Someone has opened a bottle of Drene shampoo, the smell is unmistakable . . . Ma is washing her hair in our sink by the window. She always gives me a threepenny bit to go down to Lizzie's shop and buy the small bottle with its ribbed sides for her. Lyn Thomas lets me share his basin. We both try to see in the small mirror at the same time. Now and then I glance at his face. Lucky bastard! He has unblemished, lightly tanned skin. I look at mine; pale and covered in acne. I've already nicked two of the angry, red spots. They bleed profusely. I'm near to tears. My life is nothing but a misery. God, why don't you just give me cancer like my ma and finish the fucking job?

I thought I'd been unhappy during the two months from Ma's death until coming into the Boys' Service. But at least I was still living in our house, could see my two pals, Sammy Johnston and John Purden, all the time, go to see a film at the Blythswood, sit in Cocozza's Café. Not now. My father is also in the RAF. He's given our house up. I'm hundreds of miles from where I want to be. The two spots still bleed. I fetch a couple of pieces of totally non-absorbent toilet paper from a cubicle, I don't want to stain the water in the basin. I wonder if I'd be as good-natured as Taff, sharing my shaving water with someone who's bleeding all over the place?

'I'll let you finish, Lyn.'

'Okay, Boyo. Won't be long.'

We all skitter back into the billet on tiptoes, chittering and chattering with the cold. The hut is only marginally warmer than the washroom.

'Why didn't I join in the summer?' complains a Scouse accent.

'They think they're toughening us up,' says a Jock.

'I'll be fahking dead soon if it dahn't warm up,' states a Londoner.

'Southern softy.'

'Get fahked, Jock!'

'Ah'm a Geordie!'

'Same fing.'

Everybody laughs.

Minutes later we trot over to the mess for breakfast. We never do anything at a leisurely pace. As Corporal Graham informed us on our first day, 'For the next two months you'll be chased from arsehole to breakfast time.' It was the first time I'd heard that. I didn't quite understand it, yet knew EXACTLY what it meant.

There is a warm fug in the mess hall. It seems to enhance that smell which, I'll eventually find, is peculiar to all mess halls; a mixture of meals past and present with a permanent background of greasy washing-up water. There is always a long queue. Almost every day someone drops their china mug. At the sound of it smashing on the concrete floor, a cheer goes up. It costs a shilling to get a new one from the quartermaster's stores. I decide to have porridge. I've been brought up to put salt on mine. And milk. The RAF doesn't cater for this. The lukewarm milk in the large aluminium bowl has sugar in it. I have to take the sweetened stuff. It breaks me of the habit of eating it salted. For the rest of my life I'll put sugar on my porridge.

I sit beside Ian Douglas, an Edinburgh boy. Lyn Thomas, my shaving companion, joins us. During the last couple of weeks the three of us have 'palled-up' in the billet. Lyn is from Camarthen and is quite happy to be called Taff. He doesn't like 'Lyn' because it sounds like a girl's name. We are all to be trained in various electronic trades. I am to be a Ground Wireless Mechanic. I'm totally uninterested. As we eat our over-cooked, lukewarm breakfasts, Lyn and Ian blether away to one another. Now and again I force myself to join in. Every couple of minutes I dab my face with a hankie; the two spots are still weeping. Other boys from our billet sit nearby. They are all nice lads. Just like Ian and Lyn they actually WANT to be in the RAF. From listening to conversations over the last few weeks I find that they almost all could hardly wait to leave school and join up. I, on the other hand, didn't even know the Boys' Service existed until three months ago when my father pressured me into signing on.

After breakfast we just have time to brush our teeth before the shout goes up, 'GET ON PARADE!' The D.I.s (drill instructors) chase us out onto the parade ground and we line up in three ranks. A biting cold wind blows and there is an occasional flurry of snow. Jeez! I really do NOT want to be here. I watch as Corporal Graham, with much crunching of tackety boots, takes up position in front of us, brings us to attention, then slowly walks up and down our ranks, inspecting us. The good corporal is in his thirties; a regular. He has the hoarse voice, bristling moustache and stern persona that D.I.s are supposed to have – according to British films of the last thirty years. We are his squad and he is always around; morning, noon and night. He often wanders into the billet late in the evening just to see what's going on. He walks along the rear of my rank and stops behind a gangly youth called Ryder, who hails from the Isle of Wight. Ryder has had his hair cut really short; 'into the wood', as they say. Unfortunately it has accentuated his very thin neck and large, knobbly head. Below the leather rim of his beret there is no hair to be seen, just stubble. Corporal Graham has been standing behind Ryder for a minute or more. Just staring. He utters, 'Back of your 'ead fascinates me, lad. Like a fucking duck's arse at Christmas time!'

We usually have two forty-five-minute drill sessions a day. After a fortnight, the majority of us are beginning to 'get it together.'

Alas, there are two or three who aren't picking it up as quickly as the rest. They are normally referred to as 'the awkward squad' by the corporal. Then there is Depenning, who is in a class of his own. Depenning – nicknamed 'Tuppenny' – is Asian. Small and slim, he is consistently good-natured, excels in all aspects of his trade training, but is a disaster on parade. He is totally un-coordinated. He will turn left when the rest of us turn right. It always takes him an extra second, at least, to react to the word of command. This makes him stick out like the proverbial sore thumb. It also makes him a D.I.s nightmare. Corporal Graham appears to be on the verge of a nervous breakdown . . .

'SQUAD! Wait for it. SQUAD! Right turNN! I said RIGHT, Depenning. Cor, do you think you're ever, EVER going to learn your right from your left?'

'Sorry, Corporal. I am trying very, very hard.' This is said in Depenning's melodious Asian accent. The corporal marches over and, with a crescendo of crunching boots, halts in front of the diminutive, ever-smiling Depenning. He is greeted by flashing white teeth.

'I've just 'ad an idea that'll 'elp you tell your right from your left, lad. What hand do you use when you 'ave a J. Arthur Rank?' Graham is actually serious. We stifle giggles.

The rhyming slang is lost on Tuppenny. 'Jarther Ank? What is that, Corporal?'

Graham looks heavenwards. 'What hand do you use when you're playing wiv' yourself?'

'Oh, goodness me, Corporal. I do not do such a terrible thing.' I can hear one or two moans as a couple of guys in the rear rank take a stitch. The corporal persists.

'Well all right then. Just say you DID 'ave a bit of a toss – which hand would you use?'

'Oh please, Corporal,' Tuppenny nods his head continually, 'I cannot contemplate such a question.'

Graham gives up. 'Are you telling me you've never 'ad any kind of sexual experiences in your life, Depenning?'

Tuppenny puts on his best Peter Sellers accent 'Well, some-times I waken up in the morning, sir, and find that during the night I have been visited by a damp dream!' From the corner of my eye I see somebody fall, helpless, onto the tarmac. Corporal Graham shakes his head.

'It's a WET dream! WET dream, not fucking damp dream.' He smartly about turns and marches back to his usual position on the square, muttering to himself as he does.

Tommy Green leans toward Tuppenny and speaks out of the side of his mouth 'Ah could have sworn blind ah heard you having a wank after "lights out" last night.'

'Sorry,' says Tuppenny. 'I shall be extra quiet tonight.'

After our drill sessions the rest of the day is taken up with trade training, lectures and PT (Physical Training). Like all growing lads we are always hungry. Twice a day, Monday to Friday, the NAAFI (Navy, Army and Air Force Institute) van comes round. We only get ten shillings a week. This isn't enough to cover two NAAFI breaks per day AND buy me a snack at night in the canteen before I go to bed. I'm always hungry by late evening and would prefer to keep my few precious shillings for some supper. But, when the van comes round during the day and I see others buying mugs of tea and thick slices of 'fly cemetery' (Sly Cake), I can never resist. Consequently, I'm usually skint by Monday evening and go to bed three nights a week on an empty stomach. Just about every boy gets regular postal orders from parents or indulgent aunts and uncles. My father sends bugger all. About once a month I might get a letter in his hard to read hand. Ma isn't quite three months dead when he informs me that he and Beenie – now I know her name – are to be married when he finishes with the RAF later this year. There is no mention of me being asked. He knows I wouldn't go.

The last weekend in February we are allowed out of camp for the first time. On the notice board I spot that the film *White*

Christmas is on at the Queen's Cinema in Wolverhampton. It seems ages since I was last at the pictures. I used to go two and three times a week with either John Purden or Sammy Johnston. From my locker drawer I take out the programme for the Blythswood Cinema on the Maryhill Road. I took it as a keepsake when I left. There's an illustration of the main entrance on the front. Jeez, how many times did Ma and I pass through those doors. It's still the current programme. Just. February 1955. I sit on my bed and look at the films I've missed . . . Frank Sinatra in *Suddenly*, Elizabeth Taylor in *Elephant Walk*. Sammy will have gone to see the Sinatra one. We both like him. So much has happened since I took this from the pile by the pay kiosk at the end of January. *White Christmas* has already been on at the Blythsie. As I look at the entry in the so familiar programme I have to fight back tears. Ma and I would have been queuing up for it, we loved movies like that, 'Cheery pictures' she called them. I know: When I'm allowed out that weekend I'll get the bus into Wolverhampton and go and see it by myself.

The Queen's Cinema is located in the main square in the centre of town. Wearing my uniform, I stand on the pavement and look up at the colourful poster. I love movie posters . . . 'Bing Crosby, Danny Kaye, – Rosemary Clooney and Vera Ellen in Irving Berlin's "WHITE CHRISTMAS" in VISTAVISION!' Once I'm seated and the lights go down I can imagine I'm back in the Blythsie. I take a seat next to an older woman. If I don't look at her I can pretend it's Ma. The lights dim and the programme starts. Within minutes my pretence falls to bits. Even in the dark it's nothing like the Blythswood. The hall is too big; the proscenium arch surrounding the screen is a different style, the exit lights along the walls differ in shape and colour. The woman wears a nicer perfume than Ma ever had. If she'd been using California Poppy or Evening in Paris it might just have worked. I decide to give up trying to imagine I'm somewhere else and just enjoy the film. It's very sentimental and finishes up with

8

an all-singing, happy-ever-after ending. As the smiling audience and I leave, I wonder if I'm the only one sadder than when he came in.

After four months at Cosford I realise I'll never settle in the RAF. Sometimes I toy with the idea of making a go of it, but not for long. The main reason I want out is because of the way my father pressured me into signing on. The day after Ma's funeral he'd given me a 'choice' – I can go and live with his fancy woman or join the Boys' Service. He knows that out of loyalty to Ma I'll choose the RAF. Within two days he has buried his wife and set the wheels in motion to unload his son. I remembered how he'd gone about the house whistling to himself. Another reason I want out is the fact I've signed on for ten years; the minimum. The ten years doesn't start until I'm eighteen. As I joined up just a week after my sixteenth birthday this means that, in reality, I'm doing a total of twelve years! It's too big a commitment. A third reason I want out is simply because it'll piss him off. It'll show he no longer controls me, I've broken away. But how do I go about it? I don't know what to do. Where to start. My salvation is called Ron Mason.

Everybody knows Mason because he's always on 'jankers' (punishment). He's only a few months older than me, but wise for his years. Early one evening he's trudging back to his billet weighed down, as usual, with his full kit, the FSMO (full service marching order). He is, yet again, on jankers. When you are serving this punishment, usually for a period of three, seven or fourteen days, you have to pack all your kit into various heavy webbing packs, strap them on to yourself and, after the day's work, report to the guardhouse at six p.m. There, the Orderly Officer and Sergeant inspect you. If your webbing isn't 'blan-coed' and your brass buckles not highly polished, you might finish up getting put on a 'charge' – and receive a few more days jankers! After the six p.m. parade you have to 'double away' back to your billet, change into your denims (working overalls) and report back to the Orderly Sergeant for an hour or more fatigues. When that task is done you have to return to your billet, put all your kit on once more and be on parade back at the guardhouse for nine p.m. and final inspection. All this is designed to take up what little leisure time you have of an evening and make you mend your ways.

I know Mason only by sight. In fact, Mason IS a sight. When you are on punishment you're supposed to keep your kit immaculate. Mason doesn't. I stop as he approaches.

'Can ah ask ye something?'

He halts, half bent under the weight of webbing. He has a long, saturnine face, dark hair and looks like a young John Le Mesurier. He gives a tired smile. 'If I can understand a bloody word you're saying, Jock.'

'Can ah ask why you're always oan jankers?'

'S'easy. 'Cause I'm wanting to get to fuck out of this lot! The only way to do it is by working your ticket, refusing to obey orders. Eventually they'll realise you mean business – and chuck you out. I hope!' He looks closely at me with his intense, black-button eyes. 'Why you asking? Do you want out?'

'Aye.'

'How old are you?' He leans back against the wall to ease the weight he's carrying. We're standing in a long, empty corridor between huts.

'Nearly sixteen and a half.'

'That's good, you've still got time. If you're over seventeen there's no good starting. The bastards just put up with you 'til you turn seventeen and a half, then they transfer you into the adult RAF and that's you stuck in that for your ten years – without a trade. If you keep causing trouble in the men's service it won't be jankers anymore – it'll be the Glasshouse!'

'Whit's that?'

'Military prison, me old Jock. Makes jankers look like a

fuckin' picnic!' He unleans himself from the wall. 'So, if you're going to do it, you'll have to start now.' He shrugs the large pack on his back up higher and hooks his thumbs through the shoulder straps. 'It's hard work, mind. See yah!' He staggers off in the direction of his billet.

That evening I lie on my bed, my mind full of the conversation I've had with Mason. At last I can see a way out. I feel better than I've done for months. The Tannoy, as usual, is tuned into the Light Programme; Sandy McPherson is knocking seven bells out of the BBC organ. Ian has finished with this week's *Rover* and passed it over; poor old Alf Tupper. 'The Tough of the Track', every time he has an important race to run next day he ALWAYS gets an urgent repair job into his workshop under the railway arch. I bet he'll just have a fish supper for dinner, the job'll take him 'til two in the morning . . . eventually I'm distracted by the furtive actions of a little Scots lad called Forsyth, who hails from Dalkeith. He's a real dour little bugger, doesn't seem interested in making friends with anybody. As Ian says, 'He wouldn't give you a nod in the desert!' He receives parcels from home on a weekly basis. Unlike most of the lads, he never shares. Now and again someone will cut up a home-made cake and pass some slices round. Not Forsyth. Often, an hour or so after 'lights out' he can be found sitting up in bed guzzling Dundee cake in the dark. I pretend to read the *Rover* but watch him from behind it. He has a hand in his pocket and there is a certain amount of movement. I don't think he's having a stand up wank. Whenever the hand stops he looks slowly around, then, if he thinks no one's watching, the hand makes a quick visit to his mouth. He then slowly, almost imperceptibly, chews. After fifteen minutes of this he ambles past the waste bin and deposits something in it from his pocket. A few minutes later I go over and look; there's a dozen or more toffee papers on top. I look at him. He never seems to be short of money. What a greedy little git. Watching him has made me feel quite annoyed. 'Hey lads!' Everyone turns to look at me. 'You'll not believe it. I've been clocking Forsyth for the last twenty minutes. He's unwrapping caramels IN HIS POCKET and slippin' them intae his gob when he thinks naebody's looking.' Forsyth goes bright red.

'Huh! That's nowt,' says 'Red' Skelton, 'I watched him peel an orange in his pocket the other night and slip . . .'

'Did not!' says Forsyth, 'It was already peel . . .' he goes even redder as everybody laughs.

'No wonder us Jocks get a bad name,' Tommy Green shakes his head in mock sorrow.

'Howay then, pass them round.'

'There's only three left.'

'Well, you've had your share. Pass the buggers round.'

Reluctantly, he distributes them. I don't get one.

At last it's 'lights out'. I lie in the dark, my mind buzzing yet again as I think of my conversation with Mason earlier in the evening. All round the hut guys are talking, laughing, playing tricks on one another. Jeez! I feel really good. My mind is quite clear about what I have to do. Simply refuse to cooperate. I don't think I'll be any more miserable on continual jankers than I am now. No need to cry myself to sleep tonight. Tomorrow I start working my ticket.

Anywhere But Here

It's next morning and, as usual, Taff, Ian and me sit together at breakfast.

'Ah've got something tae tell ye's, boys. Ah'm gonny start working ma ticket just like yon lad, Mason.'

Taff looks at Ian. 'What's he saying? He's speaking too fast again.'

'Tell you later.' Ian turns to me, 'It'll be tough, ye know.'

'Ah don't mind it tough for a couple of months, as long as ah know ah'm gonny get oot.'

Forty minutes later we file into the large workshop. Our instructor is J/T (Junior Technician) English, a good-natured Geordie with red hair. He's doing his two years' National Service. After a while he notices I'm drawing a German tank in my notebook. Even though I know what I have to do, I feel somewhat embarrassed about it all. He comes over and leans on my desk. He keeps his voice low. 'What are you doing? What's going on?' He's a nice bloke; I don't want to hurt his feelings. I also speak quietly, 'It's nothing against you, Mr English. Ah've decided ah want oot of the RAF, ma father forced me intae it. Between you and me, can ye put me on a charge for deliberately no' taking part in the class – or something like that?'

'Are you sure that's what you want?' He looks quite concerned. I wouldn't be surprised if this'll be the first time he's put somebody on a 'fizzer'.

'Aye, definitely.'

*   *   *

The following evening Ian and Taff help me on with my webbing. That morning I've been given seven days jankers by the C.O. I've made a start. I can't help wondering how long it will take me. Even more important, and worrying, will I be able to keep it up? These thoughts fill my head as I trudge down to the guardhouse and line up with the other miscreants for the first of the evening's two parades.

'Hello, me old Jock. Hasn't taken you long.' Mason leans out from the front rank. 'Welcome to the Land of the Sane!'

'QUIET, YOU LOT!' screams the Orderly Sergeant.

'Dear me!' mutters Mason.

It's a few weeks later. Mason, I and another three janker-wallahs line up side by side at one end of an enormous hangar. Various guys come and go on punishment. Mason and I are a constant. The five of us hold broad sweeping brushes. They've recently started using this hangar for indoor athletics, so it has to be kept clean.

'Right,' says the corporal in charge, 'sweep up to the other end, keeping your brushes together as you go, move to the side a bit, then come back down again. You won't get it all done tonight,' he gives us his version of an evil grin, 'but there's always tomorrow.'

Earlier we had lined up for the first of the two evening parades, wearing our full kit. After being inspected by the Orderly Officer we'd been told to 'Double away!' back to our billets, change into denims and report back for fatigues. We begin sweeping.

'I wrote an essay today,' says Mason, 'a minor masterpiece, even though I say so myself.'

'What about?'

'I was in the educational class. The sergeant said, "Write a piece about something in your life, past or present, that you love." So I did.'

'Whit wiz it?'

'Pardon?'

'What was it?'

'Ah! It was called "I Love My Webbing". Somehow I don't think he was best pleased.'

I start to laugh at the thought of it. Mason, as usual, is deadpan. I manage to ask, 'What did ye say?'

'Oh, it went something like . . . The reason I keep getting myself put on jankers is because it gives me the opportunity to regularly blanco my webbing and polish my brasses . . .'

I interrupt him. 'But you never blanco your webbing, you lying hound. Half the time you're put on a charge is because you've turned up for jankers wi' manky kit!'

Mason looks hurt. 'You've cut me to the quick, Jock. I always TRY to have immaculate kit. It's just that I've never mastered the noble art of blancoing.'

'You don't even own a tin of blanco.' I begin to kill myself laughing at the hurt look on Mason's face and have to stop sweeping. My fellow sweepers halt to await my recovery. At the far end of the hangar, the corporal is going 'light'. 'GET A MOVE ON. YOU'RE AN ABSOLUTE BLOODY SHOWER!' Terry-Thomas has recently become very popular on TV and in the cinema. His catch-phrase is, 'You're a shower, an absolute shower!' Every NCO in the RAF seems to have adopted it as his own.

After an hour of pushing brooms up and down the giant hangar we are sweaty and dusty. At last we're allowed to go back to our billets. We still have to parade again, in FSMO, at nine p.m. I'm no longer in the wooden huts, 'the Lines', as they're called. Along with my intake I've moved up to Fulton Block, an enormous Art Deco barracks built just before the Second World War. I grab my towel and head for the ablutions – as everybody, wrongly, calls the washroom and toilets. Corporal Graham patiently explains to us one day that, 'You go to the washroom to carry out your ablutions.' It makes no difference. The facilities in the block are far superior to the old huts. I love being able to take a shower whenever I want. As I stand, eyes shut, and luxuriate under the constant stream of hot water I think back to all the 'head to toe' washes I used to take, with just a face cloth, standing at the sink back in Glasgow after I'd boiled a kettle. Or going up to the Steamie once a week, threepenny bit in hand; towel and soap under my arm, to take a bath or a 'spray', as we called a shower. Since moving up to Fulton Block I often take a couple of showers a day. Maybe I'm trying to make up for all the ones I missed. I let the hot water run down my spotty back. How nice it would be, one day, to have a house with a bathroom like they have in the movies. Hah! It'll never happen. Only Toffs have houses like that.

There's a long weekend coming up. Easter. Everybody, even those on jankers, is allowed a ninety-six hour pass. Sammy Johnston's parents, Lottie and Frank, told me I can come on my leaves to them.

Although I get a railway warrant, I feel Glasgow is a long way to go for such a short break. Half the time will be spent travelling. Another reason I don't want to go is because I feel that, once I'm in Maryhill, I might not want to come back. If I didn't, how would I live? I'd soon run out of money, wouldn't be able to take a job. No. I decide I'll stay in camp. It'll be lovely having the billet to myself, read and sleep to my heart's content. After a solid month's jankers, I'm tired. Anyway, it'll annoy the authorities. Nobody refuses the chance to go home, even Mason's taking his ninety-six. I'll tell them I've nowhere to go. It's true. I don't have a bloody home anymore.

Lyn Thomas has other ideas. To save making big explanations I've also told him and Ian I'm staying in camp because I've nowhere to go. Lyn has taken me at my word. A few days later he comes and sits beside me on my bunk. 'I've written to Mam and

Dada. They say you can come home with me to Camarthen for Easter.' He knows my father is in the RAF and has given up our house. I don't want to spoil his kind gesture by saying that there are folks I could go to if I wanted. I feel a lump in my throat at his kindness.

'That would be lovely, Taff. I'd like to come.'

'There's grand. Oh, and I must warn you, my family normally speak Welsh. English is their second language. Though mind, I don't think they'll understand a blind word you'll say all weekend anyway!'

We travel to Cardiff by train, then take the slow local branch line to Camarthen. The coaches look as if they probably saw service transporting troops on their way to the Western Front in 1914. They are non-corridor. Lyn and I travel in uniform. On joining up you have to send your civvies home. Mine are at my father's fancy woman's in Portpatrick. I've never been there. Lyn's mam and dad are quiet, reserved folk, but make me feel very welcome. His dad drives a petrol tanker for Regent Oil. They are great friends with their next door neighbours, Mr and Mrs Morris; they too are pleased to see me. The first full day after our arrival, Lyn announces, 'We shall go round to see my grandma. Don't think she's being awkward, but she'll only speak Welsh to my sister Anne and me. She'll speak to you in English, but she wants us to keep our Welsh up. She is very strict about it.'

Grandma, of course, is dressed in black even though there hasn't been a death in the family for years. Grannies always wear black. She welcomes me in what is almost broken English: 'Ah, so you are the friend to Lyn. The Scotch boy. I'm very pleased to be meeting you.' She has great difficulty understanding most of what I say. Lyn translates when needed. I listen with great interest as she converses with Lyn and Anne. They've been brought up speaking Welsh every day. It's strange to think these are British people – but English is just their second language. As I

Easter 1955, Camarthen. Lyn Thomas on left, me on right. Lyn's sister, Anne, and neighbour, Mr Morris.

listen, I realise that I don't know anyone who speaks Scots Gaelic. I've never heard it spoken.

The couple of days in Camarthen are spent walking about the town, sitting in the local café, and going to the pictures one evening. Lyn wears his uniform all the time even though he has access to civvies. He's proud of it. We regularly bump into folk who know him and want to know how he's getting on.

It seems no time at all until we're back at the station, boarding a train. As I watch the countryside slip past I sometimes glance at Taff. He has a nice home, loving parents and sister, yet he's keen to get back to Cosford. All I have to look forward to is continual disobeying of orders followed by endless jankers and fatigues. But I have to do it. I DON'T want to be at Cosford.

I'm back just three days when I get myself on punishment, again. The brush and the big hangar await my pleasure. Mason has wasted even less time. He started another seven days yesterday.

'What kept you, Jock? I felt quite lonely yesterday.'

The Orderly Sergeant gives us dirty looks. 'QUIET IN THE RANKS!'

We have been joined by Tommy Green who's in my billet. Tommy's from Parkhead, Glasgow.

He has decided he's also going to work his ticket. He soon falls by the wayside. After his three days' jankers are up he begins to conform again.

A few days later Mason comes into my billet at lunchtime. 'I'VE DONE IT! They're going to chuck me out!'

'You lucky bastard!'

'Just had me up in front of the C.O. I'll be away next Wednesday morning. The jankers I'm on at the minute are suspended. I don't have to go on parade or to workshops anymore. I've just to stay in the billet and keep me head down. I'VE BLOODY WELL DONE IT!'

I'm pleased for him, but realise I'm going to miss him. All this time we've been a good support for one another, keeping ourselves laughing when most guys wouldn't find anything to even smile at. I'll have to go it alone from now on.

As Mason's last few days dwindle away, I often come back from the evening parades, weighed down with my kit, and glance through the open door of his billet. He's usually lying on his bed reading or sleeping. Jammy bugger! He still comes round to see me. I get the feeling he actually MISSES jankers! Then comes his last evening in camp.

'Well, I'm back to civilisation tomorrow, Jock. I can't believe it's here.' The black-button eyes look intently at me. 'You won't give up, will you?'

'Ah'm bloody sure I won't. Ah canny do eleven years or more in this lot. Ah've nae option but tae keep going.'

'Good man. You'll do it.' We've both been sitting on my bed. As he rises, I stand up too.

'Well, it's awright for you, Ron, but I'll have tae get ma kit on. It's nearly nine o'clock.'

'Tell you what, me old Jock. I'll give you a hand with it.' In silence he holds up the heavy 'large pack' with both hands. By taking the weight, he makes it easier for me to slip first one arm, then the other, through the shoulder straps. He adjusts a buckle here, a strap there, then stands back and looks at me. 'Mmmm, you're like a bag of shit! I'm glad to see you still have no intention of blancoing or polishing.'

'There's nae point, is there? If they want tae put me oan another charge, that's fine by me.'

'That's the spirit. I've taught you well.' We laugh, but it's sort of sad. 'Well', he sticks his hand out and, somewhat embarrassed, we shake.

'All the best, Ron.'

'Cheerio, Jock. Get stuck in!'

Next morning, after breakfast, he's gone.

Summer Camp

Every summer all the boys are transported to RAF Woodvale near Southport for two weeks. Jankers are suspended for the duration. We live under canvas, six to a tent, sleeping on complicated wooden-framed camp beds that appear to be deck chairs which have suffered a nervous breakdown. The weather is glorious for the entire fortnight, the sort that memories are made of. There is lots going on to occupy and entertain us; sports, games, films and firing on the rifle range. One extra attraction for me and many others is the Spitfire – the last operational one on the strength of the RAF. Fitted with meteorological instruments, it takes off twice a day to take readings for the RAF's Met. Department. The front-line fighters are now all jets. The Meteor is on its way out, the twin-boom Vampire has replaced it and the Hawker Hunter is coming into service. It's sad to think that, just ten years after the war, this legendary piston-engined fighter is now obsolete. A small consolation is that it continues to fly in the pages of my weekly comics, the *Hotspur*, *Rover*, *Wizard* and *Adventure*.

Around ten a.m. every morning I join the regular line of enthusiastic boys at the edge of the runway. As the Spitfire starts up with a series of sharp cracks and puffs of blue smoke from its exhaust, I have a strong feeling I'm back in wartime RAF Woodvale. Dotted along the grassy areas which border the runway are large three-sided 'blast pens', built from sandbags, where aircraft were parked to gain some protection from marauding, low-flying German fighters. The planes have long gone, the pens lain empty for years. The canvas has rotted away on many bags but the sand has petrified and kept its original shape. The shape of 1940.

We watch avidly as the Spit taxies to the end of the tarmac, then – for our benefit – the pilot guns the Rolls Royce Merlin engine, accelerates rapidly, lifts off, retracts the wheels when just feet off the ground and with a beautiful growl soars up and away in a power climb. Man-made perfection! The hair on the back of my neck tingles. A boy next to me, whom I don't know, says, 'I'll bet if it came to it, a Spitfire could beat a jet.'

Still watching the disappearing speck in the sky, I nod my head 'Nae bother!'

To one side of the runway, on a concrete 'hard', stand ten Seafires, the naval version of the Spitfire. Fitted with 4-blade propellers, which give extra 'bite' to get them off the short decks of aircraft carriers, these forlorn ex-Fleet Air Arm planes have their engine cowlings and cockpit hoods cocooned with an early form of polystyrene to protect them from the weather. They are for sale for £150 each. If only I was a rich man's son, I'd get my father to buy me one, then spend hours every week sitting in the cockpit reading the latest exploits of Sergeant Pilot Matt Braddock VC, in the *Rover*, ever ready to 'scramble' at a moment's notice when the Ops Room reported a swarm of bandits over the Channel. Always, in the back of my mind, would be the warning Braddock gives to all new pilots . . . 'Beware the Hun in the sun!'

Another treat available – and in great demand – is a flight in an old Anson, twin-engine transport. The 'Annie' is slow and nigh obsolete, but still a very exciting prospect for boys who haven't flown. Ian Douglas and I join four other boys and clamber abroad. It's a first flight for all of us. From where the pilot and navigator sit, the large Perspex canopy spreads all the way back and over us too. It's like sitting in a greenhouse. A flying greenhouse. We taxi to the end of the runway, the engines' note increases, and with a noise like

22

six broken cement mixers we begin to trundle down the tarmac, slowly but surely gaining speed until – the ground just falls away. For the first time in our lives we are airborne! Ian and I look at one another, bursting with excitement. The Anson gains height and makes a turn; but WE aren't turning, it's the ground that's tilting. The pilot takes us up the sunny coast at around 2,000 feet. We look down on what seem to be model towns with toy cars moving slowly along their streets. Blackpool looms out of the haze and we fly close by the famous tower. Next thing we're over Liverpool, looking down on the docks and the overhead railway that runs alongside them. After forty-five minutes we return to Woodvale, where another half dozen boys wait impatiently to have the thrill of a lifetime. For a split-second the thought comes into my head – wait 'til I tell Ma.

As we disembark we shout our thanks to the leather helmeted pilot and navigator. They look fed-up. How can anyone who flies a plane be bored?

On the Sunday in the middle of our two weeks Ian and I don our boilersuit-like denims, slip through a hole in the fence at a remote corner of the camp, and set off to walk the five miles or so into Southport. The sun beats down and the heat makes it seem twice as far. As usual we're broke. At long last, tired and thirsty, we enter the edge of town and begin strolling along the promenade, trying not to think of the long walk back. A car pulls up beside us and a window is wound down.

'IAN!'

Four adults, two couples, hurriedly climb out of the saloon. Ian can't believe it 'Uncle Bill! Aunty May! What are you doing here?' All four smother him with hugs and kisses, he's near to tears. The other couple, Tom and Betty, are close friends of Ian's family and have known him since childhood. Jeez! Imagine having relatives who own a car AND who'd come looking for you. I can't help being envious. Some boys are dead lucky. Nobody in my family has a car.

Ian Douglas sitting on my shoulder. RAF Cosford, March 1955. He and Lyn Thomas are my two pals.

'Oh, this is my pal, Robert Douglas. He's from Glasgow.'

'Hello son. Another Douglas? And from Glasgow.' Uncle Bill smiles, 'Och well, we'll no hold that against him.' He offers his hand. I wish I wouldn't go red when someone wants to shake hands.

'How did ye know ah was here?' asks Ian.

'We're doon at Blackpool for ten days. I happened to ring your Mum and she said you were at summer camp near Southport. We drove to Woodvale to ask if we could see you, but they said they'd never find you, the camp's so big and the boys scattered everywhere. So, we thought, och well, we'll just have a wee run into Southport – and we spotted you!'

'Oh, it's really great to see ye,' Ian's eyes glisten with tears again.

Aunty May looks hard at us. 'Are you boys hungry?'

Ian and I look at each other, then reply in unison, 'STARVIN!'

One hour, two fish suppers and a couple of ice-creams later it's time for the adults to go on their way. Before they do, each of the men slip Ian a nice red, ten shilling note. Uncle Bill presses a half-crown into my hand. 'Well, boys, it's time we were heading back to Blackpool.' Ian is plied with more kisses and hugs and, minutes later, we wave them off. Fortified, we decide we've had enough walking, and excitement, for one day and might as well head back to camp. By bus. En route we still can't get over our good luck. It's the sole topic of conversation. 'If your uncle and aunty had'nae found us ah think ah'd huv died halfway back tae Woodvale.'

'Me too.'

We get off the bus one stop before the camp. After some worrying moments we eventually find the hole in the fence. No one has missed us.

Later that evening a corporal comes into the tent looking for Ian. 'There was an aunt and uncle of yours called at the gate today. We had to tell them that you could be anywhere in the camp and would be almost impossible to find.'

'Oh, that's a pity,' says Ian, 'still, can't be helped.' As he speaks we avoid looking at one another. When the corporal leaves, we allow about thirty seconds to make sure he's out of earshot. At last I turn toward him. He's already looking at me – whilst biting his knuckle. We collapse onto our beds, totally helpless. The rest of the evening I just have to say, in a silly voice, 'Oh! that's a pity!' and we go into fits of laughter for another five minutes.

I'd really enjoyed my two weeks at Woodvale. For the first time since Ma died I'd had some pleasure out of life. But summer camp isn't the RAF. Especially the adult service. It's tempting to think, should I give it a go? Start toeing the line? There'd be no more jankers for a start. But what happens if, say four years from now, I decide I've had enough of the RAF? I'd be just twenty, with eight years still to do – and no way out. No, it's too big a commitment. I still want out. When I get back to Cosford I intend to step up my efforts to convince them I'm never going to settle. But this time I'm going to try something new. I'm going to go further than Mason ever did.

King of the Road

'Where are you off to?' Ian watches as I put on my uniform jacket, greatcoat and peaked hat.

'Ah've decided tae grant maself a spot o' leave.'

'You're not!'

'I am. Ah'm gonny go AWOL for a few days. They think they'll sicken me with continual jankers, so ah might as well get punished for something.'

Taff puts down his book. 'He could be right. It'll let them see he's determined.' He turns to me, 'I hope you're not going to somebody whose address is on your leave sheet. That's the first place they'll look.'

'Ah've already thought of that, Taff. Ah'm going tae an uncle who lives in West Lothian. They don't know aboot him.'

'How are you getting there, train or bus?'

I laugh out loud 'Taff! Where would ah get the money for that? Ah'm going by this. . .' I hold up my thumb. 'Ah'm gonny hitchike.'

'It's a long way, mind you. How far is it?'

I shrug my shoulders 'Huv'nae a clue. Maybe 300 miles?'

'It's mad you are. Have you hitchhiked before?'

'Nope.'

They look at one another. 'How much dosh have you got?' asks Ian.

'Aboot six bob.'

'Here!' A two shilling piece bounces on the tightly stretched blanket covering my bed. Seconds later a half-crown from Taff joins it. There's a lump in my throat. I cough to try and clear it. 'Thanks a lot, boys. You're really good pals.'

'Can't 'ave you collapsing from hunger halfway to Scotland, boyo.'

Just as at RAF Woodvale, Cosford also has its hole in the fence. Up behind the married quarters. It's mostly used by adult servicemen as a short-cut to a nearby pub. The early part of my journey is the slowest. In 1955 there are no motorways. Stretches of dual-carriageway are few and far between. The road system of Great Britain is almost exclusively single-carriageway.

I set off around one p.m. I have to cover almost a hundred miles to get to my first target – the A1. During the first part of my journey I quickly find out that, when you're in uniform, getting lifts is not a problem. I also experience the exhilaration of being on my own and heading, literally, into the unknown. Until coming to Cosford I'd hardly ever been out of Maryhill, let alone Glasgow. Now here I am, at sixteen, setting off to journey 300 miles along the highways and byways of middle England with just a few pencilled notes to guide me on my way to Scotland.

In a combination of short lifts and frequent walks I skirt Wolverhampton and Birmingham and head for Nottingham. From there I take the A52 until, near Grantham, I step onto the A1 – the Great North Road. I love the name. Even I have heard of it. This is the road on which, 200 years ago, travellers and mail coaches made their way from London to Edinburgh. It still follows the same route, ploughing straight through town and village.

One of the lads in the billet, Harry Dougan, has primed me about my trip. 'Up until ten o'clock thumb only private cars, you'll make better time. After the pubs shut, the cars peter out. That's when you start on lorries.'

Most heavy goods vehicles in the fifties are slow, the majority fitted with a 'governor'. This limits them to 50 mph to save fuel.

In reality, most of the older wagons would be hard put to reach 50 even if going downhill – with a following wind.

I make a good start on the A1. A private car going to Doncaster. The driver obligingly goes out of his way and lets me off on the north side of the town centre. 'Joost tha keep straight on, son. You'll pass Doncaster Rovers football ground on t' one side of road and racecourse on t'other. Good luck, lad!'

Even though I'm still in the suburbs, I keep my thumb out. I've hardly gone two hundred yards when a Ford Dormobile pulls in ahead, sounding his horn as he does. I trot up to him. The driver leans over the broad bench seat and slides the passenger door open 'I'm just going a few miles up t'road to Adwick Le Street, but it'll get tha clear of Donny.'

I assume 'Donny' is the locals' name for the town. 'That'll be great. Thanks a lot.'

'Nowt's a bother. Ah never pass a lad in uniform. Used to hitch a lot when ah were in t'army.'

As it slowly grows dark, towns and villages I've never heard of slip by into the night; Ferrybridge, Wetherby, Boroughbridge. I'm left with snapshots of similar main streets, stone terraces, pubs and pedestrians. In between towns it becomes hypnotic as I sit in the dark cabs of a succession of lorries. Our world is bound by how far we can see with the headlights. The Cat's-eyes in the middle of the carriageway always look as if they're about to peter out. But they never do. As our headlights sweep the road in front, one by one they seem to switch on just in time, always the same fixed distance in front of us.

Some time after eleven p.m. I'm being driven straight through the middle of Newcastle upon Tyne. It reminds me of Glasgow city centre, all shops and department stores with their lights on, and couples strolling along the pavements. The driver turns to me. 'Ah'll drop yee alang here a bit. Just keep thumbing. With yee being in uniform they'll kna' yer gannin' north. At this time o' night there's plenty 'trunk' drivers heading for Edinburgh and Glasgow. They ahll want tae get there for six or seven in the morning when the markets open.' He gives a hand signal out of his window and begins to slow down. 'Ah'll let yee off here. And another thing, hinny. It'll gan quiet aroond three or four in the morning. Some o'them park up for a few hours kip, or get themselves into an all-night cafe for summat tae eat. Ah hope it keeps dry for tha. Cheerio.'

By two a.m., just as he'd forecast, it has become really quiet. I'm somewhere between Morpeth and Alnwick. I keep on walking into the darkness and have a strong feeling of being in the middle of nowhere. Yet I'm enjoying myself. It's dry, I'm warmly clad, and I've never been in the countryside at night. I've hardly been in it during the day. It's full of strange noises, most of them unidentifiable. I stand still and listen. From out of the blackness comes the distant lowing of cattle and the bleating of sheep. Birds flutter in bushes now and again. At least I think it's birds. Hope it's birds. There are regular scurryings and rustlings. There's not a light to be seen, only a thin crescent moon. I must be miles from anywhere. Sometimes one of the few clouds in the sky covers the slice of moon and it becomes so dark I have to stop walking. Almost pitch black. For no particular reason I look up – and catch my breath! The sky is a mass of bright stars. Millions of them. Because the peak of my skipped hat is pulled low over my eyes I hadn't noticed them. I never knew they could be as bright as this, nor that there were so many. Sometimes, in the comparative darkness of the tenement back courts, I would look up, see some stars, and wonder. But never at this intensity. There was always light spilling out from dozens of windows, putting a haze between them and me.

This is the second time in my life when something has made me catch my breath. The first was on walking into the Bluebell Woods at Milngavie. I take off my hat – and almost catch my breath again. The moon has obligingly stayed behind a cloud. The sky is the blackest of black velvet strewn with brilliant-cut diamonds. The night now seems to be silent.

After a while my neck begins to ache with the continual craning upwards. I can't get enough of this splendour. I stamp my feet on the ground to frighten off any horrible beasties then, feeling a bit silly, I lie down on the grass verge and put both hands behind my head. There are no nearby trees or buildings to encroach on my view. I can see nothing but star-filled sky. It is dazzling. Occasionally, lying there with my thoughts, the immensity of it makes me a little frightened. I'm alone in the night. Isolated. Floating in space.

Ten minutes later. Or is it an hour? A flicker of light catches my eye. Reluctantly, and feeling a little tipsy with the wonder of it all, I get back on my feet. To my right there are occasional flashes of light on the horizon as a vehicle, still a few miles away, follows the undulations of the road. Sometimes its headlights shine up into the sky like searchlights then abruptly vanish as it drives into a dip. It takes ages to get to me but I don't mind, I just keep looking up, drinking in the heavens until my neck aches again. I'm filled with a sense of well-being. It's good to be alive.

Eventually the lorry turns onto the stretch of road I'm on. I stand facing it, left arm out, thumb up, as it trundles toward me. The driver flashes his lights; he's seen me. He pulls up just short and I run forward, reach up, and open the passenger door. He looks down. 'Ah'm going tae near Edinburgh, bonny lad.' The warmth spills out from the cab and makes me realise I'm a bit chilled.

'That's great!'

'Climb in. Ah'm only going as far as Haddington, that's aboot 18 miles frae the toon.'

'That'll be smashin'. Thanks very much.'

We've been driving for about quarter of an hour when he turns to me. 'Are ye hungry?'

'Starvin'!'

He laughs. 'There's an all-night café a few miles up the road. We'll stoap an' huv a wee bite.'

Thirty minutes later we pull off the road onto a cinder-covered parking area. Another six or seven lorries are already there. Welcoming lights shine out from the one-storey, jerry-built café. As we enter this makeshift building the smell of bacon and eggs goes round my heart. Suddenly it's the most inviting place, probably on a par with The Ritz. I've had nothing to eat since a couple of cold meat pies many hours ago. I can hardly wait for the woman to fry my late supper. Or is it an early breakfast? My driver nods to the others. A soldier in uniform sits with one of the drivers. We smile at one another, instantly connected by our shared experience. For a second I wonder if he marvelled at the stars tonight while between lifts.

We take a seat in the far corner of the large room. There are three women amongst the customers. All wear too much make-up. One is in deep conversation with two of the drivers. Where can they be going at this time of night? Her friends sit at a table. My driver nudges me

'Ye can hae one o' them for afters if ye want!'

'Eh?' I'm busy watching the cook, willing her to hurry up.

'The weemin. They're oan the game. They're here maist nights o' the week, doing business.'

'Jeez! Are they?' I look at them with interest. It's the first time I've seen prostitutes. I've never been with a woman. Never even been with a girl. Had the odd feel now and again in the back court. I wonder what it would be like to go with one of them? They look a bit . . . hard. I find that makes them EXTRA sexy. I recall what my pal, Sammy, used to say if we passed a woman who looked a bit brazen; over made-up . . .

'Did ye see her? She'd suck ye in and blaw ye oot in bubbles!'
Then we'd go into fits of laughter.

At last the woman brings me my meal. As I try not to guzzle it –
it's one of the finest fry-ups ever cooked – I find I can't take my
eyes off the women. They're probably all in their thirties. I spend
most of my time looking at their legs. And tits. Their skirts are
quite short. Two of them have real good legs, and one of them
wears black stockings. Jeez, I bet she'd let you put your hand up
her skirt. In fact I bet she'd let you see it. For as long as you want.
Even if you have to pay her, so what? It would still be nice. I feel
myself getting aroused. So hard it's throbbing. The three of them
don't seem to have a care in the world, laughing and joking with
their potential customers. One of the trio rises . . . MAMMY,
DADDY! She's coming over to us. I stop in mid-chew, my face
goes red, the hard-on vanishes. Jeez! Does she know what I've
been thinking? If she says 'What are you staring at?' I'll crap
maself.

'Any of you boys looking for a short-time?'

'No thanks, flower,' says the driver, 'Ah'm sorry tae say, ah
have'nae got the time or the money.' I can feel my face is still red.

She looks at me. 'What about you, Squadron Leader?'

I go back onto 'full red'. 'Eh, no thanks,' I manage to squeak,
'I'm skint tae.'

She sighs. 'That's the story of my life.'

As she clip-clops back to her friends the driver and I watch her
go. He leans toward me and speaks out the side of his mouth,
'She probably huz a hole in her knee for laddies like you!'

Twenty minutes after setting off I can't keep my eyes open. The
driver notices me nodding.

'Lean tae the side and coorie doon on top o' the engine
cowling. Use the blankets.'

Nearly all lorries are the 'flat-nosed' type. The engine is in the
cab, between the two seats. Almost every driver carries two or

three ex-army blankets, folded up and lying on the metal cowling covering the engine. I half lie-on my side and use the blankets as a pillow. The warmth and vibration percolate up from the engine and, within minutes, I'm asleep.

Moments later – so it seems – I'm shaken awake. 'It's the parting of the ways, son.'

Bleary-eyed, I sit up. Jeez-oh! It's daylight! I yawn, stretching my arms and legs out in front of me, trying to shake off the tiredness. 'Ohhhh! That was a good wee sleep. I really needed it.' We fork to the left for Haddington then pull up. I open the door. Crisp morning air breezes in. I climb down onto the verge then look back up into the snug cab. 'Thanks a lot, that was a great lift.'

'Nae bother. The traffic will pick up, shortly. All the best, son.'

As I watch him drive off I pull up the collar of my greatcoat against the breeze. I look up at the sky. It's a solid gray. The stars have long gone. But I know they're still there.

I get a lift into Edinburgh then walk west for a while through the suburbs to get onto the A8. I'm beginning to feel weary, I could do with my bed.

One hour and two lifts later finds me, at last, in Blackburn, West Lothian, knocking on my Uncle Jim's door. I look at the familiar aluminium handle and letterbox. The last time I stood here was with Ma. Jim, oldest of her three brothers, opens the door. He looks for a moment at the bedraggled figure in RAF uniform, not recognising me, then, 'In the name o' the wee man! Whit urr you daeing here?'

'Ah got the chance of some leave, so ah've hitchhiked up the road. Can ye put me up for a few days?' I hate lying to him. Jim and Jenny have four kids, all younger than me. Will they have room? He gives me the smile I've known since I was a bairn.

'Och, ah suppose we'll squeeze ye in somewhere.'

Services No Longer Required

The Wing Commander looks me in the eye. It's plain he doesn't like what's in front of him. I look at what's above his left breast pocket. Underneath his pilot's wings are two rows of medal ribbons. From the colourful poster hanging up in the NAAFI I recognise the first two as the Air Force Cross and the Distinguished Flying Cross. He speaks: 'Obviously the previous punishments you've received haven't worked, so let's try something new. Seven days' close confinement. March him out.'

I swallow hard. Well, you've done it now. Seven days' cells. I'm marched out of his office at the double. 'LEFT RIGHT LEFT RIGHT!'

After four days at my Uncle Jim's, I'd hitched my way back to camp. Once more I really enjoy being 'on the road'. The wonderful feeling of freedom. Travelling hundreds of miles with just a few bob in my pocket. The certainty of UNcertainty. When someone drops me off I watch them drive away, then turn and face the oncoming traffic KNOWING I'll get another lift. I never have a moment's doubt. My uniform is my ticket.

Just before one p.m. the following day I approach the camp's main gate. The window of the guardroom is slid back. 'I'm Boy Entrant Douglas. I've been absent without leave since last Thursday.'

The Duty Corporal looks at me. 'Oh, you have, have you? Right, what billet are you in?' I tell him. 'Just go back to your room. The Orderly Officer will come and see you later.'

I'm a bit disappointed. Is that it? At the very least they might have turned out the guard; grabbed hold of me; something.

The billet is almost empty as I walk in. The midday meal is being served. There are two or three 'Hello, Jock's'. I get my mug and eating irons from my locker and, in great anticipation, slip into the mess. Ian and Taff are at our usual table. I'm feeling tired after my overnight journey, but the thought of surprising my two mates buoys me up for the moment. I manage to approach without being seen. 'Awright, boys?'

'Yah bugger!'

For the next quarter of an hour I regale them with 'Tales From the Highway'. But behind the bravado, there's the nagging thought of what will happen to me tomorrow. Up on another 'fizzer' – this time for the more serious offence of being AWOL. Well, I've done it, so I'll have to take the consequences . . .

After receiving my seven days' cells I'm marched, still at the double, back to the billet. I'm allowed to take only essential kit, toothbrush, razor and, surprisingly, my few paperback books. Everything else, military kit as well as personal, I have to pack up and take, still under escort, down to the quartermaster's Stores. It'll be lodged there for the duration of my sentence. That done, I'm then double-marched to the guardhouse. As it comes nearer I try to give my spirits a boost by thinking about Frank Sinatra – Private Maggio in the movie *From Here To Eternity* – being marched to the stockade where Sergeant 'Fatso' Judson waits for him. If Frank can do it, so can I. I just hope to fuck there's nobody like Ernest Borgnine (Fatso) on duty!

Arms swinging, I'm marched into the presence of the two duty SPs (Security Police – the RAF's military police). The pair of them, both corporals, look at me. One takes charge. 'Just keep marking time. AT THE DOUBLE! Swing those arms

SHOULDER HEIGHT!' He walks round me, points at my knees. 'HIGHER! WAIST HEIGHT!'

I comply. No good antagonising them. If you try to be smart they'll just mess you about. Bullshit baffles brains (BBB).

'Take that bloody grin off your face. DO YOU THINK IT'S FUNNY?' he screams.

'No, corporal.'

They leave me marking time for a few minutes and talk among themselves. Then one cries, 'HALT!' I halt. I'm then marched down a passage with shiny linoleum on the floor and a row of heavily studded doors. He opens one and I'm marched into a cell. 'This is your 'ome for the next week, lad. I'll leave you to ruminate.'

I'm sorely tempted to say 'I've already had a pee, corporal.' But, as usual, I haven't the nerve.

'Thank you, corporal.' He exits, banging the cell door loudly behind him.

I'm quite taken with the cell! It's small, cosy and not too uncomfortable. The bed is a wooden dais, raised about six inches off the floor. It's covered with a slim, firm mattress. After years of lying on the three lumpy cushions of my bed-chair, back in Maryhill, this is de luxe. As I look around my small cell I realise what else I'm going to like about it. It's quiet. And it's warm. I lie down on my hard bed and begin to read. Jeez! This is better than jankers. It's going to be cells for me from now on. The best laugh is, this is supposed to be the tougher punishment. I read on for a few more minutes until the warmth, and the voices of the SPs drifting along the corridor, get to me and I drift off to sleep.

'LET'S BE 'AVING YOU!' It's a couple of seconds before I realise where I am. I jump up and stand to attention. BBB. 'Do you want some supper, lad?'

'Yes please, Corporal.' Supper? Jeeesus! This is punishment? He hands me a plate with a large currant bun on it, also a mug of cocoa made with a mixture of milk and water. 'Thank you, Corporal.' In the SPs there is no one below the rank of corporal. As soon as they finish their training for the RAF police they are promoted to that rank to give them some authority.

'It's 'alf past eight. I'll be back in twenty minutes to let you out to the bogs to 'ave a wash, etc.'

'Thank you, Corporal.' This is bloody great! Most nights of the week I go to bed hungry because I'm always skint. Here I am, in cells, and I'm going to bed with a full stomach. Old Mason never thought of this. It's definitely the cells for me from now on. I eat just over half the large bun and secrete the rest under my pillow for later. I'll have it after 'lights out'.

The next seven days are a doddle. The SPs obviously have instructions not to treat the boys as harshly as the adult prisoners. There is just one airman on punishment. I see him now and again in passing. He does get chased 'from arsehole to breakfast-time', but even so, it's mostly verbal. I could handle that no bother. We get a certain amount of doing things at the double early in the day. By noon things slacken off and we spend most of our time out of our cells in the guardroom buffing up almost spotless floors or polishing the brass taps and pipes we did yesterday. And the day before. If you happen to annoy one of the corporals on duty he'll usually make you run on the spot for five minutes or so. I always do what I'm told and never aggravate them. Remember 'BBB'. It works. By late afternoon we spend most of our time locked up. For me, that ain't punishment. I just lie and read – when I'm not kipping. I soon devour the few paperbacks I brought with me, but the SPs have quite a few in a drawer and let me borrow one when needed.

At least once a day there is an interruption to the smooth running of the guardhouse when the Orderly Officer, accompanied by the Orderly Sergeant, gives the place, and any prisoners, a cursory inspection. I'm lying, totally absorbed in *How Green Was My*

Valley, when the peace and tranquillity of the guardroom is broken as, with much stamping and clashing of studded boots, the two corporals on duty come to attention and report: 'Two prisoners in cells. Guardroom ready for your inspection, SAH!'

The young Pilot Officer enters my cell, the sergeant and one SP behind him. I leap off the bed and come to attention. He's trying to look as if he knows what it's all about. I'd take a bet he's a National Serviceman on a 'short service commission.' University students are deferred from the call-up until after they graduate. Because they have a degree they are offered the chance to become an officer during their two years.

'What's your name?'

I'm already standing at attention, but I visibly stiffen. They like that. BBB.

'Zero five four five, Douglas, SAH!' Always pronounce 'sir' as 'SAH!' It's a British military tradition. Shows willing.

'Everything all right?'

'Yes, thank you, SAH!'

'Any complaints about your treatment?'

'No, SAH!' The thing is, not to go overboard. If I say I'm being treated very well I'll get the SPs into bother. I'm not here to be treated well, I'm supposed to be on punishment.

'Are you getting enough to eat?'

'Yes, thank you, SAH!' As I say these multiple 'SAH!'s I sound increasingly as though I'm from 'way down south'; Louisiana or somewhere. As usual my imagination runs away with me and I begin to picture me bursting into a chorus of 'The Camptown Races' while doing a soft shoe shuffle on the highly polished linoleum. As I look at the well-scrubbed, boyish face of the young officer I wonder what his reaction would be – and those of the sergeant and corporal. I can't get the scenario out of my mind; jeez, if they don't bugger off soon I'm going to start giggling, then I'll be put on a charge for 'dumb insolence', that wonderful catch-all offence.

Mercifully he decides to go. 'Carry on.'

'Thank you, sir. SAH!'

They exit from my cell and the door is clanged shut. 'Ahhhhh.' I stretch out on my bed and get stuck into *Somebody Up There Likes Me*, the biography of former World Middleweight Champion, Rocky Graziano. I'm really enjoying it.

It's around six-thirty in the evening. Rocky and I are ahead on points against Fritzi Zivic, the former welterweight champ. American boxers have great names; Sugar Ray Robinson, Joey Maxim, Jake LaMotta, Willie Pep. They couldn't be anything else BUT fighters with names like that. The door to my cell is quietly opened. A man, in what looks like RAF uniform, comes in. As I go to rise he holds a hand out, fingers spread. 'Just stay where you are, no need to get up. I'm Captain Wright. We're allowed access to lads in the cells.' He sits on the solitary chair.

'Oh, hello.' Should I have saluted him? They have Group Captains in the RAF, but not Captains. That's the army. He starts talking and it doesn't take me long to figure he's some sort of 'Holy Joe.'

'May I ask why you're in here, Robert?'

'Well, ah went AWOL for a few days, sir.' I'm not sure if he's entitled to a 'sir'. He's definitely NOT going to get a 'SAH!' Might frighten the crap out of him.

'Mmmm, goodness. Why did you do that, Robert? Trouble at home?'

'I don't have a home, sir. My ma died last December and my father gave it up. He's in the Air Force, too.'

'So why DID you go AWOL, Robert?'

I shrug my shoulders. 'Because anywhere's better than Cosford.' We chat for a few more minutes, during which time I put him in the picture about my father – without using any bad language. He looks at his watch. 'Before I go, Robert, would you like to kneel and say a short prayer together?'

I feel my face go red. Would I fuck, I think to myself. I'd feel really stupid. 'I'd rather not, sir.'

'Oh, may I ask why?'

'Nae offence tae you, sir, but I used tae pray a lot at one time. I believed there was a God. Yet he never stopped my Ma dying, or my father being a bad little git. Or me having tae leave Glasgow. So ah've sort of gave Him up – or mibbe it was Him who was'nae bothered aboot me?'

'Well, the Lord sometimes does his work in ways that are hard to understand. We can't always see what he intends for us.' He smiles. 'A little prayer might help.'

I begin to feel annoyed at this stranger pressuring me into praying. 'Aye, well, since December last year aw' the Lord seems tae have intended for me is a load of misery.'

'Yes, I'm sure it must seem that way. Anyway, I'll say goodnight to you, Robert. And I'll say a prayer for you later.'

'Thanks very much.'

His footsteps have hardly faded from the corridor before I'm back in Madison Square Garden. It's the third round and Rocky's having a lot of bother with Tony Zale. Jeez, that's another great name. I find out later my visitor is a Church Army Captain, known locally as 'Creepin' Jesus'.

My seven days' rest cure over, I draw my kit back from the quartermaster's stores and return to the billet. My metal-framed bed lies empty, the black and white striped mattress folded in half. Through the springs I can see bits of 'oose' (fluff) lying on the floor. I soon get my stuff back onto the shelves of my locker then get the brush and sweep up the oose.

As I lie on my bed Ian and Lyn sit either side of me and quiz me about the cells. They seem to think I've been through some sort of ordeal. I have a terrible job convincing them it's better than jankers. 'Honest, it's a doddle for us boys. Ah've had a bloody good rest. Did nowt but read.'

They look at one another. 'Trying to be 'ard, he is,' says Lyn.

'You don't need to be brave wi' us.' Ian looks at me sympathetically.

'Ah'm not! Straight up. As long as ye can stand being in a cell for long periods it's nae bother. Never read so many books in ma life.'

That night as I lie in bed, I decide it's cells for me from now on. No more jankers. Too much like hard work. I reach up and put my reading light out. Might as well start again in the morning, do something to get me another dose of cells.

'C'MON, GET ON PARADE!' Corporal Graham crunches up and down the length of the billet. We've had breakfast, given the floor a quick sweep, left our beds tidy. It's now time for workshops. As the lads begin to exit, the corporal with them, I make myself comfortable on my bed and find my place in *A Tree Grows In Brooklyn*.

'Are you starting, already?' Ian stands at the foot of my bed. Lyn joins him. I try not to laugh at the looks on their faces. They both worry about me.

' 'Tis mad you are.'

'Ah'm not, Taff. Ah have tae keep it going.'

The two of them hurry away. I watch as they disappear through the door, chattering to one another. Sometimes I envy them, they're doing what they want to do. I wish I was. I can hear the roll being called. Minutes later Corporal Graham comes noisily into the quiet billet. 'Why aren't you on parade?'

'Ah don't want to, Corporal.'

'You know I'll be putting you on a charge?'

'Ah do, Corporal.'

Without another word he marches back out. He doesn't think much of me at all. I wish I could tell him how I came to be in the Boys' Service. I like Graham. In his thirties, he's married and lives in quarters on the camp. Now that we've been here nearly nine months he's built up a good relationship with all the lads in our intake – except me. Well, it'll just have to stay that way. I've always been a well-behaved boy, ready to do what I'm told. All this disobedience goes against my nature. But being obedient won't get me out of the RAF. I try to strike a balance between being un-cooperative without being insolent. I feel I do it well. Sometimes I wonder if I should explain to those in charge why I want out. But I'm worried that when they discover I've no home to go to, they'll get their heads together and decide 'for my own good' to keep me here until I eventually get used to the RAF and settle down. I decide I can't risk that happening. I'll have to keep on 'working my ticket'.

I settle back on the bed with my book. Must try and get a loan of some good ones for my next spell in the clink.

Next morning, cap off, arms swinging, I'm marched into the C.O.'s office. Once more he looks disparagingly at me. 'We've decided that keeping you here any longer is a waste of taxpayers' money.' My heart gives a leap. Is this it? 'You are to be discharged on 19 November under what is known as "Services No Longer Required".' My heart gives a double-leap! 'Wipe that smile off your face! I don't know why you bothered to join us in the first place.'

I look at him. I take in, yet again, the pilot's wings and double row of medal ribbons. I really hate it that this fine man thinks so little of me. If this were the movies, now would be the moment when James Stewart or Spencer Tracy would make an impassioned speech to explain themselves. I say nothing. He gives me the same warning he gave Mason, 'Just stay in your billet most of the time until you're released. You're excused parades, workshops and lectures.' He begins to shuffle his papers together, then he looks up. 'And be aware, when you turn eighteen you are still liable for two years' National Service. This wasted nine months doesn't count. Dismiss!' I'm double-marched back out.

'Cap on,' says Graham. 'Right, just go back to the block, and as the C.O. says, keep out the bloody way!'

Even though I'm frustrated that these people don't really know me, it doesn't dampen my elation. I'VE DONE IT! It was Mason's turn a couple of months back, now it's mine. They're going to let me out. I'm not going to be stuck in the RAF for the next twelve years. I want to do a jig, shout and bawl! Instead, I walk back up to

Fulton Block, my mind buzzing. So, okay, I still have to do my two years' National Service. But that's all it is; two years. When I do that I won't be causing any trouble. Everybody has to do it. It'll be a chance to show I can knuckle down and make a good job of it. All the square-bashing and rifle drill I've done here should give me a flying start when I get called up. From out of the blue, the thought occurs to me – where the hell am I going to go?

By the time I get back to the billet I've decided there's only one place I can go. My Uncle Jim's. What if he says he can't take me? I sit at the table in the middle of the billet and quickly write two letters so as they'll catch the noon collection. One to Uncle Jim, asking if he can put me up for a few weeks until I get a job, then I'll find permanent digs. The second is to my father to tell him I'm being chucked out, and will he send my civvies down to me right away. I enjoy writing this one. During all the time I've been working my ticket I haven't told him anything about it. He thinks I'm settled in the RAF. Well, to use a favourite phrase of his – 'You've got another think coming!'

I'm lying on my bed, too excited to read, when the boys come back to the billet for their eating irons. As my two pals come through the door, Lyn spots me. 'He's 'ere! I thought you'd be down the cells, boyo.'

I look up. 'Aw'right, lads?'

'Have they just given ye jankers this time?' enquires Ian.

'Nope.'

'They canny have given ye the guardhouse,' he reasons, 'or you'd already be in the cells. Have they let ye off?'

'Nope.'

'There's turned into Gary Cooper, he has,' says Lyn.

'I'VE DONE IT! They're chucking me out. I'll be away on the nineteenth.'

They both congratulate me. Ian looks at Lyn. 'Trouble is, I think we'll miss the daft Scots git.'

'Oh, I dunno,' Lyn pauses, 'well, I s'pose we will.' I can tell they mean it.

Less than a week later, I take my leave of Cosford. And my two pals. It's my first experience of the close friendships that can be made in the forces. To work, play, sleep and eat with your mates close at hand, twenty-four hours a day, replacing family, forges a bond that doesn't exist in 'civvy street'.

The support of Lyn and Ian, even though they themselves were happy to be in the RAF, was a big help in my quest to be discharged. I've never forgotten them. We were all just sixteen years of age. Over twenty years later I managed to track Lyn down and we met up again; but I'll keep that story for another time. I've made efforts to find Ian – including ringing all the Ian Douglases in the Edinburgh phonebook – but alas, no luck.

At last! I've worked my ticket out of the RAF Boys' Service.
I'm free. November 1955.

Looking For Somewhere

Charles Dickens would have felt at home had he seen the working conditions on the 'tables' at Polkemmet Colliery in 1955. They could give the Blacking Factory of his childhood a run for its money. The screens – to give them their proper name – are where stones are hand picked from coal just brought up from the pit bottom. The red brick building stands on concrete pillars, allowing railway wagons to run underneath and be filled with the newly-picked coal. This is where I'll work until I'm old enough to go underground.

I've quickly settled in at Uncle Jim and Aunty Jenny's. My four cousins are all younger than me; Marion by four years, then come Dennis, Tommy and William by 6, 8 and 11 years respectively. They'll be joined in 2 years by Alec. Marion is Jim's step-daughter, though that grim-sounding term is never used. Jim treats her as his own. She was born Marion Boon, the daughter of Jenny's first husband, Jack Boon. Sadly, Jack was killed in a road accident in North Africa during the war.

Their three-bedroom, semi-detached house in Murrayfield Terrace seems like the height of luxury to me – it has a bathroom AND toilet. Built in 1948, these houses are known locally as 'the steel houses' because they've been assembled from large metal panels, which were then pebble-dashed.

Less than a year ago I was still living in our tenement single-end, sharing a lavatory in the close with another two families. To find myself living in a house with all mod cons is really something. Jim and Jenny also have another object of desire – a television. Until the novelty wears off, I sit happily for hours watching anything that's on . . . *Andy Pandy*, *Muffin the Mule*, even the test card. The background music's nice.

A week after my arrival in Blackburn, I go for an interview with the NCB (National Coal Board). I ask if I can be given a job at Polkemmet because my uncle works there. This is granted. As I leave their offices I think back to that day in 1951, just four years ago, when my class from Springbank School in Maryhill had been taken on a day trip to Linlithgow and Edinburgh. As we'd driven through the Lothians I'd stared out of the window at the many pit heaps and winding gears that littered the area. I'm about to start work at one of them.

The arrangement at my uncle and aunt's is supposedly until I get settled in a job, then I'll look around for permanent digs. I suggest they let me know when they think it's time for me to move. It all seems to work out well and I stay longer than expected. My starting wage at the pit brings me, after offtakes, just over four pounds a week. I give Jenny two pounds 'dig money', leaving me just over two for myself. For a sixteen year old whose main vices are reading, going to the pictures, and eating sweeties, this is ample.

One dank morning in early December 1955, I present myself at Polkemmet Colliery. Jim has supplied me with some old clothes . . . 'Anything does for yer work, especially oan the tables. There's dust fleeing everywhere. Ah've given ye one set for working in and one for shifting.'

'Whit's "shifting"?'

'Changing. Ye wear one lot for travelling back and forth oan the pit bus and ye keep yer working claes in yer locker in the bath-hoose. When ye come tae work ye change intae the dirty ones. When ye finish yer shift ye strip off, put the dirty claes in the locker, have a shower, then put the clean yins oan for coming hame. Got it?'

'Aye, fine.'

I realise that stripping off in the pit baths every day is going to be an ordeal. Everybody will get to see my back and chest, which sport the worst case of acne in the Western hemisphere. The only way to spare myself this daily embarrassment would be to travel back unwashed and bathe at home. That isn't really an option.

One of the pit-head foremen leads me up the stairs to where the tables are located. As we near the door there is a throbbing, grinding noise. He opens it and the sound doubles. We step inside and it doubles again. A few heads look up. He puts his face to within an inch of my ear. 'THIS IS IT!' he bawls. I can barely hear him. The charge-hand comes over and they converse in a mixture of lip-reading and hand signals. It reminds me of the riveting shop at the North British Locomotive Company in Springburn; my first job. I look around. The three screens, or tables, are 4 feet wide conveyor belts. Conveyor belts with a difference. The 'belts' are metal rods and look like moving railings. They trundle along on small metal wheels, making the most dreadful noise, metal upon metal grinding and screeching. Every few minutes there's an avalanche at the end of the shop as a couple of 'hutches' (coal tubs) tip their loads of freshly-dug coal down metal shutes onto the tables. The extra weight makes the rails and wheels scream louder than ever. The fall of coal takes place behind stretches of rubber belting which hang and sway from the ceiling, supposedly to contain the dust which swirls up at each new delivery. It doesn't. Soon, like everyone else, I'm spitting black. Between the tables are small, rubber conveyor belts, 2 feet wide and protected by metal sides. As each fresh batch of coal vibrates along past them, the workforce set to with a will. Bent over on either side of the three tables, they rhythmically hand pick any stones they spot amongst the advancing coal and send them flying the few feet into the small conveyor belts which carry them away on the start of their journey to the 'bing' (pit heap).

Now and again a large boulder comes jiggling along, its weight making the metal wheels and rails screech like a banshee. If it is too big to fit onto the smaller belt, one of the older lads walks alongside it smashing furiously at it with a sledgehammer as it traverses the room. As he progresses, one by one the pickers step back to let him pass and continue his running battle with the rock. It becomes a point of honour to break it up into manageable pieces and remove it. It musn't be allowed to fall off the end of the table and down into the coal wagon. Now and again a stone will prove to be too big and hard. As it approaches the end of the screen it will be wrestled off the conveyor and onto the floor; later it can be attacked and reduced at leisure. As I look around me on my first day, I'm reminded of Chaplin's masterpiece, *Modern Times*. Except Charlie's world was silent. And there wasn't the dust.

So, this is to be my workplace. I take off my ex-army haversack, which contains my flask and piece (sandwiches) and hang it on one of the many nails hammered into the dirty, whitewashed walls. Taking a position at one of the tables I await my first load of coal. Soon I'm stamping my feet and thrusting my hands deep into my pockets as cold December draughts blow in from various corners of the large, unheated room. Through the dusty atmosphere I eye my new workmates. They are a mixture of the very young and very old. All are clad in the most raggedy of clothes; jackets with torn lapels, ripped seams and pocket flaps hanging. The older men all wear bunnets (cloth caps), the youths a mixture of bunnets and woolly hats. They look like a collection of tramps – tramps who've fallen on hard times.

I'll later find that almost all the older men have worked for years underground until retirement, then, finding they can't afford to retire, have taken this 'pit-heid job' to supplement their meagre pensions. The majority of youngsters, like me, are waiting until they are of age to go down the pit. Three or four of the older lads, usually the ones who wield the sledgehammers, have no wish to go down below. This is a permanent job for them. At last the coal starts flowing again and I realise why my workmates set to so energetically – it's to warm themselves up.

I quickly adapt to life on the tables. The young lads soon accept me as 'one of the boys'. It seems to be a help when word gets around I'm from Glasgow. Immediately it's assumed I must be tough, having been brought up in the city. I try not to shatter their illusions, but also hope I won't be called upon to prove it. The older men are all sociable and helpful. When our thirty minute piece-time arrives it's a wonderful relief, as the screens are stopped during the break and we can have a conversation. When, all too soon, they start up again, they seem louder than ever and it's back to communicating by lip-reading and mime.

I soon find we have a great character amongst us in the shape of 'Wee Sammy from Fauldhouse'. Around sixty years of age, unmarried, and standing well under five feet, Sammy has worked on the tables for years. Stockily built, and with a reluctance to wear his dentures, he nearly always has a shortened clay pipe clamped between his gums. This gives him a marked resemblance to Popeye. It is his habit to immediately break off two or more inches from the stem of each new 'penny pipe' he buys (nowadays penny pipes cost threepence). He prefers them short. Like many old folk, he claims a clay pipe gives the finest smoke of all. It's a regular sport for the young lads, when we're not busy, to chip an occasional small piece of coal at him when he isn't looking. Without fail this causes him to yell an unheard 'Whaes chipping?' and also usually causes the pipe to fall from his mouth and smash on the floor. He immediately flies into a rage, grabs a stone and races up and down his side of the screen, threatening to throw it at whoever he thinks is guilty. We all mime our innocence with a skill that would impress Marcel Marceau. A few minutes later he'll calm down, throw the stone into a conveyor, then go searching behind the girders supporting the roof, eventually emerging, triumphant, with a dusty 'emergency pipe'. He has a dozen or more stashed in between the eaves and girders. Like a squirrel with its nuts, he often forgets where he's hidden them.

Sammy has another claim to fame. Although no scholar, he has a phenomenal memory when it comes to the history of Celtic Football Club, and loves it when his skill is put to the test at piece-time . . . 'Sammy, can ye name the team who became league champions by winning the last game of the 1946–47 season?' He will reel off, without pause, the entire team, name the goal scorers and throw in the reserves. He can name the full team for every major game Celtic took part in from around 1930 to the present day. Yet in all other respects Sammy could be considered as 'not too bright'.

I'm now quite used to living at Jim and Jenny's and working at the pit. It's far better than being in the RAF. No more being ordered around. I can go out when I want, always have money in my pocket, don't go to bed hungry anymore. I'm also pleased when, at last, 1955 lets go and gives 1956 a chance. Most of the year just gone has been miserable as far as I'm concerned. My first year without Ma. The ninth of December was the first anniversary of her death. I think of her often. Of her long illness and sad, lonely death. Also I remember our good times – always when my father wasn't around. But often, too often, that last year of her life when the cancer slowly took her is what I think about. Through sheer willpower she lived an extra twelve months for me. The doctors had given her six months to live after they'd removed her breast and saw the cancer had spread elsewhere. She lived a YEAR and six months. Quite simply this was to see me up as far as she could. She knew my father would unload me as soon as possible, so the longer she hung on the older I'd be and, hopefully, more able to look after myself. I always feel I should have done more for her.

Whenever my thoughts take me back to Ma, there's just one

thing I'm so grateful for. When I saw her for the last time, not knowing that's what it was, I gave her a goodnight kiss. It was a kiss goodbye.

I carry on an intermittent correspondence with my father. He's now out of the RAF and living in Portpatrick with his new wife. They married a few months after Ma died. I regularly try and figure out why I keep in touch with him. This is the bad little git who, when he was around, made my childhood a misery, I was always in fear of him. This the man who told Ma, just weeks before she died, 'I'm jist waiting for you tae die so's ah can get married again – so fuckin' hurry up, will ye!' Why do I continue to write to a pig's melt like that? Is it because he's a last link with Ma? With the life I've lost? Or because I'm no longer afraid of him? I really don't know.

Return to Sender

On 9 February 1956 I turn seventeen. Jim and Jenny have still not made any mention of me finding digs. The job on the pit-head goes well and I'm very much one of the lads and get on fine with my workmates. Even so, I haven't yet teamed up with anyone who could be considered a pal; not like Sammy Johnston or John Purden had been back in Maryhill. One of the main problems is that none of the boys on the tables comes from Blackburn. They are from other surrounding towns and villages like Whitburn, Armadale, East and West Calder. When not at work I don't have occasion to mix with any local lads. At home I spend most of my time reading, watching TV, or playing games with my younger cousins; draughts, snakes and ladders or snap! Once or twice a week I'll make the 3-mile bus trip into Bathgate – the biggest town around – if there's a good film on at the Regal or Pavilion. I still love the cinema.

Blackburn is a typical Lothian mining village, i.e. it's dead. Every day is Sunday. Half the residents think the Avon Lady is a film star. The next most exciting event – after her cry of 'Avon Calling!' – is when the NCB lorry comes round to drop each miner's 'free coal' allowance on the road outside their house. When the men come home after their shift they have to set to with shovel and wheelbarrow and cart it round to the concrete bunker in the back garden. Many wives and kids, sporting an array of buckets, baths and barrows, make a joint effort to shift it before dad's return. Neighbours watch from their windows, awarding points for style and delivery. The black mounds cleared, the village settles down for another month of enforced tranquillity. Used to a busy Maryhill Road, with its rows of shops and constantly moving trams, lorries and pedestrians, it takes me a long time to adjust to this slow-paced, quiet life.

There are just two pubs in Blackburn: The Crown, known as 'The Croon', and The Turf. At the cross is the only shop; a café cum tobacconist cum general store. And that's it. The needs of the residents are mostly met by a daily succession of vans; grocer, baker, fish man and 'Johnny aw' things'. These come round at their own set times, announcing who it is by sounding their horns in their own individual way. Uncle Jim has solved the problem of the twice a day ice-cream van. He's told the kids that when you hear the chimes, that means he's sold out and is on his way back to the depot!

Supermarkets are way off in the future. Private cars are at a ratio of just two or three per street. When a married couple go into Bathgate on a Saturday their purchases are limited to how much they can carry on the bus. Plastic bags haven't yet put in an appearance. Brown paper carrier bags are the norm. Without fail, one or more of the string handles will cut through the bag long before you get home, or the bottom will split. Either way, folk picking up spilled shopping is a Saturday scenario. Bags seem to have an ability to know when you've just boarded a bus and regularly deposit the day's shopping on the platform or in the aisle.

Buses are the most used form of transport; taxis are only hired for weddings, funerals or emergencies. A trip to the 'big city', Glasgow or Edinburgh, is normally only undertaken once, at most twice, a year. Holidays abroad are only taken by toffs. Working class families, if they can afford it, will spend a week, maybe ten days in the likes of Largs, Rothesay or Saltcoats on the Ayrshire coast. Lately some have been known to splash out on a fortnight at Butlins! Since the end of the war Billy Butlin has been expanding his holiday camp empire, especially in the north of

England at coastal resorts like Blackpool and Skegness. With the end of hostilities in 1945 and the consequent demob of hundreds of thousands of servicemen, dozens of camps became redundant. Butlin snapped up those in good locations at bargain prices and began to adapt them to give cheap accommodation, fitting them out with facilities such as bars, swimming pools and dance or concert halls. Always situated near the seaside, they began by offering 'cheap and cheerful' holidays. As the years have gone by they have become more sophisticated, but still offer low priced, communal holidays which appeal very much to working class folk.

Another aspect of Blackburn life I'm trying to get used to is the fact that every guy I pass in the street, young or old, greets me – even though I've never clapped eyes on him in my life. I'll be taking a walk down to Blackburn Cross – just for a bit of excitement – and I'll pass some middle-aged man. 'All right, sur?' This is usually said with a nod of the head. The first one of the day nearly always catches me unawares. 'Oh! Aye, hiyah!' A few minutes later a young lad around my own age goes by. 'Hello, sur.'

I nod and smile. 'Hiyah.'

Then, there's the bus scam. The main services in West Lothian are run by the green-liveried SMT (Scottish Motor Traction). It takes me a while before I twig what's going on . . . It's a Saturday, I'm on the Bathgate bus and it's just pulling away from a stop, having taken aboard six or seven passengers. I watch with interest as the conductor goes around taking the fares. I'm wondering if this thing will happen again. Sure enough! He approaches one of the new passengers. 'Single tae Bathgate. Don't bother wi' a ticket.' I watch even closer. The fare is fourpence, which is held out in an open palm. The conductor takes TWO pence, which he slips into his jacket pocket, then moves on. No ticket has been issued. The passenger puts the remaining two pence back in her purse.

Over the next few months it becomes a way of passing the time when I go into Bathgate – carrying out my field study on the 'Great SMT Fare Scam'. The results of my investigations show that, on average, one in four conductors take part in it. Perhaps one in five passengers. The montony of the journey is often broken when the driver spots an inspector waiting at the next stop and gives his mate 'the wire'. If we're on a double-decker, this results in the conductor flying round at breakneck speed to revisit the ticketless passengers, collect the balance of the fares and issue tickets at such a rate I could swear I've seen sparks fly from his machine on occasion.

I'd never came across such a thing in Glasgow. Perhaps the 'country yokels' aren't as slow as we city folk think.

It's a pleasant spring afternoon as the pit bus wends its way toward Blackburn. Jim and I, fresh from the baths, sit companionably together.

'Ye know what ah think ah'll dae oan Saturday, Jim?'

'No. Not unless ye tell me.'

'Ah think ah'll have a trip intae Glesga. Ah hav'nae been back for more than a year.'

'Aye, why not. Will ye be havin' a run up tae Maryhill?'

'Oh, aye. That's ma main reason for going. Tae have a look at the auld place and try and see one or two of ma pals.'

The following Saturday I'm up bright and early, shave without leaving the bathroom like an abattoir, and catch an early bus to Bathgate. From there I take the Glasgow service. The journey will take around an hour and a half. I find that sitting upstairs at the front, as the bus wends its slow way toward Glasgow, seems somehow conducive to thinking. I've brought a paperback with me to help pass the time, *The Great Escape* by Paul Brickhill. The book lies open in front of me, but I'm not reading it. As the bus sways and jerks its way along, I'm looking out the window but seeing nothing, my eyes aren't focused. I think about where I'm going with my life. If anywhere. It would be nice to have a steady girlfriend. But who wants to go out with someone with a face full of acne? I miss having a pal. Somebody like Sammy or John. I don't know anybody in Blackburn; never mix with any local lads. It shouldn't be long until I go down the pit. I'm quite looking forward to it. The screens are okay. We have a good laugh. But they're murder polis in the winter. Be better off down below – and I'll make more money. Jim says there's regularly the chance to 'lie-on' and do a double-shift. I'll be game for that. I might as well earn some money. I'm too old now, at seventeen, to learn a trade – they like to get you straight from school. If Ma had lived I'd have been well into my apprenticeship at NB Loco up in Springburn. I'll have to go through all my working life now as an unskilled man. The best I can hope for is semi-skilled. Get a job where I can learn welding or something. We're passing through Airdrie now. The number 23 tram used to run all the way from Maryhill to Airdrie. I think that was the longest non-stop trip. They lifted the lines a while back, they don't come out this far now. Shouldn't be long until we're into the city; butterflies take flight in my stomach. If I go down the pit I won't have to do my National Service. But I WANT to do it. I want to prove to the authorities . . . No I don't, I want to prove to *myself* that I can do it. The authorities won't even know, won't give a shit. I WANT to do my two years in the army or navy – they probably won't have me back in the RAF – and prove that I can knuckle down just like any other lad and make a go of it.

At last the bus crosses the city boundary, passes Calderpark Zoo and heads for Baillieston. I'm back in Glasgow! Butterflies take wing again. All thoughts of the future vanish. I begin to see old friends. Trams. Jeez! I have a lump in my throat. Their numbers increase; I drink in every detail, whether it's auld tram or new 'Coronation'. The cream, green and orange livery, the splendid Glasgow coat of arms emblazoned on the sides of every one. Destination boards with district names on display. Drivers and conductors in smart, bottle-green uniforms, many sporting long-service badges. It makes me realise how much I love this bustling city – and miss it. My city. Will I ever be able to come back and live in it again?

We head down Duke Street past the womens' prison, then into the first area I really know, George Square, with its array of statues of long dead worthies. The City Chambers stands at one end, built in the days when Glasgow was the Second City of Empire.

I get off the bus near Argyle Street just so as I can walk under the Central Bridge – the 'Hielan Man's Umbrella'. Minutes later I hop onto a number 29; Swing Low Sweet Chariot! The pleasure it gives me is immeasurable. Once again I'm on a tram heading for Maryhill. As it makes its way north-west through the city the sights become more and more familiar until, at last, we shoogle over the multi-track crossing that is St Georges Cross – and start up the Maryhill Road. There are bees as well as butterflies swarming in my stomach now. Nothing at all has changed since I was last here . . . there's the wee Electric Cinema, a relic from the days of silent movies. Further along is the Tabernacle with its cast-iron canopy stretching out over the pavement. In the window the large Bible still lies open, an arrow pointing to today's text as it has done since my childhood – I wonder if it's from 'The Prodigal Son'. Oh Jeez! Now we're passing the Seamore Cinema. How often were Ma and me in there? My eyes smart with tears as I take in that familiar facade. There's the Tramway Vaults with its model of an 1890s horse-drawn tram hanging above the door. The red sandstone Methodist Hall hoves into view. I remember the Sundays my pals and I used to attend – not with any religious fervour, but because they had a 16 mm projector and, after the service, they'd give us a sticky bun and a cup of tea while they ran a couple of fifteen-minute comedy 'shorts' from the 1930s, usually *Our Gang* – a bunch of American kids who got up to all sorts of mischief. My ma would quite happily give me the penny needed for the collection plate, and that was me out from under her feet for the next hour and a half.

I rise and make for the platform, strap-hanging all the way as I find I'm not as adept at keeping my balance as I used to be. Like a sailor, back on board ship after a long spell of shore leave. I get off at the so familiar stop, glancing at the red sign with its black lettering – Trams Stop Here If Required. I stand on the pavement and let the tram pull away, unveiling the other side of the street. Here I am at last. Right in the middle of MY bit of Maryhill Road. This is where Ma did her daily shopping. Everything is exactly as it was. The Blythswood Cinema, Cocozza's Café. MAN! How I've missed them. Can you get arrested for hugging a café? Patting a cinema? I run my eyes along the shops, trying to take them all in at the same time. They're all there . . . McGregor's the fishmonger, Maryhill Road Post Office, Wilfrid's the barber, Colman's Bakery, Craig the butcher. Ma was in and out of them all the time. I will her to step out of one so's I can shout 'Ma!' and give her a wave then dash across the road, kiss her – I wouldn't be shy now – say 'Hiyah, Ma. Ah've been looking for ye. Here, ah'll carry yer bag . . .' My eyes focus again on the shops. Every single thing is here, everything in its place. Except her. She was the main ingredient. It will always be incomplete now.

I decide to go up to Frank and Lottie's first. I hope Sammy's in. It's just a few yards from the tram stop, 375 Maryhill Road, the close next to Kinnaird's the fruiterer. They've got their usual display of produce out front. On the wall hangs the familiar bronze sign: 'D.W. Weatherstone. Dentist. First Floor.' I enter the close, it's as dark and gloomy as ever; still with the familiar damp smell. I go up the spiral stairs two at a time until I reach the second floor. My heart gives a wee leap, I'm standing at Sammy's door again. The clear plastic nameplate with the tartan background and F. Johnston, is still there. I ring the bell; sounds like it always did. C'mon, be in. As usual, Sally, the little black terrier, runs the length of the lobby and starts giving me cheek through the door. Great! I can hear footsteps. I hear Frank's voice shushing Sally. The door opens, he peers at me. 'Hiyah, Frank!' He leans forward for a better look. I don't wait for him to speak 'Have ye gone blin' since ah last seen ye? It's Robert Douglas.' Sally prances round my feet, she knows who it is.

'Oh, for goodness' sake, ah did'nae recognise ye, son. Come away in.' As he speaks, Lottie's getting fed up waiting to know who it is. 'If it's somebody selling something, we're no' wantin' any!'

Frank sighs, looks at me and shakes his head. 'It's Robert Douglas come tae see us,' he calls.

'Fuck me!' she says. Always the apt phrase from Lotisha.

I look at Frank. Just thirty seconds into my visit and already he's about to go into 'Stan Laurel' mode. I've been coming around to Sammy's since I was eleven years old and we became pals. His ma and da have the ability to make me helpless with laughter. They're a double act. Frank is the gentlest of men, a male nurse at Ruchill Hospital. He neither smokes, drinks nor swears. Lottie does the lot! She also does her best to hide a soft heart by being, apparently, short-tempered and snappy. Mostly with Frank. Whenever she starts on him he always goes into what I have christened his 'Stan Laurel mode'. When Lottie gets onto him he becomes more and more bewildered and, to my eyes, looks just like Stan Laurel does when Ollie's getting onto him, and any minute now he'll start scratching his head then burst into tears. I enter the lobby and wait as Frank shuts the door. I breathe in. Proust got it right. I'm almost dizzy from the familiar smell; the fetid dampness from the little lavatory on the left mingles with Lottie's cooking – she's had the frying pan out again. The aroma of old Sam's pipe tobacco – so he's still going strong – the smell of Sally, and Toby the cat. Yeah, I'm in the Johnstons'. I've never knowingly caught a whiff of Chanel No. 5, but you can keep it. Just bottle this for me. As we pass old Sam's room, Frank gives a wee knock and slightly opens the door. 'Robert Douglas has called in tae see us, Faither.'

I hear Sam clear his throat. 'Aye, ah'll be through in a meenit.'

Frank smiles, 'He's just havin' a wee lie doon.'

We enter the kitchen. Lottie's in her chair, she has a Woodbine on as usual. She smiles. 'Hello, tumshie heid,' (turnip head).

'Hello, Lottie.' I give her a kiss.

'Pit the kettle oan,' she says to Frank.

'Ah wiz jist gonny. Gie us a minute, will ye'.

'You're no' quick enough,' she snaps. 'It's action we need aroond here!' She winks at me.

Frank turns on the solitary cold water tap and starts filling the kettle. He turns his head 'As ye can see, nuthin's changed – especially that wumman!'

'Piss up ma kilt!' says Lottie, from behind a cloud of smoke. I could cry. It's so wonderful to be back. Time has stood still. I feel that if I get up now and run round to Doncaster Street, Ma will be in the house.

An hour or so later I reluctantly drag myself away. I won't be able to see Sammy, he's working and won't be home until late. Old Sam, a Boer War veteran, has joined us and I'm gratified at how pleased he is to see me. He's beginning to look a wee bit frail.

We say our goodbyes and I leave after promising not to wait too long before my next visit.

I emerge from the close into a busy Maryhill Road. As I cross the street I'm pleased to see that George Porter is in his usual spot – the corner outside Cocozza's. Since I was an infant George has stood there day in, day out. The Porters live 'one-up' across the street from my close. He has one leg shorter than the other, but won't wear one of those grotesque surgical boots to even things up. Consequently he has a pronounced limp. I don't remember George ever having a job. To pass his time he stands outside Cocozza's, usually with George Gracie and Mr Aitken, two retired men. I suppose George must be pushing sixty. His wife, Eileen, has little charring jobs cleaning toffs' houses, just like Ma used to. They probably have less income than any other family in the street. I remember calling up for their son, Albert, one day and being invited in to wait until he finished his dinner. There was no oilcloth on the table, just newspapers. Eileen drank her tea from a cup with no handle. George sipped his from a jam jar. Yet he is a fairly well-read man and articulate. As I grow up he never seems to alter. In winter and summer, for ever in his old gabardine mac, he stands at Cocozza's corner, often pacing back and forth to ease his legs, sometimes leaning on the green junction box to take the weight off them.

What I've always liked about George Porter is that he is so approachable; he never treated you as a kid and listened to what you had to say. I especially remember how concerned he was when Ma was ill. I suppose the neighbours knew she was dying.

Maryhill Road, 1950s. Looking from Hopehill Road up toward Queens Cross. This is how it always was – full of people, trams and shops. Life!

It was obvious to everybody. Except me. They would also have known my father wasn't in the least interested. During that last year I'd often wander round to Cocozza's and stand talking to George. First thing he'd always ask was, 'How's your mother, Robert?' Not just for the sake of asking. He'd look at me with his brown eyes and I'd see the concern in them.

He's leaning on the junction box as I approach. The old mac is more worn than ever.

'Hello, George.'

He turns, pauses for a second, then gives me a big smile. 'Robert! Well how nice tae see ye, son. Ah've often wondered how you're gettin' on. If ye'd been jist five minutes earlier ye'd have caught George Gracie. He's jist away up the stairs tae make his dinner. Are ye on leave?'

'Naw, ah came out o' the RAF.' I proceed to bring him up to date with what I've been doing since he last saw me. Then I change the subject: 'Where's your other auld pal, Mr Aitkin?'

'Aw, he died, son. Aboot six months ago.' He shakes his head, 'Aye, he's a miss. We're no' the three musketeers anymore. Jist two of us left tae haud up the corner.'

'That's a shame. He was a nice wee man, Mr Aitkin.'

'Aye. But he was a lonely wee sowel since the wife died. He did'nae half miss her.'

'Anywye, ah'm just gonny have a wee wander roond tae the street, George. See if ah can spot anybody ah know.'

'Right, son. Well ah'm pleased ah've seen ye. Ah'll let wan or two know that yer daein' all right.'

I walk the fifty yards along Trossachs Street and left into Doncaster Street. MY street. I stand at the corner, outside Lizzie's shop, and look up the length of it. Again, like the Maryhill Road, nothing's changed – except it's got smaller! I always thought my street was big. Some kids are playing football. I'm surprised wee Mrs Docherty isn't hanging out her first-storey window ready to give them a tongue-lashing if the ball comes anywhere near her. Maybe she's pegged out. I decide I'm going to stand at my close-mouth, I don't care if folk think I'm mad. I just want to stand once more at my close and watch people go by like I used to. Say 'hello' if I know them. I lean against the wall, hands in pockets, and look up and down the street. What a funny feeling it is being here again. I feel slightly embarrassed, but I don't care, it's worth it. Behind me, the close wends its way through to the back court. I take a walk halfway along and look at the three nameplates. Kinsella's is still there. So is Barlow's. I look at 'our' door. A small brass plate says 'Noble'. Don't know that name. I can still see the mark where our combined letter box and nameplate was. My father must have taken it with him. The door used to be dark brown; it's now light brown. I look at it again. Just over a year ago, the day Ma died, I was standing behind that door, breaking my heart, my face pressed into Ma's coat to try and catch the merest scent of her. I walk back out and stand at the entrance again. Across the street, one up, George Porter's wife, Eileen and their two kids, Albert and Eileen, have spotted me. They've pulled the curtain to the side. I give them a wave, they smile back. Probably thinking . . . 'Pour soul!' They eventually get fed up looking and let the curtain go. Now and again someone I know, always an adult, passes by and stops for a wee blether. When I'm on my own I pretend I'm still living in the street. Any minute now Ma will open the door, step out into the close and say, 'Ah, yer there. Here, away and get me a quarter of Brooke Bond Dividend Tea, will ye.'

A familiar figure approaches. It's my cousin, Ada Ure. Ada's four years older than me; she was brought up round the corner in Trossachs Street. She's really my second cousin. Her mother, also Ada, and my ma were full cousins. I'd heard Ada had got married. As she nears the close she recognises me. 'Hello Robert, how are ye? Huv ye been waiting for me?'

What a funny question. 'Eh, no. I wasn't. Why would ah be waiting for ye? Ah would'nae know ye'd be coming this way.'

'Ah thought mibbe somebody had telt ye, Murdie and me have got your auld hoose.'

'Oh! Naw, ah did'nae know that. Hey, that's great, you living in oor auld hoose.'

'Aye, we got it a month or so efter yer faither gave it up. C'mon in and huv a cup o'tea. You'll no' recognise it.'

I walk behind her and stand for a moment while she finds her key. Jeez! This is going to be strange. She opens the door. MY door. As I step into the single-end it's ALMOST the same – yet it isn't. The double windows still look out onto the back court. The recess bed is there, of course; not much you can do with that. Our old pulley still hangs from the ceiling. But everything else has changed. The coal bunker has been taken out. So has the range – no more black-leading and polishing steels – a modern tiled grate with a fitted gas fire stands in its place. The door of the press (larder) has been removed, a couple of the lower shelves taken away, and a gas cooker stands in the space. The decoration is quite different, a lot lighter. I know I'm in my house, yet somehow I'm not.

As Ada busies herself making a pot of tea, I sit and look around. My mind's a whirlpool of memories. Snapshots. The happy times spent in here when it was just Ma and me. The rows, shouting and bawling, violence, when that wee bastard was drunk – and when he was sober. The all too brief fun when Uncle George was on leave and would bring his pals, male and female, back from the pub to play cards. Jeez, I wish I knew where he was. The countless evenings when Ma and me would sit with the wireless on, having a good laugh at *ITMA, Ray's a Laugh, Take It From Here*, or listening to a play on *Saturday Night Theatre* and *The Man In Black*. She loved the dance bands, Geraldo, Henry Hall and Edmundo Ros. I wonder if these stone walls have absorbed it all and someday, way in the future, they'll invent a machine . . .

'Would ye like a sandwich, tae?'

'Ah wouldn't mind, thanks. Ah've got at least a two-hour bus journey tae get back oot tae where ah'm living.'

Yet again the minutes go twice as fast as they should. How come, if you're waiting at the dentist's or the doctor's, time goes as slow as can be? I have a good blether with Ada and, when he comes in from work, meet Murdie, her postman husband. He's a nice, stockily built lad with curly hair; a typical Glasgow fella with a good sense of humour, always poking gentle fun at Ada. Her usual reaction is . . . 'Aye, that'll be right!' Or she hits him a futile punch on the shoulder. Sometimes both. It must be nice to be married. I wonder if I'll ever get wed?

All too soon I have to take a tram down the city and catch a bus to Bathgate. I've really enjoyed my day back in Glasgow. Yet it has left me sad. Everything is exactly as it was, except for Ma. It's now fifteen months, but I still miss her so much. How I wish I had an older brother or sister to share that loss. Today has reminded me, yet again, that when she died I lost everything. I'm away from Glasgow and losing touch with my two pals. We're rapidly growing up – and apart. I haven't even had time to see if John Purden is around.

I've got a lot of pleasure from my run into the city and I'll do it again, soon. Yet I know that every time I visit there will be that sadness. That's what I am now. A visitor. I don't belong to Glasgow anymore.

The Deep

I had already put my name forward to go down the pit when I was of age. When I turn seventeen and a half I receive a letter informing me I'm to attend the NCB school at Sauchie, near Alloa, for the mandatory period of 'underground training'.

It's an August day in 1956. Carrying a suitcase borrowed from Jim, I report at the gate of the training centre. It's a former army camp, last used by Polish troops, and the accommodation and classrooms consist of the ubiquitous Nissen Huts of Second World War fame. By early afternoon, the former barrack room I'm allocated to has received its quota of twenty trainees. In many ways it's reminiscent of my first few hours in the RAF – except I'm happy to be here. At regular intervals guys carrying suitcases make their entrance, nod greetings to those already in residence, then find themselves a vacant bed-space. Very quickly we all relax and gradually begin to get to know one another. Most of us are in our late teens, but there are a few in their twenties and thirties who've left less well-paid jobs to join the Coal Board.

Within a short space of time this group of strangers begins to sort itself into types . . . The Joker; the Quiet One; the Know-all; the Blether. I wonder how I'll be classified? They come from a variety of towns and villages in the central Scotland 'coal belt'. We soon settle down to being a fairly amicable group. After all, it's only for a month.

I discover that some of the lads my age have decided to become miners for just one reason – to avoid having to do their two years in the forces. I've already made my mind up that when I register for National Service, I'll tell the authorities I DON'T wish to claim deferment because I'm working underground. There is such a shortage of miners that, provided I stay working underground, I wouldn't be required to go into the forces. Perversely, I'm more and more determined that I will do my two years. I knew I hadn't done myself justice in the Boys' Service, but that was for a good reason. It still rankles with me when I recall the contemptuous looks Corporal Graham and others regularly gave me when I was working my ticket, and my frustration at not being able to explain how I came to join in the first place – and why I wanted out.

This first afternoon at Sauchie we're issued with a blue crew neck jersey with the embroidered badge of the training school on it. No doubt it's meant to make us feel part of a team. I'm extra pleased about it as it's better than the worn-out jersey I already own. After the course is finished we can keep it. It'll be fairly easy to unpick the stitches and remove the badge.

The next month proves to be a doddle. The NCB feed and water us while we train, as well as paying our wages. Riches indeed! This first week we attend daily classes on the history of mining, first aid, and mining techniques. From the second week onward we're regularly taken by coach the few miles to Muircockhall Pit, near Dunfermline. The Training Pit. This is an old 'worked-out' mine and ideal for introducing new recruits to the experience of being underground. I find I have no problems being down below. I also become quite interested in seeing how the theory we've been taught in class has been carried out in practice . . . the way the coal face advances on a broad front, and the roof is systematically allowed to collapse behind it – except for the 'roads' (tunnels) which are shored up with girders and give access to the ever-receding face. The controlled use of explosives down a pit. The methods used to extract the coal, from coal-cutting machines to picks and shovels – then the job of transporting this 'black gold' from face to surface and on to the markets, be they coal merchants or power stations.

There is another bonus to being at Sauchie. A few of my fellow trainees like dancing and soon discover there are a few dances held within striking distance. Not least of them the Sauchie Miners' Welfare on a Monday night. For some time now, especially when I hear a good record on the radio, my feet have been itching. Having not yet acquired a pal in Blackburn, I haven't quite worked up the courage to go on my own. This month at the training school is my chance, and I quite happily tag along with the bunch a couple of nights a week. Ma would be pleased. She always wanted me to go to the dancing and enjoy it as much as she did. Although my dancing won't have improved since my first faltering attempt at Glasgow's Dennistoun Palais two years earlier, I feel that my extra couple of years will have given me the confidence to ask a girl to dance. I also discover there seems to be some mysterious correlation between intending to go to the dancing and acne. Without fail, if I've decided to go dancing on a Saturday night, on the Friday one or two boil-like entities will erupt on my face. How do they know? I'm never able to resist trying to improve the situation by squeezing them. Result? They won't burst. Instead they become irritated, growing larger and redder as I watch. Often, near to tears, I decide not to go out. An hour before dance-time I usually change my mind and there then ensues a frantic attempt at camouflage using one of the flesh-coloured, patent acne creams which I always have in stock. They never really work. How can you hide a lump? It's also around this time I make the decision that when I die, and supposedly appear in front of God on Judgement Day, before He can open his mouth I'm going to say, 'Why did you have to give me acne?'

Another constant when I'm going anywhere special is the increase in the amount of cuts when I'm shaving. At any given time I have plooks on their way down, plooks in their prime, and new plooks on their way up to replace the first two categories. When I shave in preparation for going somewhere special, the number of nicks increases dramatically. These seem to have lost the ability to clot, and bleed profusely for long periods. It's a regular occurrence for me to be standing looking at myself in the bathroom mirror with four or five little Japanese flags sticking to my face. Whenever I think the bleeding's stopped, I find these pieces of toilet tissue are now welded to my chin. Removing them always starts the bleeding again. I now have to make another decision – will I wait until the bleeding finally stops and then do my 'make-up', in which case I'll probably arrive in time for the last dance. Or should I get there early with the pieces of toilet tissue in situ – and tell them I'm a convert to Shinto and I'm celebrating the Emperor's birthday?

My life is dominated by acne bastarding vulgaris. Lots of guys get spots. I had to get them in spades. I hate being a teenager. With all the things that have happened to me this past couple of years I'm beginning to feel that when there are good things handed out in life, I'm always near the back of the queue. If it's barrow loads of shit – I'm well up front. If it meant getting rid of my acne, I'd quite happily give up ten years of my life and jump from seventeen to twenty-seven.

During my month at Sauchie I don't bother coming home at weekends. I average two nights a week at the local dances and find I take to it like the proverbial duck to water. Ma would be delighted. I also realise it's the ideal way to meet girls. I'm becoming increasingly interested in the lassies and would love to get myself a 'steady'. By the time my stint at the training school is over I've not only acquired some of the skills needed to become a miner, but my dancing apprenticeship is finally underway and I've made my mind up to try and get myself a girlfriend. Three cheers for Sauchie!

*　　*　　*

I'm back to Blackburn and Uncle Jim's just a few weeks when I get a letter informing me I'll be putting the training to use and going underground. The screens have been an easy enough job, but I'll be pleased to get away from the incessant noise. It also means I'll be down the pit by the time winter arrives. The ramshackle building which houses the screens is draughty and can be a cold place for an eight-hour shift, especially in January or February. 'You'll be a lot warmer doon the pit,' Jim assures me. I hope he's right.

Since coming back from my training I haven't yet ventured to the dancing. I just don't want to go on my own. Whenever I hear a good swing record on the radio, especially the stuff from the forties that Ma liked, Artie Shaw's 'Begin the Beguine' or Tommy Dorsey's 'Sunny Side of the Street', I always find my feet are tapping. I'm raring to go. I just wish I could find a pal in Blackburn who likes going to the dancing.

The great day comes. I'm going down the pit for the first time. By good luck, Jim's on day shift, so he'll keep me right – where to go, what to do. Self-consciously I follow him as we walk into the baths and head for the lamp cabin. I'm given a brass numbered tally – and immediately hand it back to the attendant in exchange for a lamp which is attached by a black, rubberised cable to its heavy battery. From now on, if that tally is hanging up that means my lamp is 'out' and I'm down the pit. I loop my leather trouser belt through the metal clips on the battery and Jim moves it round so it hangs over my left buttock. 'Now, let's get the lamp ontae yer helmet.' He slides the torch-like lamp into the holder on the front of the lightweight, black helmet, then leads the cable through its fitted clips so it runs down my back to the battery. He gives me a smile. 'Right, sir. That's you ready.' I sometimes feel very close to Jim. Ma would be pleased at the way he looks after me.

*   *   *

We make our way across the yard and on up the incline to the large red-brick building over which Polkemmet's twin winding gears stand sentinel. For almost a year now I've watched these large wheels turn swiftly and silently, first one way then the other, as at the beginning and end of each new shift one of them lowers white men down the shaft, and eight hours later disgorges the chorus of the Black and White Minstrel Show! The other winding gear continually brings up coal for my mates and me to pick clean. I'm finished with that laddie's job. I'm a miner now.

We stand in the queue waiting our turn to board the cage. I can feel butterflies stir as, with much clanging of metal gates and safety rails, the double-deck cage appears at regular intervals and unloads another gang of Al Jolson look-alikes. It's then filled up with an equal number of day shift men. As the different shifts pass one another there are all sorts of greetings and comments, from the civil to the ribald . . .

'Mind and give it a good wash if yer thinkin' o' getting yer leg ower this morning, Alec.'

'Aye, dinnae worry,' says Alec, ''cos it's your missis ah'll be slippin' a length tae!' There's a roar of laughter from those around.

A man in front holds out his hand to stop one of the 'loused' (finished) men. 'Was it any better doon therr last night, Erchie?'

'Naw, jist the same. It's a bloody wet face, that yin. We were pumping non-stop the whole shift.' I listen intently to these half-understood, very masculine conversations. I have a strong feeling I'm about to enter a man's world. Jim interrupts my thoughts by giving me a nudge.

'Listen tae these two auld lads when they pass yin another,' he whispers. 'This is Windy Willie and Terrible Tam,' he motions for me to look to my front. I watch as an elderly man makes his way from the cage. He is last off. As he approaches, he catches sight of another veteran, waiting in the queue . . .

'It's windy, Willie,' the first man says, as he passes the second.

'Aye, it's terrible, Tam,' acknowledges his friend.

A few of the men waiting for the cage shake their heads and give indulgent smiles. Jim leans nearer to my ear. 'That's Windy Willie and Terrible Tam. Willie's constant day shift and Tam's permanent night shift. They pass each other every morning that God sends, winter and summer, rain, hail or shine, and that's aw' they ever say. Ah don't think they know they dae it.' As he speaks, the cage suddenly rises into view. The butterflies in my stomach are doing overtime. I'll be going down with this batch. With some more clangs and rattles, the overseer clears the way. Trying not to slip or trip on the rails underfoot, while making sure I don't lose sight of Jim, I make my way onto the large cage along with seventeen or eighteen other men. Underneath us the same number are making their way onto the bottom deck. I can feel the cage sway with all this weight and movement. Jeez, I hope the cable's in good nick. The men around me are having casual conversations about kids, football, gardening. Between their heads and shoulders I can see and hear the cage being closed. There's a last glimpse of daylight. A bell rings. Oh my Gawwwwd! We drop, literally, like a stone. My stomach moves up into my chest. For a moment I feel lighter as the cage seems to drop faster than I do and I haven't caught up with it yet. I'd thought it would be a bit like the lift in Lewis's department store in Argyle Street. I turn my head; Jim and his pal George McAdam are looking at me, smiling.

'Fuck me! Ye might huv telt me.'

The two of them laugh. 'It fairly draps, disn't it?' says Jim.

I put on a brave smile. My stomach has just about returned to its rightful place.

'Och, it would have spoilt the fun,' says George.

We continue to drop, accelerating all the while.

'How deep is it?'

'Three hundred fathoms.' I do a quick sum. Jeez, that's 1800 feet!

A few men had switched on their lamps as we'd boarded. I

look through the metal framework that makes up the cage. The sides of the shaft whizz by, giving a fast-moving kaleidoscope of steel runners, slats of wood, girders, patches of concrete and, occasionally, the stone and earth through which this vertical tunnel has been dug. The further we fall, the more I begin to imagine, in my mind's eye, a picture of this heavy, double-decker cage with nearly forty men aboard, hurtling deeper and deeper into the earth on an ever-increasing length of slim cable. At last we begin to slow, then come gently to a stop. All the clanging is done in reverse, the gate opened, and we troop out into the pit-bottom. A few stragglers from the night shift brush past us and board the cage. The warning bell rings and I just catch sight of their legs as they're whisked up and out of sight on their way back to the real world far above. Will I ever see it again?

I look around me. I'm in the hall of a medieval castle! The pit-bottom, being a permanent fixture from which various tunnels have been built at different times is a large cavernous area whose walls, ceiling and buttresses are all a dirty white-painted brick. There's nothing to show we are deep underground, no stone, earth or girders to be seen. Electric lights burn brightly. This isn't at all what I expected. Those who work here have their lamps switched off and are well wrapped up. Bunnets, knotted scarves and gloves are the norm. Within a few minutes I find out why. It's cold. The twin shafts at Polkemmet are the most important parts of the ventilation system. Cold air is being drawn down this shaft from the surface, giving a constant, chilly draught.

'Ah thought you said it was warm doon the pit?'

Jim looks at me. 'No' at the pit-bottom, pal. Once your away fae here in yin o' the sections you'll see the difference.' He goes over and has a word with one of the oversmen. The two of them look at me.

'Robert Douglas, son?'

'Aye.' I give him the standard blush. He'll be thinking, never seen anybody in ma life wi' plooks like that!

Pushing tubs toward the cage at the pit bottom.

'Right, you'll be working doon the Main Sooth,' he looks around. 'TOMMY! This lad's for the Main Sooth, show him the way, will ye. Andy Smart knows he's coming.'

As they speak, I make a mental note to remember to say 'sooth' instead of south. I find it interesting how, just 25 miles from Glasgow, not only is the accent quite different but many of the words are pronounced in their own way. In Glasgow we just say 'south'.

Tommy and I set off down one of the roads towards the section. Once away from the pit-bottom the mine then becomes what I'd expected – long tunnels with curved girders every couple of feet, the space between them, especially above my head, spanned by thick battens of wood. The further in we travel, the more irregular and higgledy-piggledy becomes the girders and wood packing. Within the first hundred yards I bang my head two or three times; the helmet doesn't give much protection. Tommy laughs, 'You'll get used tae it. You'll soon learn tae walk half-bent AND keep an eye open fur anything sticking doon fae the roof.'

'Ah hope yer right. How far is it intae the section?'

'Nearly a mile and a half.'

'Jeez! That's a long walk every day – when yer bent in half!'

'Aye, and it's a longer walk at the end o' a shift.'

The deeper in we go, now and again we come across places where the top arch – where two curved girders meet and are bolted together – has buckled downward because of tremendous pressure from above. In some places large rocks are trying to force their way between girders. I continue to bang my head with painful frequency, usually when I'm talking to Tommy and forget where I am. It often stops me in my tracks, driving my head into my shoulders, sometimes dislodging my helmet and lamp. 'Oohyah! Ah'll be fuckin' punch drunk by the time we get tae the Main Sou . . . Sooth.'

As we progress along the road, our lamps lighting the path, Tommy and I blether away to one another. He's in his late twenties, from Whitburn, married with two kids. Now and again my mind strays and my vivid imagination presents me with a picture as seen from the surface, of our two isolated figures hundreds of feet underground, walking along a narrow tunnel with just the dancing beams of our lamps for comfort. BANG! 'Jesus wept!' This dramatic picture vanishes as a bent girder stops me in my tracks. 'These buggerin' helmets don't gie ye much protection, dae they?'

Tommy smiles in sympathy – or is he trying not to laugh? 'You'll learn.'

As Jim forecast, the further we've travelled away from the pit-bottom the warmer it's become. Now and again we have to step into a safety manhole, gouged out the side of the wall, as trains of four or five 'hutches' (tubs) full of coal trundle past us on their way to the cage. The front hutch is clipped onto a moving cable which runs between the rails, the other hutches coupled onto one another behind it. As we come nearer to the workings, the rails stop. The coal is being carried from the face by a series of conveyor belts to a loading point, where the rails start, and it can spill off the end of the belt into the hutches.

At last we near the face and Tommy hands me over to the man in charge, Andy Smart, who is a *Deputy* and shotfirer. A small, grey-headed man with no time for small talk, Andy looks to me as if he must be around sixty. He always seems to be busy – and expects everybody else to be too. As well as being in charge of the men in the section, he's also responsible for placing the gelignite and detonators in the holes drilled in the coal face after the coal-cutting machine has been along to rip out the bottom of the face. With that channel cut, the coal has somewhere to fall when it is blown. After clearing the area and giving warning, he'll fire his shots. When the dust and smoke has settled, face workers like Jim go back in, make sure the roof has settled, then start shovelling the coal brought down onto the first of the conveyor belts to begin its journey via hutches, cage, screens and railway wagons to the market-place.

As I'm too young to work in the face, or even go into it until I'm 18 *and* 'face-trained', I'm allocated to one of the small teams responsible for keeping the hutches running, conveyor belts clear and roadways clean. If we find the roof forcing its way down between girders, or bending them, we let Andy know and two or three 'brushers' will be sent for. They will carefully bring down the stone that's causing the trouble then break off (known as 'brushing') any other loose material. All badly bent girders will be replaced and the space between them spanned with wood.

Once more I find I get on well with my new workmates. The majority, like me, are waiting until they turn eighteen and are old enough to move on to more adult, better paid jobs. Just as there are surface workers who've no intention of going down the pit, there are also underground workers with no inclination to work in the more dangerous face. Me? I'm daft enough to work anywhere – if the money's good.

* * *

I start off on the three-shift system – day shift: six a.m. to two p.m.; back shift: two p.m. to ten p.m.; and night shift: ten p.m. to six a.m. Except for day shift, the other two give little time for a social life. Even days don't give that much scope. With a start time of six a.m. I have to rise just after five to give myself time to get ready, have breakfast and catch the pit bus. If I'm out in the evening and I'm late back, which I usually am even if I just go to the cinema, it means I'm not getting enough sleep. At seventeen, one thing I do need is my bed. Lots of it! After another bleary-eyed morning I always promise myself I'll have an early night. I rarely do. There will usually be something on TV I can't resist staying up to watch. On the rare occasion I do go to bed before ten it's usually because I'm reading a good book and can't wait to get back to it. I then lie quite happily, totally absorbed, until nearly midnight. Reluctantly I'll put the book down and the light out, then wake up with Jim shaking me . . . 'C'mon, sir. Are you gonny get yerself oot o' that bed?'

'Mmmmm!' I lie there, bone-tired.

Since my return from Sauchie I haven't yet plucked up enough courage to go to the dancing on my own. Reading and the cinema are still my two great pleasures. Since childhood I've devoured the *Dandy* and *Beano*, graduated to the *Hotspur*, *Rover*, *Wizard* and *Adventure* – the 'boys' papers'. At age eleven I'd read my first 'real' book, *A Child of the Jago*. It had been heavy going, but I'd finished it. Some three years before that, I'd joined the children's section of the Woodside Library down in St George's Road. There I'd cut my teeth on the adventures of Arthur Ransome's *Swallows and Amazons* and other children's books. Since I no longer have my father regularly snatching a book or comic out of my hands with his usual, 'Every time ah see you you've got yer nose stuck in a fuckin' book!' my pleasure in the written word has increased. I can, and regularly do, lose myself in a book. As I read, it all unfolds in my imagination as though I were watching a film; the characters have faces, I can see their surroundings. While I turn the pages, missing Ma, having acne, living in digs – all are banished temporarily as I identify with the hero or heroine. Thank goodness paperbacks have really caught on these last few years, as publishers like Pan and Corgi have flooded the market with cheap editions of popular books. I like to browse the shelves and read the 'blurb' on the back covers to see if they'll interest me. I also look at the front covers. If the critics of newspapers or magazines say good things about it, that's usually enough for me to buy a book. I especially love the spate of wartime memoirs that have come out during the last ten years or so – fighter pilots, commandos and, best of all as far as I'm concerned, the stories of those POWs who continually tried to escape from German camps and make their way, with forged papers, across occupied Europe to freedom. These are far better than fiction. I can't get enough of them. In two or three sittings I've devoured epics such as *The Colditz Story* and *The Wooden Horse*. I literally can't put them down, reading them on the pit bus, at meal breaks and in between programmes on TV. A close second to 'escape' stories are the tales of secret agents. Men and women who parachuted into enemy territory to organise resistance groups. I race through these too, then I'm so disappointed when I read the last page and reluctantly have to close the covers. Stories of bravery and comradeship, whether on page or screen, regularly move me to tears.

It isn't too long until my reading and cinema-going are at last joined by another absorbing pastime – or two. 'Going to the Dancing' and 'Chasing the Girls!'

New Digs

'Robert, there's something ah want tae talk tae ye aboot.' My Uncle Jim looks a bit embarrassed. I know right away what it'll be, so I try to make it easy for him – and Jenny.

'Is it time ah was looking for new digs?' I smile, hoping he'll see it isn't a problem.

'It is, actually. If ye would'nae mind. The reason is, Jenny's pregnant again.'

'Oh, that's great! Look, it's nae bother. The arrangement was supposed tae be that ah'd stay with ye until ah got a job, then ah'd look for digs. It's been nearly a year. Longer than ah expected. Anyway, it's been a lot of extra work for Jenny, so ah'll just ask around and see what digs are going nearby.' I smile again. 'It's your ain fault ah'm still here, you've made me too comfortable.'

'Are ye sure it'll be okay?' He looks really serious.

I decide to gee him up. 'Well, it isn't really, ah'd rather carry on staying here, thanks very much!'

He laughs. 'Yah bugger o' hell, ye.'

I can tell it's been difficult for him to bring it up. After all, I'm his only sister's son. So, I'll have to start looking for digs. Trouble is, I don't know that many folk. Who can I ask?

As I travel back and forth to Bathgate, usually when I'm going to the pictures, there's a Blackburn lad often catches the same bus. He always gives me a nod, and as time goes on sometimes sits beside me and we have a blether. He works at Bathgate Foundry. Our conversations are always short, just the fifteen minutes it takes the bus to make the trip. After a while it has got to the stage where he'll sit next to me and we carry on the conversation from last time. We don't, as yet, know each other's names. Shorter than me, slim, dark haired and sharp featured, he tends to speak quite fast and I often have trouble understanding his strong, West Lothian dialect. I assume he finds me of interest simply because I'm a Glaswegian. In 1956 we're thin on the ground out here. I decide to ask him, next time I see him, if he knows anyone who takes in lodgers . . .

'Ah'm gonny have tae find maself new digs, it's getting a bit crowded at ma uncle's place. Dae ye know anybody who takes in lodgers in Blackbu . . .' I don't get the chance to finish.

'Ye can move intae oor hoose if ye want!'

'Had ye no' better ask yer parents first?'

'Och, it'll be aw'right. Anywye, get aff the bus wi' me and have a walk up tae the hoose and meet Auld Jock, and see whit ye think. It'll be okay.'

'Who's Auld Jock?'

'That's ma faither. We live in Riddochill Road. It's no' the tidiest hoose, mind, but the grub's good.' He smiles, his dark eyes dancing.

'What about yer mother? She might huv something tae say about it.'

'She's no' ma mother, she's ma stepmother. Och, Lily will be aw'right.'

I have another thought. 'Just in case ah dae finish up at your place – it might be a good idea if we knew each other's names! Ah'm Robert Douglas.'

He looks at me. 'You're right, we don't. Ah'm Chic Wright.' He holds out his hand. 'Hello.' We shake. 'Hello,' I say. We both give embarrassed laughs.

We get off the bus together and saunter up Riddochill Road. 'How auld are ye, Chic?'

'Eighteen. Whit aboot you?'

'Seventeen.'

As we amble along I tell him why I'm having to find new digs, then a little of how I come to be in West Lothian. He nudges me with his shoulder. 'This is us.'

We walk up the path toward a semi-detached, red brick council house. All the lights, upstairs and down, are blazing. The front door, which is on the side of the house, is already ajar. Chic pushes it fully open and we enter. Gene Vincent is going full blast with 'Be Bop a Lula' on the radiogram, four or five adults and a couple of bairns are spread around the downstairs rooms and I think there are more upstairs. My initial impression is that you're not allowed to talk to folk in the same room – you can only shout to those those in adjoining ones. Low volume conversations are apparently forbidden. As we pass the kitchen I glance in. An older, heavily-built woman stops what she's doing and looks at me quizzically. Chic speaks loudly to her

'This is ma pal, Robert. He might be coming tae lodge wi' us. He's looking for digs. Will that be aw'right?' I get the impression she maybe didn't catch all of that. She smiles and nods.

'Aye, aye.' This is said in the sort of resonant way that some deaf people speak.

As we walk along the lobby the smell is just like Sammy's house back in Maryhill; a mixture of cooking and the mustiness of a lived-in house that's excused too much cleaning. I like it. I always like houses like this.

I'm ushered into the presence of Auld Jock. He holds court from a heavy, dark brown armchair by the fireside. Short, round and with the darting eyes of his son, he reminds me of a wee fat owl. He hasn't bothered to put his dentures in; they're on standby on the mantlepiece. At regular intervals his tongue flicks along his lips. As we enter the living room we've interrupted him in the middle of attempting to set a new world record – for smoking a Woodbine down to the shortest dowt. 'Whaes this?' He looks at Chic.

'This is ma pal, Robert . . .' Chic pauses. . . . 'It's Douglas, in't it?' Auld Jock's tongue does a couple of circuits. 'Sombloo . . . pal . . . know'sname, eh?' This is said so rapidly I barely get the gist of it; compared with his father, Chic has an impediment. I'm also surprised Chic hasn't mentioned his da is Polish!

'He's looking fur digs, Faither. We can put him up, kint we?'

'Aye, huvty . . . sh'bed . . . you.' Auld Jock pauses for a moment while he goes for the record. Holding the miniscule dowt between thumb and index finger, he places all three between his lips and actually manages to extract a final puff from the unseen remains of the Woodbine – burning the tips of his fingers in the process. 'Yah buggah!' He goes through the motions of throwing what's left of it into the fire. There's nothing to be seen.

'You'll huv tae share a bed wi' me. That aw'right?'

'Aye, nae bother. As long as you're no' wantin' a goodnight kiss.'

Chic goes all prissy. 'You're safe enough, ah belong tae another. When dae ye want tae move in?'

'Whenever ye like. Ah hav'nae got much stuff tae bring.'

'Might as well move in the night if ye want.'

I give it a moment's thought. 'Aye, why not. Ah'll go hame tae my Uncle Jim's, huv ma dinner, then bring ma stuff roon'.'

While we speak, the rest of the family plus visitors – and possibly one or two passers-by, come into the living room to see what's going on. Chic does the introductions. 'This is ma aulder brother, Robert.' Robert is in his late twenties, strongly-built and tanned. Not a holiday tan. 'He works on a farm. He dis'nae live here – but ye'd never know it!' Robert throws a gentle punch, Chic dodges it. 'This is his wife, Jean.' I say my 'Hello's. A young man, perhaps a year or two older than Chic, enters the room. Dressed in a suit and tie, he looks out of place. 'This is Eddie, Lily's son. He lives here as well.' Chic points: 'The bairns are Robert's. They're a nuisance like their faither!' This time the punch connects. Chic turns to his father, 'How much are ye gonny take for dig money, Da?'

Auld Jock's tongue does a couple of laps. 'Three . . . 'ound-sawee . . . 'right?'

Chic turns his head. 'Three pounds a week. That okay?'

'Aye, fine.' I've also realised, by carefully listening to Auld Jock's last utterance, that I'm mistaken in thinking he's Polish. He hails from well to the west of there. West Lothian. 'Right, ah'll away and get ma dinner and see ye in aboot an hour or so.'

The leave-taking at Jim's is fairly low-key. They're surprised at how quickly I've got fixed up, and the speed at which I'm moving out.

'Well, ah might as well. They're quite happy for me tae move in right away. Anywye, it's no' as if ah'm going very far. Ah'll still be coming roon' for a blether, and ah'll be seeing you regularly on the pit bus, Jim.'

'Och, aye.' I can tell, that all things being equal, Jim would have preferred me to stay. But with the new baby coming it'll be all for the best. I finish my dinner, clean my teeth, then gather my few belongings together. I actually need TWO carrier bags this time. Things are certainly looking up.

Dancing the Night Away

It doesn't take long to settle into Chic's. Thirty seconds, tops! I find it to be the most harum-scarum house. Untidiness is the order of the day, but the important thing is I fit in straight away. And feel welcome. Chic and I soon become great pals and I find him to be an easy-going and constantly good-natured lad. Nothing bothers him. We usually come in from work, have our dinner, then head out somewhere. Anywhere. Not that there's that much to choose from; one of Bathgate's two cinemas, The Regal or The Pavilion, or just sitting in the only café playing rock'n'roll records on the jukebox. Eventually, having had enough excitement for one day, we head back to Blackburn. Always, as the day ends, we lie side by side in the dark blethering away to one another. Chic smokes and is having a last cigarette as we talk. The end of the fag glows brightly as he takes a draw; the sound of the TV drifts up from the living room as Auld Jock sits watching it until, as Chic puts it, 'the last wee dot fades from the screen' when the station closes down around midnight. I begin to feel sleepy, my eyelids heavy. 'Well, ah'm ready for some shut-eye, Chic.'

'Aye, me tae.' He takes a long, last draw then reaches his hand up over the headboard and lets the fag end, still lit, drop onto the linoleum. A few sparks fly up, then it burns itself out amongst the others, leaving another brown mark on the lino. I smile to myself in the dark as I drift off. Never seen a house like it.

I've been living here about three weeks when I find out that Auld Jock actually has a job.

'Ah did'nae know yer faither worked.'

Chic smiles. 'He tries not tae. But occasionally he's forced tae go intae The Lady (Whitrigg Colliery) tae dae 'miner impressions' for a week or two. He's usually oan the sick. He's got a great doacter. Well, ah say 'doacter', he's mair like a bookie – always writing lines. Sick lines!'

We've come into the house in time to catch Auld Jock making reluctant preparations for his imminent return to work. A loose roll-up hangs from his mouth as he sits on the front edge of his chair, directing operations. 'LILY! Huvloo . . . see . . . boots'right.' Fag ash drifts down and forms a snowy mantle on his trousers and the arms of the chair. He looks up as we enter the room '. . . 'rightboys?' Enter Lily, stage right, holding a pair of dusty, almost new boots. 'They're here.'

Auld Jock gives them a dirty look. 'Gonny . . . bit . . . clea . . . eh?' Lily looks at us, shakes her head and the loose curlers that hang from it in resignation, then silently retreats to the kitchen.

Minutes later the sound of brushing, punctuated by the occasional 'cling-ting' as the Cherry Blossom tin falls on the floor, drifts through to the living room.

'Huving tae turn oot for a spell of forced labour, Faither?'

'Fukabassards!' exclaims Auld Jock. He looks beseechingly at me. 'M . . . back . . . n'standit. Coo . . . deatho'me!'

As Chic and I leave the room, I enquire, 'Whit did yer faither say there, Chic?'

'Fucked if ah know!'

It's 1956 and rock'n'roll is King. Bill Haley and the Comets, Little Richard and Elvis blast out from the radio constantly. My feet are raring to go. Chic supplies the push I need . . .

'Dae ye go tae the dancin', Robert?'

'No' regularly. But ah'd like tae.'

'There's a dance oan every Friday night in Blackburn Welfare.

It's pretty good. Trouble is, it's a wee hall and dis'nae half get stowed oot. Fancy going?'

'Aye, ah'm game.'

We enter the small bar of The Turf at Blackburn Cross preparatory to making our entrance at the Miners' Welfare, which lies a hundred yards up the Bathgate Road.

'Whit are ye gonny huv?' Chic nonchalantly extracts a ten bob note from his wallet.

'Eh, ah don't really drink.' I'm already feeling very daring at being in a pub and me not yet eighteen. 'Whit would ye recommend?'

'Have a sweet stout. They're quite good.'

A bottle of Sweetheart Stout and a half pint glass are placed in front of me. I pour it at the wrong angle and soon hold a glass of brown froth. Most of the stout is still in the bottle.

'Fuck me!' says Chic. 'Here, ah'll show ye. Try and get some o' that froth oot the glass. I hold it to my lips and suck. Very little comes out. I'm no more successful with my tongue. 'Ah could dae wi' a spoon.'

'Ask for yin and ah'm oot o' here!' We dissolve into laughter. He takes the bottle and glass and shows me how it should be poured. He looks at his watch. 'We'd better no' be long. By eight o'clock they'll be stopping folk gettin' in.'

'Okay.' I buy another round, which we quickly see off, then, feeling pleasantly light-headed, I accompany him to The Welfare. The sound of music drifts out into the street as we approach. The retired miner on the door takes our half-crowns.

'Ah! It's yerself, Chic. How's Auld Jock?'

'No' very weel. He starts back oan Monday.'

'Poor sowel!'

We enter the crammed hall. I feel a little frisson of excitement. All I can see are a mass of bobbing heads. A pall of blue smoke has settled just below the low ceiling. The seven or eight members of the band fill the small stage. They're making a very good job of playing 'In a Persian Market Place' to a rock'n'roll beat. They all wear the same light gray, double-breasted jackets with black slacks. The leader steps up to the mike and begins to sing. He is short, stocky and fair haired and I really like his voice. Very much along the lines of Bill Haley. I turn to Chic. 'Hey! What a great band, and I like the singer.'

'Aye. That's Wee Sanny.'

'Whit dae they call the band?'

'Wee Sanny's Band' says Chic, deadpan.

'Seriously?'

'Aye.'

The girls stand along one side, the boys along the other. This leaves limited space in the middle. Most couples dance very close, one arm round each other, the other held ramrod straight down their sides, hands clasped. This is called 'doing a moonie' (Moon Dancing). The four corners of the dancing area have become the place where the rock'n'rollers try to find some room to jive. The hall is crowded, smoky and warm. Just how it should be!

I haven't been dancing – or held a girl close – since I did my training at Sauchie a few months back. Still under the powerful influence of my two sweet stouts, I decide to waste no time in getting up. After the statutory three numbers from the band, which makes up a round, the dance floor clears. Wee Sanny consults with his boys for a couple of minutes, no doubt to give them a 'blaw' (a break), then announces the next dance: a quickstep. My speciality! I've already got my eye on who I want to dance with; a thin gamine type wearing a broad-striped polo neck, whose hair is styled in a short urchin cut. It's a pity she's not wearing a beret – then I could request 'Maestro' Sanny to strike up an Apache Dance – and throw Ma'mselle aw' ower the Miners' Welfare. Sometimes my imagination fair runs away wi' me!

When the band goes into the next number there's an immediate surge by the male population. Rather slow off the mark, I have to swim through a tide of criss-crossing guys, often being swept in the wrong direction. Suddenly I spot that the object of my desire has been snapped up. I divert slightly and head for a quickly chosen substitute. Just four feet from her I'm cut up by a guy who comes out of nowhere and beats me to her. Jeez! It's dog eat dog in here. Wee Sanny and his troubadors are now well into the number and most people are dancing. Me and another two or three no-hopers are stranded on the female side. The UNdanced females – Wallflowers United – are watching us with, I suspect, a certain amount of glee. I look at the diminished choice of girls. In a last ditch attempt to save myself the humiliating walk back to the men's side, I approach someone who, without being unkind, could definitely be listed under 'plain'. I have the good grace to entertain the passing thought that this is a bit rich coming from the Acne King of Central Scotland!

'Would ye like tae dance?'

Not being in great demand, she has no doubt had time to watch my failed attempts to reach first and second choices. It's possible she hasn't had a spin so far tonight – but she's still not ready to be considered as a last resort.

'Naw thanks.'

Aw', man! Ah'm doomed. The men's side looks awful far away. Because of the dancers I'll have to go the long way round. I set off on The March of Shame.

'Whit happened therr?' Chic joins me, face flushed after dancing with Jean, his 'getting to be steady' girlfriend.

'Ah wiz too slow.'

'You've got to be quick off yer mark in here. When ye think the band's aboot tae strike up, if ye see three or four guys setting off – you're already too late! It's aw' aboot timing. If they've already started playing and ye huv'nae moved – forget it.'

'Right! Got it.' I'm determined to do better this time.

* * *

I'm keeping an unwavering eye on Wee Sanny. Once or twice he's approached the mike, only to veer off. Each time I've mentally put myself on starting blocks. This is nerve-wracking. At last he steps up to the mike, I hear him draw breath – I'm off like a bullet; I'm already halfway across the floor heading for the French yin. There's nobody near me. Wee Sanny speaks:

'We'll now take a ten minute interval!'

Oh, Mammy Daddy! Where can ah go? Oh, my God, they've turned on the main lights! Why don't they just put a spotlight on me? 'Here we are, ladies and gentlemen – 'Eegit of the Week' just crossing the floor now to claim his prize. Give him a big hand!' I'm waiting any second for Wee Sanny to say that. Then it comes to me – a flash of genius. I walk straight up to the 'objet' of 'mon desire' . . .

'I've tried tae dance wi' you a couple of times, already,' I make sure she can hear the Glasgow patois, it'll add a certain 'cachet' to my persona. Unless of course she was watching my antics earlier. 'Jist tae make sure ah don't miss out again, could ah huv the first dance efter the interval?' Cary Grant couldn't have got out of that situation any better. She looks into my eyes.

'Aye, aw'right.'

Ten minutes later I amble over and, at last, hold her in my arms. As we moonie around the floor I ask the usual questions. Her name is Dinah and she comes from Bell's Quarry. Tres romantique! By the end of the evening I've danced with her quite a few times, and as she doesn't seem to have an aversion to acne, a few nights later I squire her to the pictures at the Bathgate Regal. We spend the last hour or so snogging in the back row. Things are looking up. Ooh la la!

Hellzapoppin!

It was Aunty Jenny's fault. Definitely. Although I'm soon well established at Chic's, I continue to go round at least once a week to Jim and Jenny's for a blether. Like many things that go wrong, it started with the best of intentions.

'Them boils of yours are'ny getting any better.' Jenny peers at my face. I wish she wouldn't. I hate people looking at them.

'If ye remember, Aunty Jenny, they're no' boils. They're what's called acne, except mine are bigger than just the normal spots. Ah've got whit's called acne vulgaris.'

She continues her inspection. 'Well, they look jist like boils tae me. Ah'll bet ye a course o' sulphur and treacle would dae them the world o' good.'

'Sulphur and treacle?'

'Aye. It's an 'auld wives remedy. The sulphur gives ye a good purging, and the treacle just makes it easy tae swallow. Cleans oot yer system. Would ye like tae try it?'

'Might as well. Ah'll try anything if there's a chance it'll dae some good. Anywye, it'll no' dae any harm.' This last statement would prove to be less than accurate.

A bus trip is made to Bathgate to get sulphur powder from the chemist, followed by a tin of Tate and Lyle's finest molasses from the Co-op. Later in the afternoon I watch in interest as Jenny mixes the bright yellow powder with a few tablespoons of thick, black treacle.

'Therr ye are. Take three teaspoonfuls a day 'til it's done. That should sort ye, gie ye a good cleaning oot.'

Sometime later that day I have a brain wave. I decide to take DOUBLE the dose for the first twenty-four hours. Get things working quicker. This is another mistake.

On the second day of taking Aunty Jenny's remedy, I turn out on the Sunday night to start a week of night shift. As the pit bus jolts and sways its way up the lane toward the colliery yard the first symptons begin to manifest themselves – my stomach feels distended and there seems to be actual movement, as though a hard ball of wind is trapped down there. And it wants out.

As usual I'm working down the Main South. Sometime after midnight the deputy, Andy Smart, rings me on the internal phone. 'Come further in toward the face and give a bit hand, will ye? There's nine or ten hutches ran away doon yon steep bit. It's a right bloody mess. Some are oan their sides, others are jammed the gether up against the roof and there's coal everywhere. Make sure ye bring a shovel.'

I'm the last to arrive on the scene. It certainly is a mess. I stand at the bottom of the steep brae and look up the roadway. Ten or eleven guys are hard at work. Silhouetted by each other's lamps they busy themselves disentangling the piled up hutches, lifting them back onto the rails, and filling them with the spilled coal. The arc of girders supporting the roof frames this activity. Until it's all cleared up, production at the face is at a standstill. As the guys work away there's the usual banter . . .

'Ah see that team of yours got a right skelpin' oan Setterday, Alec.'

'Aye, we were a bit unlucky.'

'Unlucky! Since when wiz gettin' beat four-yin unlucky?'

Being at the foot of the hill I'm marginally nearer to the pit-bottom. This means I'm upwind of my workmates. This is a bad place for me to be. The ventilation of the pit is such that there's a continual movement of air circulating from the main shafts, through all the roadways, and deep into the pit. This moving air travels very slowly; perhaps one mile per hour.

As I work, I find all the bending and straining is adding to the problems brought on by my recent intake of sulphur and treacle. My stomach is now quite distended and hard, due to the amounts of wind being produced by this ancient tincture. I'm beginning to get sharp pains. I straighten up and, unmindful of the ventilation system, let go an enormous, but silent, ball of wind. As the soft breeze carries it off up the brae the effect is instantaneous. The guy nearest me gives a gurgle and drops his shovel. 'Fuck me!' he says. 'Where's that come fae?' The fellow next to him jerks upward, bumps his head on a girder, then spits two or three times. 'Huz somebody shit thursel?' Seconds later it's the turn of the next two up the line. They're working side by side and are struck at the same instant. Both stop shovelling. 'Wiz that you?' says one to the other. 'Yuuuch! Ah'm bloody sure it wiz'nae. Huz something crawled up somebody's arse and died?'

By now I'm leaning against a girder, helpless with laughter. Unfortunately this causes me to let go another one. The aroma from hell continues its meandering way up the brae, seemingly undiluted. The next two victims stop work and look back down the slope, obviously wondering what's causing the commotion. They soon find out . . .

'Jesus wept! That's evil.'

'Huz somebody's arse jist fell oot?'

It reaches the next in line. 'Whae'ever did that should see a doacter.'

'Wiz that you?' enquires the next guy.

The pains in my stomach have gone for the moment; now I've got a stitch. 'Ah've been taking sulphur and treacle,' I manage to gasp.

'Sulphur an' shite, ah think,' says a voice from the gloom.

'That huz got tae be the worst fart ah've ever smelt in ma life!' says another.

'Here, c'mon oot o'there. Away up the top of the brae and work so's it'll blaw away from us. Ah could'nae manage another yin o' them.'

Shovel in hand, unable to stop laughing, I climb the steep hill and run a gauntlet of punches on the arm, plus derogatory remarks on the state of my digestive system, underpants and ancestry.

'Ah'll stop taking it, honest!' I promise.

Once working at the top, I feel safe enough to break wind to my heart's content. Half an hour later Andy Smart approaches from the direction of the face to find out how long it'll be until we're done. As he's about to set off again, he turns. 'When ye's are clear, a couple of ye take a slow walk along the road in this direction. Aw the lads at the face are complaining aboot a bad smell drifting intae the seam. Ah think there's mibbe a deid rat lying somewhere.'

Nancy

I've taken the chance to 'lie-on' (work a double shift) from day shift to back shift. Around nine p.m. the deputy allows those of us who've worked through to have an early louse. It's a Friday evening. I make my way to the pit-bottom, surface, have a quick shower and as it's too early for the pit bus, I walk down to the road end and catch the service one. As I board, a voice from the top deck hails me.

'Up here, Robert!' It's Chic. I clamber up and sit beside him. He's busy talking to two girls seated behind him. 'Dae ye know Robert?'

The girls shake their heads. Chic does the introductions. 'This is Nancy and Betty, they're fae Seafield. This is ma pal, Robert Douglas. He lodges wi' us.'

'Hello.' At the same time I give the mandatory blush. I feel at even more of a disadvantage. Chic and the girls are dressed up; I'm in my 'shifting claes' with ex-army haversack slung over my shoulder. As we make small talk, I keep looking at Nancy. She's very attractive, lively and I especially like her hair which is in a fashionable 'bubble-cut'.

'So, where have youse been?' I look at my watch. It's quarter to ten. 'Or should I say, where are youse going?'

'Hame!' the girls chorus.

Nancy explains, while lighting a cigarette. 'There was a dance oan at Whitburn Miners' Welfare,' she pauses. 'Cigarette?'

I shake my head. 'Naw thanks. Ah don't smoke.'

She continues, 'It was absolutely mocket! So we've left early.'

'Where are youse off tae, now?'

'Naewhere. There's nothing on anywhere else, and anywye it's too late. So it's hame time.'

Chic interrupts, 'It's oor stop next, Robert.'

I look at Nancy. 'Ah might see you around sometime. If it's at the dancin' ah'll come ower and gie ye a dance. Okay?'

She draws on her cigarette. 'Aye, that'll be fine.'

'See yah, girls. Cheerio.' We make our way downstairs and step onto the pavement. A cool wind blows, but it doesn't bother me. 'Ah quite fancy that yin. That Nancy. Dae ye know if she's got a steady boyfriend?'

'Don't think so. Ah usually jist see her wi' her pals.' He looks at me. 'She's a good bit aulder than you, mind.'

'Is she? How auld is she?'

'Ah think she'll be aboot twenty-three or so.'

'Och, if ah ask her oot ah'll tell her ah'm twenty. Mibbe twenty-one. Ah'm always gettin' told ah look aulder than ah am. She dis'nae look twenty-three mind, diz she?'

'Naw. Twenty-eight!'

'She DIZ'NAE!' I give him a dig on the arm.

'Hey! You don't half huv a fancy for her, dain't ye?'

'She's aw'right.'

'She's nearly always at the Bathgate Palais oan a Setterday night. She loves the dancing.'

As we walk along a deserted Riddochill Road, a few spots of rain begin to fall. We quicken our pace. 'Fancy going tae the Palais the morra night?' I blush, unseen, in the dark.

Chic laughs. 'Therr's a surprise!'

I keep up my badgering. 'C'mon, Chic. We're gonny miss the Bathgate bus. If we're no' therr by half seven we'll no' get in.'

As the rock'n'roll phenomenon sweeps on through '56 it does wonders for attendances at dance halls – and the music industry. Records are being produced for a new market – teenagers! The 'Big Band era' had lasted through the thirties and forties until succeeded by the 'next big thing' – crooners. Sinatra, Dick

Haymes, Eddie Fisher, et al. These had been aimed at a record-buying public which was almost entirely adult. There was no such thing as a teenage market. By the mid-fifties, this has changed. Teenagers now have money in their pockets. Not much, but enough for movie makers and record companies to realise there's a market out there, and to start catering for it. Then comes rock'n'roll. It is aimed directly at teenagers. It's *our* music. Along with the records come the movies: *The Blackboard Jungle*, *Rebel Without a Cause*. Things will never be the same again. Teen movies, teen records, teen magazines. The entertainment industry has changed for ever.

I'm seventeen, the perfect age to be. Every time I hear Bill Haley and the Comets on the radio I can't keep my feet still. When the first few bars of any Little Richard record comes over the air waves and I hear that voice, the hair on the back of my neck stands up. When I sit in the darkness of the cinema and watch Elvis, I think, 'how can one guy be so lucky?' To be so handsome. Not just good-looking – handsome in a classical, Roman way. To look at Elvis and Marlon Brando in profile. When did the Romans land in America? Has anybody checked it out? Not only is Elvis unique in his looks, but what about that voice? I find his records aren't as danceable as the other rock'n'roll stars. For me, Elvis is for listening to or, even better, watching up on the screen. He is not of this world. Definitely from another galaxy. I sit in the stalls of the cinema and watch this *god* perform. I read in the papers of the muti-million-dollar deals for records and movies. Every time he comes out with a new record, because of advance sales it ALWAYS goes immediately to number one on the day of release.

But then the movie finishes, I go back to my digs, my mind still full of Elvis – and I glance in the mirror. Looking out at me is a face with skin like a pan of lumpy porridge. Thanks a lot God. For fuck all!

* * *

We get into the Palais just on seven-thirty. It's heaving. As is the norm, it's girls on one side, boys on the other. As we make our way through the throng I walk on tiptoe now and again to get a better look at the ladies. My heart gives a little leap. I prod Chic in the back. 'Ah've jist spotted that Nancy from Seafield. Ah'm straight ower for her at the next dance.'

'It wid be a rerr laugh if she said no!'

'Thanks pal.'

Seconds later the band begins to play. I cut straight through the mass and make for Nancy.

I'm a few feet away when she sees me and smiles. I'm almost there when a guy beats me to it

'Would you like tae dance?' Awww, man!

She points to me. 'Sorry,' she says to him, 'Ah've already promised this fella I'd dance with him.'

'Oh well!' he moves on.

I feel great. Nothing like this has ever happened to me before. I stand in front of her. 'I hope I'm the fella you're talking about.'

'You are.' She blushes.

We filter into the mass of dancers and bump our way gently round the floor. The band still plays the normal programme of waltz, quickstep and foxtrot but no longer are they exclusively the old favourites from the Big Band days. To show they're 'with it', they've adapted many of the rock'n'roll hits. When it's a quickstep being played, half the dancers jive to it instead of the old 'one, two, chasse'. Things are a'changing.

As we dance, I try to make small talk. 'Well, I told you ah'd give ye a dance first time ah saw you.'

'You did.'

'I was really hoping you'd be here tonight.'

'Yeah. Ah thought ah might see you.'

'Where's your pal, Betty?'

'She's no' mad keen on the dancin'. She jist comes now and again.'

Up until the interval we have just about every second dance. After the break I begin going over for every one. She seems quite happy about this. Before the end of the evening we're dancing cheek to cheek. It's wonderful. In no time at all, it's the last waltz.

'Eh, would ye like tae go tae the pictures next week?'

'Aye. That would be nice.'

I think my heart's gonny burst. I can tell she means it. I'm in love. Instantly!

Chic and I lie in bed. There's the usual flurry of sparks as his dowt hits the lino.

'Ah wish it wiz next Thursday.'

'That when you're meeting her?'

'Aye, ootside the Pavilion at seven.'

'Ye know it's *Rock Around the Clock*? You'll huv tae queue.'

'Aye, but it's in its second week, and we're going midweek. We should get in aw'right.'

'You'll still huv tae queue.'

'Are you going oot oan Thursday?' I ask.

'Don't think so.'

'Gonny let me borrow that black drape jacket of yours?'

'Dae you think ah'm a branch of Moss Bros?'

'Can ah take that as a "yes"?'

'Aye.'

We lie silent for a minute or so.

'Anywye, it suits me better than it suits you!'

'Cheeky git!'

'G'night, pal.'

'G'night, toerag.'

I turn on my side. I still feel a glow from the dancing. Well, from being with Nancy. I really think I'm in love. In fact, I'm pretty certain. I've had big crushes on lassies, but I think this is the real thing. I've only had a few dates. Very few. This might be my first steady girlfriend. I feel Nancy could be 'the one.' As I lie there in the dark, eyes open, a little warning voice intrudes now and again . . . 'You don't have to fall in love with the first girl who goes out with you more than once. You're so keen to have a "steady" that the first one who shows an interest in you – you're in love!' I try to ignore it; it's spoiling my daydream. Or is it because it's speaking common sense? I very much want to be in love with somebody – and have them love me. I'm not in the market for little warning voices.

Going Steady

I'm beginning to wish I'd never mentioned it. I'd told Nancy I loved Elvis's 'Heartbreak Hotel'.

'Ah've got the record. When ye take me hame the night, ye can come in and ah'll play it for ye.'

Up until now, whenever I take her home we usually do a little bit of courting (snogging) a few blocks away from her house. I'm not yet ready to meet her folks. Not nearly ready.

'Och, ah'll no' bother. Your mother and faither will'nae be wantin' tae hear Elvis at nearly eleven o'clock at night.'

'It's Setterday night, they'll still be up.'

I knew she'd say that. I try to think up some other excuse. Nothing comes to mind; we're approaching her house; I'm getting desperate. 'Look, ah really hate meeting new people. Ah'll just stand here at the door and listen.'

She looks at me. 'Well, okay. Seems daft tae me.' She goes inside, leaving the outside and living room doors open. Minutes later, Elvis and 'Hearbreak Hotel' – at full echo – flows out into the street. I'm not aware of it, but her dad's a great kidder. His voice rises above Elvis. 'Whit the buggerin' hell's going oan? Is the hail street gettin' tae hear oor records fur nuthin'?'

Outside, on the front step, I'm mortified. Oh, man! Why did I have to tell her I like that bloody record?

'Wheesh Faither!' says Nancy, 'Ah'm jist lettin' this fella hear a record.'

'Well tell'm tae come in. There's a draught blawin' through the hoose that wid fell an ox. We'll aw' be doon wi' pneumonia in a meenit!'

The cause of all the trouble!

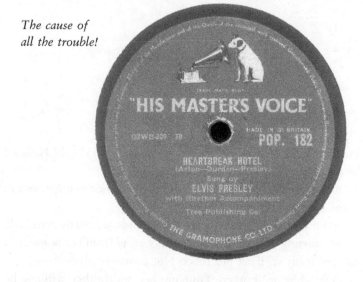

"HIS MASTER'S VOICE"

G2WB-209 7B MADE IN GT. BRITAIN
POP. 182

HEARTBREAK HOTEL
(Axton—Durden—Presley)
Sung by
ELVIS PRESLEY
with Rhythm Accompaniment

Tree Publishing Co.

THE GRAMOPHONE CO. LTD.

I can hear Nancy trying not to giggle. She appears at the door and has some difficulty saying 'Ma faither says would ye like tae come in?'

'AH DID NOT!' says a voice from the depths of the house. Nancy tries to suppress a cough, or something. I've broken out in a cold sweat, I can feel new plooks emerging as I stand here.

'Naw, it's aw'right. Ah'll be getting away hame when the record finishes. Ah'm up early in the morning.' How long does this bloody record last? It's been on for at least ten minutes.

Nancy returns to the living room. 'He has'nae got time. He'll be going hame when the record finishes.'

'Thank God fur that. Ah canny feel ma feet!' I can tell he's having difficulty not laughing.

Nancy's choking. 'See you! Faither! Nae wonder ah canny bring anybody tae this hoose.'

At last Elvis finishes; that has got to be the longest single ever made. Nancy reappears. 'Jist come in for five minutes.'

'Naw, honestly. Ah'm murder polis at getting up in the morning. Anywye, will we go tae the pictures on Thursday?'

'Aye, that'll be nice. What's on?'

'Ah think it's a Dean Martin an' Jerry Lewis picture at the Pavilion. Ah'm no' sure what's oan at the Regal.'

'Aye, the Pavilion will do. What time?'

'Seven-thirty?'

'That's fine.' I give her a quick kiss then scuttle away before her da says anything else.

Eventually I'll have to meet her folks. But not tonight. Not for a few nights, I hope. I bet when I eventually meet him the first thing he'll say is . . . 'So this is the fella who likes tae stand oot in the street listening tae oor records!' Jeez, the trouble this bloody acne causes me.

I don't have too long to wait. The following Thursday, when we meet outside the cinema, almost the first thing Nancy says is, 'Oh, before ah forget. My ma says you've tae come for your dinner this Sunday.'

'Oh, that'll be nice,' I lie. 'What time?'

'Ye can come along aboot five-thirty. We usually eat roon' seven.'

Oh, man! This is the first time I've ever been asked to somebody's house for a meal. Jeez! It's adults who do things like that, not boys. I won't know where to put myself, what to say. Everybody'll be looking at me when I speak, even when I'm not speaking. Should I just not turn up? Just stop seeing Nancy? Why can't you just take a girl out without having to meet her folks? This'll be pure torture.

Sunday's come. I get off the bus in Seafield and make my way down to Cousland Crescent. It all looks different in daylight. Up to now I've only seen the house late at night when I bring Nancy home. It's a well-built, 1930s semi. I descend the few steps from the front gate down to the path. I've a feeling I'm being watched through the bay windows. As I knock on the front door I'm acutely aware of the couple of big spots which have put in an appearence for the occasion. How do the bastards know when I'm going somewhere? Of course, squeezing them hasn't helped.

Thank God the lights aren't on in the living room, they might not be too aware of my awful blushing. Nancy introduces me to her mother, father and sister, Betty. As I go through my usual routine when meeting new folk, face red, eyes watering, I wonder, 'what must they be thinking to themselves?' After the introductions I sit on the sofa, Nancy beside me. That's Phase One finished, I'll now go onto Phase Two; every time someone speaks to me, or I have to speak, I'll repeat all the Phase One symptoms! Is it EVER going to end? When I'm into my twenties, will I be as bad I am now? Even more important, will my acne have calmed down by then?

As I listen to the small-talk, I look at Nancy's family. Her dad is stockily built and quite bald. Her mother homely and rather quiet. Betty, her sister, has long black hair and looks nothing like Nancy, who's fair. Betty is to be married soon. Eventually I relax and begin to enjoy myself – I'm doing plenty of listening, very little talking. Nancy's dad, known as 'Sanny' – short for Alexander – is full of fun. I find out much later he's a First World War veteran. He joined up, underage, in 1917. Later that year, at Dinant in Belgium, he was wounded in the thigh and taken prisoner. For most of the next fifteen months he was made to work in a German coal mine at Recklinghausen. Nancy's mother, Sobina – always called 'Beenie' by her husband, same name as my new stepmother – had been in service at a large house. They'd met and married in the late 1920s. They have four children; Alec, the oldest, then Nancy, followed by twin sisters Betty and Isobel.

We go through to the kitchen and sit round the pale green, Formica-topped table. A 'proper' Sunday dinner of roast beef with all the trimmings is served up. Nancy's ma prides herself on her cooking – and so she should. The Scotch beef just about melts

*Nancy, on left, me
and friend. Ayr,
1958.*

in my mouth. I sit back in my chair. 'That's the best meal I've had for a long time, Mrs Nicol. I really enjoyed that.'

She smiles with pleasure. 'Thank you.'

'He's jist saying that tae keep in wi' you,' Sanny's eyes twinkle.

'You be quiet!' says his wife. She turns to me, 'Pay nae attention tae that auld D'eil (Devil).'

'HERE! Less o' the auld,' protests her husband.

Nancy shakes her head. 'He'll be delighted he's got somebody new tae torment. At least it'll gie us a break.'

Sanny's now in full flood. He puts on a serious face. 'Jist watch whit youse are saying. Remember, ah'm the boss in here. The breadwinner.'

Mother and daughter give derisive snorts. 'Ye could'nae win a raffle,' says his wife.

'He'd be too miserable tae buy a ticket in the first place,' says Nancy. She and her mother go into fits of laughter. Sanny looks at me.

'See how ah get treated. Me, the head of the hoose.'

'Mair like a head of cabbage,' says his spouse. Nancy had been about to take a mouthful of tea; she splutters into her cup, almost choking. Mother and daughter become helpless with laughter. I sit there laughing, too, mainly because Nancy and her ma are having such fun. It just reminds me how Ma and I also used to spark each other off into fits of laughter at the most innocent of things.

'Are you no' gonny support me?' enquires Sanny, trying to look hurt.

'No,' I manage to say, 'you've brought it on yourself.'

'Why yah buggah! Well, nae good me staying here, ah might as well gan through the living room wi' the paper.' He starts to rise.

'Don't know whit good that'll dae ye, Faither.' Nancy turns to me, 'He'll be sound asleep in less than five minutes.'

Sanny rises from the table and disappears into the next room. Nancy shakes her head. 'He does this every night that God sends. Sits doon wi' the paper – and three minutes later he's off. Takes him aw' night tae get the *Courier* read.'

Beenie starts to clear the table. 'He's an awfy man. You'll no' have tae be thin-skinned if yer gonny visit this hoose.'

His voice comes through from the living room. 'Ah hope youse aren'y talking about me.'

'Sole topic of conversation, Faither.'

'If ah huv tae come through there, mind, there'll be trouble!'

'Get tae sleep and gie us peace. Silly auld fool,' says his wife.

'Yes, flower.' He chuckles away to himself.

Mother and daughter look at each other. Nancy turns to me, 'That's not just for your benefit, ye know. He's like that every mealtime.'

Sunday nights like this are now a regular feature of my life. For a few months, anyway.

The Kings of Rock'n'Roll

I've caught Nancy doing it once or twice when we we've been having a night out. If we're sitting in the lounge bar of a pub, as the evening goes on I'll become aware she's 'giving the eye' to some fella sitting in another part of the room. It seems to be a game with her. Adds to the pleasure of the evening out – to be sitting with one guy while making eyes at another. So far I haven't said anything. At seventeen, I'm too inexperienced to know what to do about it, so I tend to sulk, hardly speak to her.

Chic and I board the Bathgate bus and climb to the top deck. It's early Saturday afternoon so it's crowded. Chic pulls out a ten packet of Player's. 'Ye want yin?'

'Naw, thanks.' Sometimes I do have one, but in reality I find the idea of smoking is better than actually doing it.

He finally gets his petrol lighter to do what it's supposed to, and we're surrounded by a slowly moving abstract in blue smoke. I quite like the smell of a newly-lit cigarette.

'Are ye going oot with Jean the night?'

He takes a draw. 'Naw, we've fell oot.' As he speaks, the smoke spills out of his mouth in time to the words. 'Are you oot wi' Nancy?'

'Naw, we've fell oot as well.' We both laugh and shake our heads. I feel sort of grown up when I talk about things like this. Reading books, watching movies, having a steady girlfriend, all make me think I'm getting to be an adult. In reality I'm just kidding myself on. In more ways than one, I'm still a virgin.

Maybe Chic will agree that what I've done about this problem with Nancy is the right way to handle it.

He looks at me. 'Whit did ye's fall oot over?'

Now's my chance. 'She has this maddening habit when you're sitting in a bar or club, she looks roon' the place 'til she catches some guy looking at her, then spends the rest of the night giving him the glad-eye.'

'Never!'

'She diz. She must think it makes her look good or something. Makes me feel really stupid. She knows ah know whit she's daeing, but she jist carries on, real blatant.'

'Have ye done something aboot it?'

'Aye. Wait 'til ye hear this – then ye can tell me if ye think ah've done right. We were in the Kaim Park Hotel the other night, and she's daeing it. Her and this fella smirking away at one another. Ah'm sitting next tae her, getting madder and madder, and ah'm no' wanting tae cause a big disturbance, yet at the same time ah want tae dae something aboot it.'

'So whit did ye dae?' Chic's hanging on my every word.

'Well, it jist suddenly came tae me. Ah leaned ower tae her and ah said, "Ah hope ye know that guy quite well, the one ye keep giving the glad eye to. 'Cause he's gonny have tae take ye hame the night!' then ah jist got up and left her sittin' therr."

Chic looks at me, wide-eyed. 'Ye did'nae?'

'Ah did!'

'Well, good for you. That wiz perfect.'

'Dae ye think ah did right?'

'Definitely. Whit else could ye dae?' He takes a draw on his Player's. 'Have ye seen her since?'

'Naw. Ah'm jist gonny let her stew. Ah'm on back shift next week, so ah would'nae be able to see her anywye.' I look at him. 'Whit did you and Jean fall oot about?'

He purses his mouth and lets the smoke trickle out. 'The usual. Still no' let me go aw' the way.'

'Well, they never dae, dae they? Ah've been taking Nancy oot for three months now – never even had my hand oan it! Get a bit tit, that's ma lot. They like tae get ye aw' worked up, then cut ye aff.'

'Tell me aboot it.'

'Fuck them!'

'Ah just wish we could!' We kill ourselves laughing. We sit in silence for a while. As the bus turns left onto the main road and passes Bathgate Academy, Chic turns his head. 'Will we buy a record the day?'

'Aye. We'll go half stuff, eh?'

'Aye. Dae ye fancy an Elvis yin?'

'We've been saying for ages we'll get "Don't Be Cruel". Will we definitely get it the day?'

'Right. Definitely. Mind, we'd better wait 'til jist before we get the bus hame. If we stoat aboot the toon aw' efternoon carrying it, it's a cert tae get broken.'

'Good thinking!'

We disembark in Bathgate centre and look around. The town is busy with shoppers. Chic stands there; black finger-tip drape jacket with a 'link' button, 14 inch bottom trousers, thick, crepe-soled brogues. The hippest Teddy boy in West Lothian. Bar none! I have 16 inch bottom jeans and wear brothel-creepers too. I can't afford a made-to-measure jacket like Chic. It cost him nine guineas. We both have the mandatory Tony Curtis quiff falling onto our foreheads, the hair at the back of our heads is combed into DAs (duck's arses). We are beyond cool.

'Where'll we go first?'

'Ower tae the café, play the jukebox, eh? There might be some talent in.'

'Let's go,' says Chic.

We order our milky coffees then sit at one of the tables with their bright red Formica tops. The jukebox is already playing. I hand Chic a shilling. You put a shilling tae it. You pick the records.

'Ye want anything in particular?'

'If Bill Haley's "See You Later, Alligator" is still therr ye can put that oan – or anything by Little Richard. Ah love him.'

'You and Little Richard.'

Chic returns from making our selections and sits opposite me. The sun streams through the window. He sighs. 'Ah jist hope ah can handle the excitement of another Setterday in Bathgate!'

'Me tae.'

Around five-thirty we get back to Chic's. Eddie, his quiet step-brother, is already in the living room, reading a book. The radio plays softly.

'We've bought a new record,' says Chic, 'dae ye mind if we play it?'

'Aye, fine. Ah wasn't really listening tae the wireless.'

Chic switches the radiogram to '78 rpm records. As the needle settles in the groove he turns the volume up. High. He winks at me. 'Don't Be Cruel' blasts out at around two decibels below the pain threshold. Eddie winces visibly. A cup and saucer on top of the radiogram begin to jiggle their way toward the edge, until rescued. There's a loud bang from above our heads. 'Fuck me!' says Chic, 'ah think Auld Jock's fell oot the bed!' I begin to giggle at the thought. Folk in the street, passing the window, turn their heads as they go by; the walls are probably throbbing. Eddie doggedly tries to concentrate on his book. Chic plays the record again and again and again. Then some more. He has just put it on for maybe the seventh time when Eddie shoots up out of his chair, shouts something we can't hear, then storms out the room. Chic and I roll with unheard laughter on the sofa. Now that Eddie's gone, he goes over and turns the volume up some more! The door to the room is thrown open. Auld Jock, toothless, holding his jammies up with one hand, stomps in. He points dramatically at the radiogram and mouths something. Chic goes over and turns it down. My ears pop with relief. Auld Jock speaks; 'Wh . . . daein' . . . ni'shift . . . wink . . . fickin' . . .

sleep!' He looks at us in turn while hitching his jammies up higher; his tongue does three quick laps round his lips.

Chic tries to look serious. 'Oh, sorry Faither. Ah did'nae know the doacter had signed ye off.'

'Aye, . . . bastid. No . . . wellman. Oan . . . 's'heid . . . badhappens!' With a last tragic look he about turns and exits, stage left.

I have to jam my knuckle into my mouth so's Auld Jock won't hear me laughing. Chic shakes his head. 'That man could win an Oscar, so he could. Anywye, that's the early evening entertainment buggered. Will we jist get ready an' go tae the dancing at Armadale?'

'Aye. If we start gettin' ready right away we should get there for eight o'clock. They had tae shut the doors before then last week.'

We go upstairs and start the lengthy preparations for going out, all the while kidding each other on. Sometimes we laugh too loud. Auld Jock's muffled voice comes from the bedroom 'Dae . . . chance . . . sleep . . . bastids!' Chic, standing outside his father's door in his shirt tails, skinny legs akimbo, gives him a vigorous, but silent, double-handed 'V' sign. I have to bury my face in my pillow AND hold my side because I'm in pain.

I really do like lodging at Chic's.

Blacker Than Black

I'm on night shift, working on my own at a corner where two roadways and conveyor belts meet. I'm a quarter mile or more from anybody else.

One belt brings coal from the face, and at this corner, drops it onto the second belt to be carried away to where the hutches wait to be filled. Sometimes there's a break for some reason and the belt from the face stops. I switch off the other one. Quiet descends. But not complete silence. Now and again there's a creak or groan, sometimes a sharp crack, as unimaginable weight bears down on girders and wooden packing. I wait until a bout of noise is finished and it's quiet once more. I switch off my helmet lamp. Instantly the deepest black it's possible to find envelops me. I'm 1800 feet underground, a mile from the pit-bottom, and on the surface it's night time anyway. This must be the blackest place on earth. As I sit there, unseeing, I know there is something there. It is real. The slight movement of air from the ventilation system adds to the strange feeling. It seems that the blackest of black is caressing my face. It is very strange to sit with my eyes wide open, the darkness stirring around me, yet I can't see a thing. After a minute or two it becomes eerie. There's definitely something there, I can feel it touching me – but I can neither touch, nor see, it.

Often, when I'm with other lads, I'll persuade them to switch off their lamps. Without fail, within sixty seconds someone will find it too unsettling and will click their lamp back on. I like to do it.

*　　*　　*

Tony Melissa comes by and decides he'll sit and have a blether with me while we have our piece. I like Tony and get on well with him. He's one of twenty or more Poles who work at the pit. All escaped from Poland as the Germans invaded and by various routes made their way to Britain and became part of the Free Polish Army. A large number of their units were stationed in Scotland for years. As they disbanded in 1945, many elected to stay on rather than go back to a Communist Poland now occupied by the Russians. It was a wise move. Those who did return were treated with suspicion and persecuted to varying degrees. During the years that there has been a Polish presence in Scotland, many Poles have married local girls. Now, in 1957, there's hardly a town or village in West Lothian without a few Polish–Scottish families. Sadly, however, the contribution of the 'Dashing Poles' and 'Our Valiant Allies' during the war has soon been forgotten. These gregarious, good-natured guys are often being treated as second-class citizens. Not just by their fellow workers, but by the government too . . .

Tony, a former sergeant in the Polish Army, now married to his 'Scotch lassie' and living in Whitburn, leans back against the wall of the roadway as we eat our piece.

'Tony, you know this thing where nearly every Polish guy in the pit gets called "Tony the Pole"?'

'Yah?' Tony is the exception – that actually IS his name.

'Do they no' get fed up wi' it?'

He shrugs his shoulders and turns down the corners of his mouth. 'Is only small theeng. No matter.' He pours some more strong black coffee from his flask into its cup.

'If it was me ah'd insist people call me by ma right name.'

'Not eevrybody get called Tony Pole. Lots of chap get called real name.'

'Last time ah was talking to ye, ye were telling me that you're an engineer and Stefan's a teacher. So how come ye's are working doon the pit?'

He takes a bit of sandwich and chews for a moment. 'Because after war, trade unions say they no' want Polish guys taking British guys' job. So Labour government they keep unions happy. They say that Polish, eh, what you call paper that show I am engineer?'

'Qualifications?'

'Yah. They say I have to go college and train two year. Then have exam in English and get British qualification.' He looks at me. 'So how I make enough money keep wife and weans while I go college, eh? They know it impossible. This happen every Polish guy who is trademan or teacher. So we all go down pit and forget we have trade.' He gives the Polish equivalent of a Gallic shrug. 'Fuck them!'

It's an hour or so after Tony and I have had our piece, he's moved on to do a job somewhere else. I hear a dull 'whumpf' from the direction of the face. That's the shotfirer detonating his charges. A couple of minutes later there's the glimmer of a light. 'RO-BERT!' The voice carries along the roadway.

'AYE?'

'Come and gie a bit hand. There's been a fall o' stane, Wee Andy Smart's badly hurt! Ah'm going on 'til the nearest phone tae let them know at the pit heid, so's they'll huv an ambulance standing by.'

As he hurries off, I make for the face. Minutes later I arrive to find a group of men standing around Andy. A couple kneel by him and try to make him comfortable. He lies amongst a group of large boulders, some probably weighing 5 or 6 hundred-weights. There is still a lot of dust and smoke in the air from the shots being fired. I can smell the explosives. I've never seen an accident close up before. I'm usually not very keen on blood, even if it's just a cut finger. I stand beside one of the men furthest from Andy. 'What happened?'

He shakes his head. 'He's such an impatient wee bugger. They're supposed tae wait 'til the dust clears efter the shots huv been fired, THEN go forward and huv a look. If there's any stanes hanging fae the roof they can prod them doon. As usual he went straight in two minutes efter firing his shots, could hardly see a hand in front o'yer face for dust. Aw' that lot must have been ready tae drop. Came right doon oan tap o' him.' He shakes his head again. 'It's snapped his legs in two. Ah think there's a shoulder and ribs broken, tae. If he'd jist fuckin' waited. He's due tae retire in a few months.' As he finishes speaking someone arrives with a stretcher. 'Right, lads. If we aw' get roond him and lift at the same time.'

I find myself saying, 'Ah'll get his legs.' Having recently come from the training school, the first aid course I'd done is still fresh in my mind. I clearly remember how to support broken legs when lifting. As I kneel beside him it's easy to see both are broken halfway between knee and ankle. I place my open hands, palms upward, underneath his legs on either side of the breaks. Somebody says, 'Ready, lads? One, two, three, hup!'

As we raise him I try to keep the breaks level, but the heavier upper parts move down. I can feel the ends of the broken bones prodding the edge of my right hand through his trousers.

As the stones fell on him the weight had driven him down and, literally, snapped his legs like matchsticks, the bones coming through the skin. We lay him gently on the stretcher and tuck blankets round him. As I take my hands away I see my palms are covered in blood. To my surprise I don't feel sick.

We now have to carry him more than a mile to the pit-bottom, most of the time bent forward to avoid bumping our heads. Andy has never lost consciousness during or after the accident. He'd spoken to those who'd first arrived on the scene. Even when I'd came up, five minutes later, he'd still been lucid. During the forty minutes or so it takes to get him to the cage, the shock takes over and he becomes quieter, sleepy. He's unconscious before we reach the pit-bottom.

When I come to work that night it's no surprise to find he'd died later in the morning.

Love's a Pain

I hadn't seen Nancy for a couple of weeks then, probably 'accidentally on purpose', I bumped into her at the Palais. We've been out a few times since. On one of the dates we went to see the movie *Picnic* with William Holden and Kim Novak. There's a terrific bit in it when the picnic of the title is being held. It's evening and there's dancing. On a small, floating dance floor on the lake, Kim is standing alone; a four or five piece combo plays that old standard, 'Moonglow'. Holden sees her and, in time to the music, approaches her slowly, fingers snapping. Just as they come together and start to dance, a new piece of music, specially written for the movie – 'The Theme From Picnic' – comes in, played on soaring strings. Although different from 'Moonglow', the Theme complements it. The couple dance close, looking into each other's eyes. They sway gently to the music of the small jazz combo while, from out of nowhere the romantic strings play, heard only by the lovers – and me.

Since meeting at the Palais we seem to be back 'on' and I've been along to her house for Sunday dinner a couple of times. Nothing's been said about me walking out and leaving her in the pub. It's as if it never happened. Things seem to be good again. I sure hope so. I really would like for us to go steady . . .

I'm getting madder and madder. We're sitting in the lounge of the Commercial Hotel on the main street in Bathgate. I can't believe it. I've just caught her at this stupid game again. She'd looked around the large room until she caught somebody giving her the eye, and has now spent the last twenty minutes playing 'optical footsie'. She regularly shoots little glances at him when she thinks I'm not looking. After twenty minutes I decide I've had enough.

'Dae you think I'm stupid?'

She quickly takes her eyes off him. 'What?'

'That fella you've been giving the glad-eye to. Do ye think ah don't see ye? Ah told ye at the Kaim Park about playing that silly game of yours. Why do ye have to do it? Do ye think because ah've started taking ye out again after the last time, that it means I'm prepared tae put up wi' it?'

She reaches into her bag for her cigarettes.

'You've got no answer, have ye?'

Blue smoke spirals up into the air.

'Does it make you feel good sitting with one guy while gettin' the eye off another? Is that why ye do it? Don't ye realise how stupid it makes me look? You seem tae think, because you're older, ye don't have tae show any affection for me. Ah have tae do all the running.'

We sit in silence for twenty minutes. I look across the room. The guy, who's at least in his late twenties, is blatantly staring at her again. I glance at Nancy. She's staring right at him, a half-smile on her face. From the corner of her eye she must have seen my head turn, the smile is switched off, she looks down at the table and shuffles a couple of beer mats around.

'Aw, fuck it!' I stand up. 'Ah'm away.'

I decide I'm going to avoid dances where I know Nancy will be. On one occasion we do finish up at the same hall – Whitburn Miners' Welfare. It was very hard to resist the temptation to dance with her, especially as I'd had two or three bottles of sweet stout. But all I did was just think of her playing her stupid game. Even so, I really miss her company. We'd been going out for a few months and I thought it was great having a steady. I miss my Sunday evenings at her house, too. Sitting at the table while Auld Sanny torments the life out of me. Sometimes I'd feel I was almost getting to be one of the family. Jeez! Why did she have to spoil it. Did she really think I'd put up with this thing of hers, which she obviously enjoys? Though, if I'm honest with myself, it isn't JUST that. When we're together I'm the only one who shows affection. Not her. She never takes my hand, I have to take hers. She never kisses me, I have to kiss her. Not once has she ever told me she loves me. I have to ask her. Even then, the answer is always 'Of course I do'. If she REALLY loved me she'd do these things naturally, just as I do. I think it's mainly because I'm so much younger than her. The thing is, she thinks she's just four years older than me. It's actually seven! When we started going out last year I told her I was twenty. She was twenty-four. I've only just turned eighteen.

The feeling I want to see her again won't go away. I really miss her. Yet I'm not going to go out with her at any price, let myself be humiliated. It's all making me feel really miserable, I think about her all the time. She was my first real girlfriend. My rotten acne never seemed to bother her. When I was with her, even I forgot about it. Why did she have to spoil it all?

The whole situation is still getting me down. I love lodging at Chic's, he and I are getting to be good mates. I like my job down the pit. I regularly lie-on for a double shift and I'm making good money – sometimes, after tax, I take home more than nine pounds a week! But this Nancy business is always on my mind. I've decided there's only one solution. Move away! Leave the area. Away from temptation. Where should I go? My first thought is Glasgow. My second is Portpatrick! Why would I want to go there? The last time I saw my father was the week after my sixteenth birthday, just before I went into the RAF. Two years ago. Firstly, I'm curious to see his new wife. After Ma died I'd had the choice to go and live with them, or go into the Boys' Service. Hobson's Choice. At the time, days after Ma's death, there was no way that I'd go and live with his fancy woman. Now? I'm just plain nosey. I'm also interested to see what my relationship with my father will be like now. I don't think I'll be prepared to put up with one of the regular bats on the lug I used to get. Since Ma died he's never taken any responsibility for me, I very obligingly relieved him of that duty. Why shouldn't he take me in for a while? If I move to Glasgow I could be tempted to come out to West Lothian. It's just 30 miles or so. Portpatrick is about 100 miles, maybe more. There'll be no chance of me seeing her again. It'll be the end of our relationship once and for all.

I let it all run through my mind for another couple of days, then I sit down one evening and write him a letter saying I feel like a move – can I come down to Portpatrick for a while? A few days later comes his reply . . . 'Beenie and me will pleased to see you if you want to come and stay.' Great! Already Nancy isn't dominating my thoughts quite so much.

Tales of the Unexpected

I wonder if I'm doing the right thing? I'm standing waiting for the Bathgate bus and I'm getting little stabs of fear in my stomach every time I think of what I'm about to do. Should I go? It isn't too late. If I want to, I can go back round to Chic's and they'll take me in again, no bother. I'll easily get my job back at Polkemmet, they're always short of men. Yeah, but if you don't go, within a couple of weeks you'll be back trying to bump into Nancy again. But this is a big step. Probably a stupid one! All of a sudden it's 'make your mind up' time . . . the green-liveried SMT bus turns the corner and begins to struggle up the road from Blackburn Cross. The for and against arguments are now racing through my mind, I can just step back and wave the driver on. I don't have to take it. I shoot a glance over to the council houses. Aunty Jenny's at the window. I'd popped in for five minutes to say 'cheerio'. Uncle Jim's at work. She gives a wave as the bus approaches and begins to slow down. I wave back just before it draws to a halt and comes between us. I get on! Getting on doesn't mean I'm committed, I'll make my mind up one way or the other between here and Bathgate. Plenty of time yet. I take a seat on the right-hand side and give her a last wave as we pull away. I look out the window as the bus lumbers toward the end of the village where the houses peter out and the fields begin. I've got butterflies again.

'Single tae Bathgate, please. Don't bother aboot a ticket.' The conductor's in on the scam.

When I reach Bathgate I find, to my surprise, that most of my anxieties have eased. Getting on the Glasgow bus is less fraught than the first part of my journey. As it is nearly empty I put my 'luggage' on the seat beside me. I look at it; TWO brown paper carrier bags. Jeez! I'm certainly coming up in the world. One of these days I'll need a suitcase. The conductor appears beside me. 'Single tae Glasgow, please.' It'll be all single tickets today.

The trip from Glasgow is a long one, via Ayr and Girvan and on down the west coast. Then at long last I'm on my final bus of the day, Stranraer to Portpatrick. As it makes its way down the steep, narrow road into the village I look through the front window. I can see the sea, then, as we reach the bottom of the hill, the road opens out and becomes a beautiful little harbour.

'I take it this is Portpatrick?'

'Aye, this is it, son.'

I step off the bus. That's almost seven hours I've been travelling. I take a deep breath. It's got the lot: fresh sea air, ozone, seaweed. You could cut the air with a knife. I stand and look around for a few minutes. Portpatrick is made for picture postcards. It's like a movie set for *Whiskey Galore*. A little half-moon harbour edged by another half-moon – of cottages and houses. The majority are painted white; the remainder pastel blues, yellows and pinks. And all of this nestles inside an arc of low hills. It is unbelievably twee, yet quite natural. I stand facing the sea then look up to my right. A large imposing hotel stands high on a hill, dominating the village the way a castle would. The sea front is almost deserted. I'll find out it's like this most of the year, its isolation keeping away all but the more determined holidaymakers. When folk do come it's usually for at least a few days; renting a cottage or, if they can afford it, booking into the hotel on the hill.

I stand looking around me for twenty minutes or so, until I realise what I'm doing – putting off seeing my father again for the first time in two years. And meeting his new wife, the last of a long line of fancy women. I wonder what she'll be like? I'll soon find out.

My father and Beenie live on a small council estate, which I've unknowingly passed as the bus came down the hill into the village. I get directions and stride back up, turn right at the cemetery, and walk into a small, neat council estate of around twenty semi-detached houses. I suppose they've built it in this little neuk so as not to spoil the 'olde worlde' look of the village.

Well, better get it over with. The butterflies take flight. As I descend the few steps into the front garden and make for the door I glance at the downstairs window. The light is on in the living room, I can see my father and a woman standing watching me. He half smiles and gives a wave. Involuntarily, I wave back. Shit! I didn't want to do that. I don't want him to think I'm ready to forgive and forget the way he treated Ma and me. There won't EVER be any chance of that. I'm prepared to be civil to him, but that's it.

As I approach the front door, it opens. My father stands there. 'Hiyah,' he says.

'Hello'. I try to say it without any warmth; got to make up for giving that wave. He moves back to let me enter. I stand in the lobby and wait for him to shut the door, then follow him into the living room. He looks really small. At just over 5 feet 2 inches, I'd thought he was quite big when I was a child. Now, at eighteen, I'm 5 feet 7 inches and still growing. That thought pleases me. He'll always have to look up to me from now on. As we come into the room his wife is standing at the fireplace.

'Well, this is Beenie,' says my father.

'Hello,' I don't offer my hand.

'Hello. You'll have had a long trip,' she says. She is obviously nervous. Or is she embarrassed? She sounds almost Irish. I'll later learn there are strong Irish connections, going back centuries, with the people of Galloway. So much so that they're nicknamed

'The Galloway Irish'. I look at her. She's not at all what I expected. She is a small woman, barely 5 feet, reddish hair and loads of freckles. She has a pleasant face and wears no make-up. She might be a couple of years older than my father. That's ten years older than Ma.

'I'll go and make a wee cup of tea. Will you manage a sandwich?'

'Yes, please. I hav'nae eaten for a while.'

She was a widow woman when he met her. No doubt my father's patter would attract her. She will turn out to be very much a country person; quite shy and often naive.

My father and I are left alone. 'So ye fancy a change, dae ye?' His Glasgow accent is still strong. After my stay in West Lothian it sounds even stronger.

'Aye. Ah had a girlfriend but we broke up, so ah just felt like moving somewhere else. It's a pity, 'cause ah quite liked working doon the pit.'

'Better you than me. Ah've never fancied being a miner. Ah'll tell ye what, we'll huv oor work cut oot gettin' ye a full-time job doon here. It's a bloody unemployment black spot roon' this area. Ye'd better get straight intae Stranraer oan Monday and doon tae the Buroo and sign on.'

'What are you workin' at?'

He shakes his head. 'Huh, ah'm in this chicken factory place. Gutting and cutting up chickens for restaurants and shops. It's a bloody cauld job in winter. There's nae heating, and yer workin' in watter aw' the time.' He looks at me. 'Maist nights ah come hame chilled tae the bone.' As I look and listen to him I realise he's looking for sympathy! You'll get nae fuckin' sympathy from me. When Ma was dying she got none from you. Beenie arrives with a tray. She sets it down on the dining table. 'Jist come an' help yourselves.'

As I stand up and make for the table, the nearby sideboard catches my eye. Jeez! It's our old 'Utility' one from Doncaster Street. It's like bumping into an old friend. 'Ah see you've still got oor auld sideboard.'

'Aye, ah brought one or two things fae Glesga'.' He points to a fireside chair. 'Remember that?' Hung over it is an embroidered chairback; a lady in a crinoline dress walks up a path toward a cottage. There are flowers everywhere. I remember it took Ma months to do it. Sometime after the war, maybe 1947. She'd sit nearly every evening working on it as we listened to the wireless. I'd watch her pushing the needle through from underneath, time after time after time in a non-stop rhythm. I'd begin to get sleepy after a while, so soothing was it to watch. I want to reach out and run my fingertips over the stitches. My ma made that. But not while he's around. I go to the table and choose a couple of sandwiches. There are also some fat, three-cornered treacle scones spread with butter.

As we sit and eat we try to make conversation. It's mostly rather stilted. I can't get over how strange it is to sit talking to my father like this. We've never done it before. Never had conversations. I realise he doesn't frighten me anymore. I turn to Beenie.

'Your treacle scones are great.' Her face lights up.

'Take another yin.'

'No, it's okay, I wasn't hinting. They're really good.'

She gets up and returns from the table with another one. Puts it on my plate.

'They're hame made,' says my father, 'she's a great baker.'

There's a noise and the door opens. Two young men come into the room.

'This is Beenie's two sons. This is Billy, he's a year or so younger than you.'

'Hello,' says Billy. He's short and stocky, has a nice friendly face, curly hair and quite a few of his mother's freckles.

'He gets called 'Biff',' says my father, 'named efter Biffo the Bear in the comic.'

'Now! Nane o' your cheek,' says Billy. The two of them laugh. It's obvious they get on well. I get a little feeling of resentment. I'm his only son. All I ever got was a regular supply of bats on the lug from the back of his hand. But that's not Billy's fault. The older boy, he's a man, really – looks to be around thirty – has just stood silent all this time.

'This is my other son, George,' says Beenie. She points at my father, then at me. 'Bobby's son, Robert.' She says it loudly and slowly. George just looks at me, a half smile on his face. Beenie repeats her introduction. The half smile never alters, but he gives a 'Hunff!' as if he is about to laugh, but doesn't. He looks sort of embarrassed. He turns and leaves the room.

'Ah'll go and see tae him,' says Beenie.

Once she's gone my father says, 'He's not quite right. He's very deaf and hardly ever speaks. He can speak, but seldom bothers, jist the odd word. He's no' quite a hundred per cent. Every now and again he turns a bit awkward, no' dae whit he's told. If he becomes too much trouble we get him intae a home for a wee while and that calms him doon for another spell. She tries tae have him at hame as much as possible.' My father turns to Billy, 'Ye could take Robert a wee walk roon' The Port.'

'Aye, nae bother.'

'That's what the locals call Portpatrick, Robert. The Port,' says my father.

Jeez-oh! That's twice in a minute he's called me 'Robert'. The average was maybe twice a year when I was a kid, and that was only when we had company. Otherwise it was 'you' or – on occasion – 'Yah diliterate fucker!' I've never ever found out if there is a word 'diliterate'. He brought that one back from the army. I must look it up sometime. I turn to Billy, 'Aye, that'll be great. You can show me the sights.'

'Hah! That'll take aboot three minutes,' says my father. He and Billy laugh. Once more it flashes into my mind how I was treated. Having a laugh with him wasn't part of my upbringing.

Billy and I set off round the village. He's like a puppy; all excited. He makes it obvious he's looking forward to having a sort of 'new' older brother. George can't be much fun.

'How old are ye, Billy?'

'Sixteen. Nearly seventeen. Ye can call me Biff if ye like. Everybody does.'

We make our way down to the harbour and stand looking out to sea. It's dusk. There's a lovely sky with plenty of red in it. The breeze off the water is quite cool now that the sun's going down.

'Dae ye like the picturs?' asks Biff.

'Oh, aye. When ah lived in Glasgow ah wiz never oot o' oor local halls.'

'That's good. Ah like the picturs tae.'

We stand and blether until the sun has gone. It doesn't take me long to realise I'm going to like him. He's very much a country boy. Works on a nearby farm. But he's open, doesn't try to impress me. His main hobby seems to be eating sweeties. He obviously doesn't clean his teeth as often as he should, already the sugar is beginning to take its toll on them. As it becomes dark the wind coming off the sea begins to cut through us.

'What aboot heading back up tae the hoose?'

'Aye, grand,' he says.

We turn round. The harbour-front is really dark. 'Are there nae streetlights?'

'Naw. They keep talking aboot it.'

Two or three cottages have lights on outside their doors, but they're too widely spaced to be much help. 'Jeez! Ah bet it can get really dark roon' here.'

'Oh aye. In winter maist folk carry a torch. Them hooses wi' the lights ootside usually switch them aff when they go tae bed. Noo and again if it's a really dark night, cloudy and nae moon, sometimes a visitor has walked aff the edge o' the harbour intae the watter! Naebody has been drooned, but they've had a guid soaking.'

'An' a good fright, tae, ah would think.'

We both laugh, then set off up the hill, chattering non-stop as we go.

*   *   *

Back in the house, Beenie has made dinner. By ten o'clock I'm unable to stop yawning.

'Boy! Ah'm no' half ready for ma bed. Aw' that travelling the day has tired me oot.'

'We're usually away oorselves by this time. We're early bedders,' says Beenie. 'You'll be sharing a room wi' Billy. Is that aw'right?'

'Aye, of course.'

'There's twa nice single beds in it.'

'That'll be grand.'

'Mind, you'll be lucky tae get tae sleep wi' Biffo the chatterbox in the same room.' As my father says it, Biff makes as if to grab him and they have a bit of a wrestle, laughing all the while. Surely my father must realise he never ever did things like that with me. At eighteen there's no way I want to be close to him. Not now. When I think of that, my next thought is, what the fuck am I doing down here? Once more I try to figure it out. Was it to make him take a bit of responsibility for me, something he's never done before? Let him see he doesn't scare me anymore? Have a look at his new wife? Maybe, probably, it's a combination of all those reasons. And others I haven't even thought of. I've only just arrived in Portpatrick, but the few times I've seen him laugh and joke with Biff has immediately evoked memories of how he behaved exactly the opposite with me and Ma – the way he was when 'in drink', face twisted in anger, Ma and me having to walk on eggs, always a scowl on his face whenever he spoke to me, him knocking Ma about. Every time he's had a bit of banter with Biff today, I've thought 'that's another man's son'. I was six when he came back from Italy. He never, from the beginning, made an effort to treat me the way he treats Biff. My only use was as someone to hit so as to bait Ma.

Biff and I lie in our beds. He really is a nice lad. I don't intend to let Biff's relationship with my father cause any trouble between us. It's already quite clear Beenie and him don't know the Bobby

Douglas I know. He doesn't drink anymore. He'll have stopped because he knows that 'in drink' he is a nasty piece of work. His mood, his temper, can change in an instant, and when it does there's no reasoning with him. Anyway, I'm too tired to work things out. They obviously think he's great. Why should I spoil it for them? I bet my father's worried in case I intend to tell them how he was with Ma and me.

We lie in the dark, talking, then I say, 'Biff, ah'm gonny have tae go tae sleep. Ah'm dog tired. It's been a long day.'

'Okay, Robert.' I hear him turn round in bed. 'Ah'll see ye in the mornin'. Good night.'

I lie on my side and get comfortable. Jeez! Here I am, living somewhere new again. It's definitely a beautiful wee village. I hope I get a job soon. I like having money in my pocket. Biff and me should soon be good pals. I always wanted a wee brother or sister. Then, my thoughts go where I really don't want them to . . . Nancy will probably be in her bed up in Seafield. There's one thing – I won't be bumping into her down here. It must be over a hundred miles away. I wish she hadn't gone and spoiled it all. I'd still be at Chic's, still working at Polkemmet, her and me would be going out a couple of times a week . . .

Different Folks, Different Strokes

Portpatrick is so quiet it makes Blackburn seem like Las Vegas. Especially in April. As spring becomes summer it gets a little busier at weekends, but Monday to Friday sees few visitors. Most folk who do come for the day travel by coach, There are usually not too many, simply because it takes a long time to get to this isolated village. There's no railway line, and not many working folk have a car. All these factors combine to make Portpatrick southern Scotland's 'Best Kept Secret'.

After a few days' 'holiday' following my arrival, I take the bus into Stranraer to sign on at the labour exchange, and also see what jobs are available. My father has already forecast I'll have a problem, unemployment is high around here. Because this part of Wigtonshire is so remote, there are very few factory-type jobs. The two major employers are farmers and the railway. During the summer a few jobs are created due to the limited rise in holidaymakers. Most vacancies are of the 'casual labour' type; helping with the harvest, or in the catering industry. The labour exchange proves to be like any other; a sparsley-furnished, spartan government department. It doesn't take me long to peruse the 'Job Opportunities' notice board. It contains few vacancies. None is suitable for me. Seeing as I'm here, I decide to take a walk round the town and see what's on offer. There's a cinema and a couple of cafés. Thirty minutes later I catch the bus back to The Port.

* * *

I sit in the kitchen with my father and Beenie. The two of them drink mugs of Camp coffee made with evaporated milk; their favourite. I have tea.

'There's a fellow lives in the Lochans might be able to give you some casual labour on the farms,' says Beenie.

'Ah wouldn't mind daeing that. How dae ah go about it?'

'Ah'll gie him a ring on oor neighbour's phone, see if he needs oanybody at the minute.' She rises and goes next door. Minutes later, she's back. 'He says he can give you two weeks work from Monday. Four pounds a week.'

I was earning more than twice that at the pit. Still, beggars can't be choosers. 'Aye, that'll do for a couple of weeks.'

'The lorry picks up the workers doon the harbour at eight every morning.'

'It's all buckshee,' says my father, 'he jist gives you it cash-in-hand.'

'That's fine. At least it'll let me pay you some dig money and leave me a wee bit in ma pocket.'

Monday morning finds me walking down to the centre of the village to meet the transport. The harbour is deserted except for a small group of people standing near the phone box. As ever, I'm a bit shy about introducing my plooks to new company. 'Eh, are youse waiting for the guy from the Lochans?'

'Aye, this is the queue fur the slave labour,' someone says. They all laugh. At first glance they seem to be all right. I stand a couple of feet away from them. There are seven; two lads around my age and five women who seem to be in their thirties and forties. Like me they're all wearing old clothes, woolly hats, ex-army boots and wellies. I've got my piece and flask in my old army haversack, which I've brought from Blackburn. The lads also have ex-W.D. bags, the women an assortment of well-worn shopping bags.

The breeze coming off the sea is fresh. So fresh, I hope the transport will be here soon. There is no one else stirring in The

Port. The gulls are setting up quite a racket. 'Time this bugger wiz here,' says one of the women. She turns her back to the water.

'Come ower here an' ah'll gie ye a cuddle if you're cauld, Margaret,' says one of the boys.

'It'll tak' a man – no' a shirt button!' replies Margaret. Everybody laughs. One or two shoot little glances to see if I'm joining in. I am.

The noise of a heavy engine rises over the cries of the gulls and a Bedford 3-tonner comes round the corner and approaches us. The back is covered by a canvas hood.

'At long last!' One of the women exaggeratedly points to her watch. 'Where have you been?' she mouths. The driver spreads his arms and shrugs his shoulders. We go round to the rear. The two lads take out the metal pegs and lower the tailgate. They climb on, then reach down to pull the women up. One of them is a plump, dark-headed lass in her thirties. She approaches the tailgate. 'Noo, nae laughing, mind.' She hands up her message bag, puts a toe on the fold-down metal footrest and reaches up with her hand. The biggest lad takes it. She bounces up and down on one foot to try and raise some momentum. 'RIGHT!' she kicks off hard from the ground, gets halfway, then just hangs in mid-air. The boy pulls as hard as he can, face red with exertion. 'Hup! Hup! Hup!' chant those already aboard. 'Dinnae make me laugh,' she says; as she finishes her plea she goes all weak and begins to laugh silently and helplessly. She swings from side to side like a pendulum. The boy can't hold her any longer, so lowers her to the ground and lets go. Everybody is in stitches. She gets her breath back. 'Right, wull we try again?'

'Will it be any help if ah push fae the back?' I offer.

'Aye, otherwise ah'll never get oan the day.' As the next attempt is started I unceremoniously put a shoulder under her large behind. Helpless with laughter she's finally dragged on board where she lies in a heap for a minute or two. Finally recovered, she takes a seat. One of the women looks at me. 'It's the same pantomime every moarning wi' Big Mary. Wait 'til ye see the carry-oan at the other end when we huv tae get her aff!'

We set off on the run to the farm where we'll be working. Someone tells me it'll take forty minutes. The canvas hood flaps continually in three or four places. Draughts come from every-where and whirl round the seating area. The noise is constant. I listen to the tone of the engine as the driver goes through the gears, accelerating and decelerating as we labour along country roads. I like that sound.

Cold and stiff, we arrive at the farm. It'll be a pleasure to start work and get warm. The farmer is waiting, we follow him into a giant field. 'Therr ye are, folks. It's aw' yours.' Rows and rows of never-ending green leaves, in straight lines, lead off from where we stand and are lost in the morning mist. I turn to one of the women. 'Ah'm a city boy. Ah have'nae a clue whit they are.'

She smiles. 'Tatties! You're gonny spend the next week or twa tattie-howking.'

We turn out to be a happy little band as we make our way up and down the never-ending rows of potatoes. The two lads are in the same position as me, looking for full-time jobs, but willing to take any casual work in the meantime. The five women are all married and see it as a chance to earn a little bit extra now and again.

The first few days are tough, then my back gets used to being bent most of the working day. I'm eighteen, fit, so it doesn't take long. The job itself is simplicity: take a canvas sack, start at one end of a 'drill' (row) and slowly move along, pulling the green leaved plants out of the ground. A good shake makes some of the potatoes drop off, those that remain are picked off. They all go into your sack. Repeat. The eight of us work in a line, advancing up the field together. As each sack is filled it's left standing upright. The farmer comes round now and again with the tractor and trailer to collect them. He leaves piles of empty sacks at various places.

As we progress, to alleviate the boredom we spend most of the time being rude to one another. We laugh all day long. The mix of three teenage lads and mature women is a good one. The boys are full of bravado. By the second day I've joined them . . .

'When we get tae the top o' the field ah'm going behind the hedge fur a pee. Dae ye want tae come and put your shoulder under it, Margaret?'

Margaret straightens her aching back. 'Ah imagine ma wee finger wid be enough!' She and her four pals begin cackling. What I'd have done if she'd called my bluff and said, 'Aye!' is a moot point.

We've only had two days of bad weather. During our first week we had one where it showered now and again. There's no such thing as being rained-off at the tattie-howking. If you don't work, you don't get paid. Our second last day turns out to be a stinker. It's raining steadily as we wait for the lorry to pick us up. The rain drums on the canvas hood all the way to the farm. It's still raining as we are decanted at the farm and set off to walk across the mostly harvested field. By the time we reach where we left off yesterday, wellies and boots are thick with rich, red mud and feel like diver's boots. We pick up the first of our sodden canvas sacks and set away. The day becomes interminable. Up and down the rows we move, mostly in silence. Piece-time is spent standing amongst dripping trees which give little shelter. There's practically no conversation. By the end of our thirty minutes we feel chilled and are glad to start again. At the end of that long, dreary shift, the lorry pulls up in The Port. Stiff and full of aches and pains, we disembark. 'Hey! It's stoapped raining.'

'It can go fuck itself!' says Big Mary.

Next morning it's a different world. We have a gorgeous day for our last one. The sun belts down from a cloudless sky. There's the merest hint of a breeze.

'Ye wid'nae think ye could huv twa such different days,' Big Mary shakes her head.

We go up and down the drills whistling and singing. After two weeks, our backs are used to the tattie-howking and we can work for long periods without straightening up to ease them.

'It's always the same,' says Margaret, 'ye get a couple o' weeks at the tatties and by the time yer feenished yer back's broken intae it. Then it'll be a week or twa afore ye get another spell, and ye have tae go through aw' the pain again.'

We are dropped off in the village for the last time. It's just after six p.m. on a balmy, warm evening. We're all sunburnt and look the picture of health. This fortnight of mostly sunny days has done my acne a world of good. Temporarily. I feel a little sad as I say 'cheerio'. I hope we get the chance to work together again. As I climb the hill to the council estate, I feel good. All of a sudden I realise I've hardly given Nancy a thought this last fortnight.

I'm unemployed again but, like Mr Micawber, I feel certain that something will soon turn up.

Echoes of War

My father is sitting reading the local paper. 'Ah! There's one of they ammunition boats coming intae Cairn Ryan. That's a chance of a couple of weeks work for ye, Robert.' He hands the paper to me and points to the War Department advert. 'CASUAL LABOUR REQUIRED FOR MAXIMUM OF TWO WEEKS AT WD DOCKYARD, CAIRN RYAN'

It's not quite a week since I finished the farm work. If the labour exchange don't find me a permanent job in the meantime, at least this'll bring in another few bob.

'If I get the job, what is it they have you doing?'

'It's unloading ammo. When ah first came oot the RAF' – as usual he pronounces it 'raff' – 'Ah did a couple of weeks at it. There's one comes in every six weeks or so. It does nothing else but sail back an' forth tae the Med, load up wi' munitions, and sail back again. It's a big freighter, one o' them Fleet Auxiliary ships.'

'Where does aw' the ammo come from?'

'It's stuff left ower fae the war.'

'The war! That's twelve years ago. You'd think it would aw' have been cleared by now.'

'Ah think it's stuff that wiz stockpiled in case anymore bother started. It's aw' oot o' date, so they huv tae get rid of it before it becomes unstable.'

'What do they do? Dismantle it?'

He laughs. 'Naw, it's unloaded intae auld wartime landing craft, then taken oot tae the Irish Sea. There's a deep trench on the seabed oot there. It gets dumped intae that.'

'And they've been daeing that for the last twelve years. Jeez! There must be umpteen thousand tons doon therr!'

A couple of days later I catch the bus to Stranraer. At the local Territorial Army Drill Hall I queue up with around twenty other guys to be interviewed. An army major, flanked by two civvies, sits at a wooden trestle table. The interview is a formality. A few days after it, I receive a letter telling me I've got the job and to be at the rendezvous point in Stranraer next Monday at seven a.m. to meet the transport.

I've now been living at The Port for four weeks. There's been no friction with my father; we remain civil with one another. Beenie and I get on fine. Biff and me have become good pals, regularly going into Stranraer to the pictures. Sometimes we take George. He seems totally unreachable. Just tags along, never speaks. I'm not sure whether he's taken it in yet who I am. He's not much more responsive with Biff, but all his searching looks are reserved for me. I feel he can't work out why I've moved into their house. Whenever I catch him I usually nod, There's no point in speaking. He always gives his embarrassed smile and looks away. Sometimes, minutes later, he's doing it again. It can become a bit unsettling.

A few days before I'm due to start at Cairn Ryan, Biff and I go swimming at the secluded Sand Deal Bay. This entails a walk of perhaps a mile along the rocky cliffs, then we look down on this beautiful little bay. It seems to be known mostly by the locals, and on this day we have it all to ourselves. The water is cold at first, but, after the initial shock we do a frantic crawl for a few yards and soon warm up. Treading water at the mouth of the bay I drift out just a couple of yards into the open sea. Suddenly I'm surrounded by lovely warm water! 'Hey, Biff! Come out here, you'll not believe it, the water's lovely and warm.'

He's still in the bay; he stays where he is. 'Aye, ah ken. It always is, it's the Gulf Stream!'

Instantly I'm back in Miss Ivy Ross's class at Springbank, my junior school. She's pointing to a map of Europe which includes Britain . . . 'Now if you look at these lines of latitude, children, Glasgow is almost on the same line as Moscow. Yet, we don't get the severe winters they do. And that's because of the Gulf Stream, which flows mostly down the west coast of Britain . . .' I float on my back. This is wonderful.

That evening, as Biff and I watch TV, my father and Beenie bustle about, preparing the dinner. I listen to the occasional banter between them. They get on very well. My father is, obviously, the brainier of the two. She defers to him if there are decisions to be made. He is for ever kidding her, poking fun at her 'country ways', making her laugh. Why was he seldom like that with Ma? One of the major reasons would be the drink. When in his cups my father is a mean drunk with no control over his temper. He won't want Beenie to see this side of him. This is why, very sensibly, he's stopped drinking. If he started to show any of the behaviour Ma and I had to put up with he'd probably be out on his ear! Biff and his older sister Margaret would see to that. I haven't met Margaret yet. She's married and lives in Darlington, over the border in England.

When I'd first met Beenie I'd felt, but not shown, a certain amount of resentment toward her. This is the woman who was carrying on with a man whose wife was dying. After Ma died they didn't even wait the customary year, out of respect, before getting married. Perhaps she'd expected I'd come and live with them right after Ma's death. I hadn't. Did she never wonder why? Yet after just four weeks, I realise that Beenie is a good-living, somewhat naive little country woman who doesn't smoke, drink or swear. I imagine my father will have spun her a tale in which HE was the put-upon husband with this terrible wife. The way he treats Beenie will have convinced her he's such a good man, so it must be true. She'll probably never see the Bobby Douglas Ma and I knew. He could hardly tell her how he regularly used to knock his wife and son about, carry on with other women. I've no doubt if I ever told her she'd refuse, point blank, to believe it. The man she knows is entirely different to the one I grew up with. The man I've seen these last four weeks is new to me. I've been called 'Robert' by him more times in any one of those four weeks than in the first sixteen years of my life.

Since arriving in The Port I sometimes feel my father is a little worried in case, if he and I have a fall-out, I might tell Beenie a few home truths about him. As the weeks have gone on I suspect he's beginning to feel a bit more relaxed. He doesn't know it, but I've no intention of upsetting her – and Biff – by telling them of the father I knew. Why spoil their lives? If it came to it, it wouldn't bother me to upset him. But it's obvious they think he is a decent, hard-working man. I'd be as bad as him if I deliberately caused trouble for them.

Cairn Ryan consists of one long quay with a dozen or so mobile cranes spaced along it. A single railway line runs its length. This small dockyard nestles inside the protection of the large bay known as Loch Ryan. During the Second World War it had been a busy place, frequented by cargo ships and their escorts as they gathered together before heading out, in convoy, into the Irish Sea then the Atlantic Ocean to run the gauntlet of German U-boats. Nowadays it is a quiet backwater.

I pass through the War Department Police on the main gate and, along with fifty or so others, I'm addressed by the major who interviewed us. As he tells us what the job entails, I keep glancing along the quay. A large, grey freighter is tied up nearby. I'm keen to get aboard her. I've never been on a ship. After our lecture we're split up into 'gangs' and led off to where we'll be working. To my delight I've been allocated on board, to work at the bottom of one of her large holds. We clamber up the steep gangway onto the red-leaded, metal deck. I look around. There are two or three officers and crew high up on the bridge. Even though it's daylight, lamps burn at various points on the super-structure. There is a background hum from somewhere below decks as generators and motors run constantly. The ship seems alive, busy – and exciting. A little world of its own. No wonder guys are tempted to join the Merchant Navy. I look again at this solid, reliable ship. A few days ago it had been in the Med. Next week, if someone gives the order, it could be heading for South America. Yet, for the crew, no matter where it sails, it's still their home and workplace. The view from the bridge may change, but below decks all is sure, certain, familiar.

'Right lads, down into the hold.' Our ganger breaks into my flight of fancy. I clamber over the lip of the hold. Oh my God! It's about 50 feet to the bottom. I'm not good with heights. But I don't want to show myself up. Without looking down, I grasp the curved top of the fixed, vertical ladder, step over the lip of the hold and carefully start to descend. The nearer I get to the floor, the more relaxed I become and even increase my speed. I work on the premise that the closer I am to the bottom when I fall, the less hurt I'll be. All during my descent I whistle tunelessly through stiff lips to help me concentrate – and forget what I'm doing.

The hold is almost full of variously sized wooden crates and solid-looking metal boxes. I'm standing on top of red-painted steel boxes which cover the floor. They are perhaps three feet square. I look at the black, stencilled words . . . 'Hand Grenades: Mk 4.' Jeez!

'Okay, lads. We'll clear a bit of floor space by getting rid of these grenades first.' Our ganger shows us where to unscrew the heavy steel lids. 'Now, we save the lids for scrap. But you just leave the grenades in the box, they don't get touched. Too dangerous. Box and grenades all get dumped.' He takes the lid off and I look down at the hand grenades. They lie there in neat rows, nestling between wooden battens which stop them moving around. Like eggs in a box.

'Mind your heads, boys!'

I look up. Framed by the open hold, the boom of the dockside crane cuts across the sky. About 70 feet of cable snakes down toward us. The ganger shows us the correct way to place the four hooks in the metal rings of the box. He waves his hand in a circular motion to the crane operator. We hold the cables until the slack is taken up, then, like a lift in a department store, the heavy box rises silently into the air. As I watch it, I wonder what would happen if one of the cables snapped and the grenades spilled out and came crashing to the floor. If one exploded they'd all go up – along with the rest of the cargo At least it would be quick.

After we clear the grenades we start on the Hedgehogs. These are held in wooden frames rather than boxes. I remember them from wartime newsreels; I never thought I'd get to see them close up. They were launched from long, landing-craft-type ships. Hundreds of them were stacked in metal frames and the vessel would come close inshore, then loose them off in salvoes to 'carpet' coastal defences. Around five feet long, painted green, they have a bulbous warhead about the size of a marrow. The main body is a four-feet-long metal pipe containing solid rocket fuel. Finally, there is the 'finned' tail – the only part saved for scrap. As I patiently unscrew them, I think of the times I sat in the Blythsie with Ma during the war, watching thousands of these bombarding enemy coasts.

At piece-time I come up on deck for my break. I lean on the rail and watch as a couple of fully loaded landing-craft head off into the Irish Sea to dump their cargo of ordnance.

'Ah guess the Second World War is still costing us money, eh?' One of our team, a man about forty whom I know as Willie, leans on the rail beside me.

'Aye, not half.'

We begin to talk about all this redundant ammo, which leads us on to the war, and I find out he'd been a POW in Germany.

'You were a *kriegsgefangener*, then,' I say.

'Aye, for three bloody years. Got captured in North Africa in '42.'

As an avid reader of every escape story that's been published in recent years, I'm soon plying him with questions. I think the topic is just about exhausted when he puts a foot on the rail and points to the army boots he's wearing. 'Got issued wi' these a couple of days after ah wiz liberated. The ones I'd been wearing when ah went 'into the bag' were falling tae bits. Ah wiz so used tae wearing boots, for the next couple of years ah wore them as "best" whenever the wife and me went shopping or tae the pictures.' He takes a sip of tea. 'Summer of '46 the missis and me are havin' a day oot in Edinburgh – ah'm wearing ma boots, of course – and we're walking doon Prince's Street. We're passing some roadworks when, from oot of a hole in the ground, comes a voice. "Hello, Villie, *wie gehts du*?" (How are you?) Ah recognised it right away – and the bastard it belonged to: Gefreiter (Corporal) Mewes! A shitbag if ever there wiz yin. No' averse tae giving ye a clout wi' a rifle butt, or the back of his ha—' We're interrupted by the ganger. 'C'mon, lads. Let's be having ye, time's up.'

Oh, man! 'Ah want tae hear the end of your story, Willie.'

'Aye, let's get doon below, first.'

A few minutes later we're in the hold. 'So, what happened? You were saying he was liable tae clout ye.'

'Aye. A real arrogant, Nazi bastard. First class! Ah never thought ah'd ever see him again. Him and a few dozen of the younger guards had all been pulled oot o' the camp in late '44 and put intae front-line units; Jerry wiz gettin' short o' manpower. We were aw' delighted. Ye can imagine ma surprise – he's talking tae me oot o' a hole in Prince's Street! "Nice to see you again," he says. The wife says, "Who's that?" Ah'll show ye who he is, hen. Ah walks ower tae the edge o' the hole and kicks him right in the face! Jist like taking a penalty. It wiz a fuckin' beauty. Anywye, there's a polis nearby, so he lifts me. A couple of days later ah got fined ten bob. Well worth it! Turns oot the good corporal was captured at the Ardennes Offensive, and wi' him being a Nazi Party member he wiz still being held prisoner.' He points to the toe of his boot. 'That wiz the toecap. Best ten bob ah ever spent!'

Although it's just two weeks work, the pay is good – it includes 'danger money'. I take home around ten pounds each week for my fortnight which is on a par with the pit. I give Beenie a month's dig money, in advance, and I've still got enough in my pocket to last the next two or three weeks if I go easy. Ever the optimist, once again I feel I won't be idle for long.

The Grand Hotel

'They're looking for staff at the Portpatrick Hotel!' Beenie has just returned from the shops.

'Is that the big one up oan the cliff?'

'Aye. Mrs Colton's been telling me. Seemingly they've just been running the bar during the winter for folk using the golf course. The hotel side o' things has been closed doon for nearly a year. Some new people have bought it and want tae open the rooms and restaurant again. Might be a chance for ye tae get a full-time job.'

'Ah wonder what's the best way tae go aboot it? Go through the labour exchange? Or jist have a walk up and say ah've heard there might be jobs going?'

'Och, ah dinnae think there'd be any harm in going up,' suggests Beenie, 'get in before the labour exchange start sending loads o' folk up.'

'Right!' I can feel myself getting excited; I knew something would turn up. 'Ah'll go and get ready, might as well do it now.'

Standing in front of the mirror I focus on my plooky face. Ah don't imagine they'll want tae train me up as a waiter. Put people off their dinner. Ah would think Reception will be out too! It's been just over a week since I finished at Cairn Ryan. It would be smashing to get a job in the village; no travelling time, no fares.

As I climb the many steps up the cliff, the nearer I get to the hotel the bigger and more intimidating it becomes. Its commanding position overlooking the village makes it seem more like 'The Big

House' than a hotel. Seen from the harbour it dominates everything around. 'Manderly' in the movie *Rebecca* comes to mind.

I enter via the front door and approach Reception. It's just after eleven a.m. on a weekday. My feet sink into the richly-patterned carpet. Jeez! That's softer than my bed-chair was back in Glasgow. I've never been in a hotel before. I stand at the desk for a long couple of minutes. There's neither noise nor movement. I think this is what you call 'a deafening silence'. I eye the brass bell on the counter; it's exactly like the ones you see in the movies – a round bell with a bit sticking up in the middle. You hit that with the palm of your hand – I've seen Cary Grant do it stacks of times. I'm beginning to quite fancy hitting it. They always do it twice – 'ding-ding' it'll go. I edge toward it and tentatively raise my hand. Somebody's coming! A door opens. I quickly withdraw it, hoping they didnae see me. Don't suppose I'll ever get the chance to 'ding' it now.

'Yes?' It's an annoyed 'yes'. I obviously don't merit a 'good morning'. He is short and dapper, very like Mr Ramsay who'd been my boss at NB Loco in Glasgow. A James Mason type. The tone of the 'yes' has said it all. He is a superior person – and I'm not. Lately I find I can pick up on things like that. I feel my cheeks colour, but not from embarrassment. There's a surge of annoyance at being spoken to like I was a nobody. Almost with contempt. I've never forgotten the lesson when Miss Ivy Ross taught us what 'noblesse oblige' meant. It also covers folk who don't speak to other folk civilly, because they think they are superior. What they don't realise is, by speaking to you like that for no good reason, they are actually proving they have no class. Somehow, that makes me feel confident. I don't speak to folk the way he's just addressed me. I just wish I was a bit older, more self-confident. Anyway.

'My name's Robert Douglas. Ah live in the village, and ah've heard you might be looking for staff.'

'You've heard correctly. Just come through to the office a minute.' He turns on his heel and sets off back the way he came. I follow. He leads me into an old-fashioned, traditionally furnished office and sits behind a grand desk. I'll bet that makes him feel good. I could easily laugh if I don't watch out. I stand next to a chair. He doesn't offer me it. 'Right. I'm Mr Cartwright and I'm the manager.' I bet you are. 'Now, it's Robert Douglas.' He writes it down.

'How old are you?'

'Eighteen.' I decide I'm not going to call him 'sir'.

'Have you worked in catering or a hotel, before?'

'No.'

'Mmmm. Well, all I can offer you is a position as a kitchen porter. Do you know what that entails?'

I shake my head. 'No, I'm afraid not.'

'It's mostly washing-up. Crockery, pots and pans, that type of thing. Also, keeping the floor of the kitchen clean, scrubbing draining boards, working surfaces. Peeling potatoes, sometimes helping Chef by chopping up veg. Things like that. Do you think you could handle those jobs?'

Portpatrick Hotel

Aged 17, I enjoyed working here – my first glimpse of The Good Life. Then it all went wrong.

'Yes, I think so.'

'Right. I'll take a note of your name and address. I have staff arriving over the next few days and I hope to be up and running a week come Monday. If everything goes according to plan I'll send you a card stating when you can start. Anything you'd like to ask?'

'Eh, how much are the wages?'

'Ah!' he pauses. 'Let's sayyy . . . six pounds ten shillings a week.' I think he's just been trying to figure how much he can get away with. 'That's for a six-day week.' He looks intently at me.

My first thought is, that ain't much. It's well seen jobs are hard to find round here. They think they can get away with paying washers. They can.

'Yes, that'll be fine. Thank you.' It's only good manners that has made me say 'thank you'.

'That's that. I'll be in touch. Can you find your way out?'

'Yes, no bother.' I feel pleased that not once did I call him 'sir' or 'Mr Cartwright'.

A week later a postcard arrives to tell me to start the following Monday. I sign myself off at the dole and, on the due day, enter the hotel by the staff entrance and find my way to the kitchen. The chef, Mr Gallagher, is a man in his fifties. He's dressed as a chef should be – tall white hat, white jacket, blue and white check trousers and a small, folded apron round his waist.

'When you speak to me, Robert, you always address me as "Chef". All right?' It isn't said unkindly. He's introducing me to the traditions of a good kitchen. As we speak, two other chefs enter. One is a heavily-built man in his forties, the other is young, slim and in his twenties. I'm introduced: 'This is Andy Sandilands, he is "Second Chef" and', he points to the young man, 'this is John Brady. John is what is known as a "Commis Chef". That's like an apprentice. John is just about qualified.' We shake hands, my face as red as a Loch Fyne kipper. Andy latches on to my accent. 'You from Glasgow, son?'

'Aye. Maryhill.'

'That's good. John and me are baith Glasgow men.'

You don't get any working class folk staying here. Too dear for them. When ordinary folk go on their holidays they stay at bed and breakfast places, or rent a flat. It's toffs who come to hotels like this. The sort of folk whose middens I used to rake along Wilton Street. Weekends are the busiest. Quite a few businessmen come down for the golf. A lot of them bring their wives as well. On Saturday and Sunday evenings some of the local toffs come for a meal.

By the time I start at the hotel, the boss has recruited enough staff to get the place up and running. The three chefs, as is the norm, live in at the hotel's staff quarters. Also in the quarters are Maisie, a silver service waitress and Harry, the Dutch head waiter. The cleaners and chambermaids are local women who, like me, come to work early in the morning. It's all a new experience for me and I enjoy the job. I don't have a problem working at what many would consider menial tasks. I always get stuck in with a will – and with the intention of producing spotlessly clean items. I take great pleasure in being told now and again that I'm doing a good job. Never by the manager, of course. The staff all get on well together, and I really enjoy working with the fat, balding Andy Sandilands, a natural-born comedian. I find Harry, the Dutchman, an extremely interesting guy. In his late thirties, he is quite handsome, especially in his tails. He reminds me of a young Victor Borge. Like all good head waiters he seems superior to the guests, but in an understated way. With his cultured manner and European accent he brings class to the dining room. More than a few of the female customers find him of interest, often engaging him in long conversations. Harry, of course, gives no sign he's aware of this.

As I get to know him and watch him at work, I begin to realise that a big part of his attraction isn't just his continental charm.

He has an indefinable air – a poise, a gravitas – which seems to say, 'I know something you don't know'. As if he's had experiences which have made him untouchable, sure of himself. He is capable of handling the most insufferable, snobbish guest without raising his voice, let alone losing his temper. He will leave them pacified, yet in no doubt they have been bested.

In time, with my innate curiosity, I'll find out what has, almost certainly, turned him into the type of world-weary character normally only found in fiction. I never get anywhere near the full story, but wheedle enough out of him to know he'd been much involved with the Dutch Resistance. Like many men who've had an interesting war, everything after 1945 is anticlimax.

I also enjoy being in the kitchen and watching the chefs at work. Most of the cooking is done on what looks like a triple-size Aga. This large, coke-fuelled stove is always covered in various types of pots and pans. There is also a four-ring gas cooker, used if small amounts of something – say, a sauce – is needed, or a dish requires an exact amount of heat. I watch in fascination at how quickly a chef can chop vegetables using, what seems to me, a large lethal-looking knife. I find out that in the really top hotels there are chefs who prepare main courses, others who do mostly desserts, still others who make sauces – not just for savoury dishes but also for puddings. I'm for ever asking questions . . . 'Why do ye put broken eggshells on top of the soup, Andy?'

'Cause when it starts tae boil, any wee bits of dirt or grit that haven't been washed oot the veg are attracted tae the eggshells, and ye can jist scoop them oot.'

'Why are ye sieving that broth, John?'

'Ah'm making consomme.'

'Whit's that?'

'It's clear soup.'

'CLEAR soup! Who wants clear soup? Whit happens tae aw' that lovely veg?'

'It jist gets thrown oot.'

'That's a waste. Aw' that veg is the best of it. Can ah have it for ma piece?'

'Aye. Away and get yerself a bowl.'

'Can ah ask why ye put salt intae that dessert, Chef?'

'Because, believe it or not, a pinch of salt brings out the sweetness in sugar.'

'Jeez! Imagine that.'

Now and again I discreetly take a look into the dining room. Saturday nights are best. There are maybe a dozen tables in use; somewhere between thirty or forty customers – 'covers', as they're called in the trade. It all looks so elegant. It is. The lights are low. Candles burn on the tables, the soft light glints on various glasses and silver-plated cutlery. Harry and Maisie serving or standing discreetly by, ready to glide into action at a signal – Harry ignoring anyone who hasn't the class to realise that snapping your fingers is *not* how you attract a waiter's attention. On Saturday evenings the ladies mostly wear long dresses, their escorts a smart suit. Conversation is a murmur. I feel no envy or resentment as I watch these folk enjoy that most civilised of all pleasures – a meal in a good restaurant. I wonder if someday I'll be able to eat at a classy restaurant. Then the thought comes to me. If ever I'm well enough off, no matter how far in the future, I'm going to come here one weekend . . .

'Robert!' It's Andy. 'The roasting trays are piling up in your sink, son.'

'Oh, sorry. Ah'll get stuck intae them.'

I take a last look at the dining room, try to get back into my daydream. Yeah. One weekend, I don't know when, I'm going to come back here as a guest! That's a promise.

One Step Forward, Two Steps Back

I wish I could stop Nancy continually coming into my mind. And refusing to go. If I'd found another girlfriend it might be different. But I haven't, and there doesn't seem much chance either. The Port's so isolated, there's no dancing for miles around. There's nowhere to meet a girl. I don't go to pubs, not on my own. Anyway, I grudge spending money on drink. My social life centres around going to the pictures in Stranraer now and again with Biff – a round trip of twelve miles. When we're there we occasionally go into the café, have a coffee, and splash out a couple of bob on the jukebox. Otherwise it's just walking round The Port, or having a swim out at Sand Deal Bay.

Now and again I'm really tempted to write to Nancy, then I think, what's the point? We're living too far apart now. I'd never see her.

It's the end of May '57. I've been at the hotel a month and feel myself very much part of the staff. You get plenty of afternoons off; it's mornings and evenings when you're needed. If it's a sunny day I usually sunbathe for a couple of hours. For the first time in my life I've got a tan. It ain't half doing my acne a lot of good.

I've recently realised that most of my socialising takes place at the hotel. It's with my workmates that I have most of my fun and laughter. If you have a job where you spend a lot of time laughing, I think that's great.

'Robert, have ye heard, the boss is gonny be looking for a breakfast cook? As ye know, he's been daeing it himself since we started up. He's getting fed up wi' it, so he's gonny advertise for one.' Andy expertly whisks eggs in a metal bowl as he speaks.

'Aye, ah know. You're no' suggesting ah put in for it, are ye?'

'I am. It's a doddle.'

I laugh. 'Aye, if everybody orders boiled eggs!'

'Ah would show ye whit tae dae. Breakfasts are the easiest meals oan the menu.'

I rinse the soapsuds off some plates. 'Do ye think ah could really dae it?'

'Nae bother. If he gives ye the job ah'll run ye through the whole thing and ah'll come in wi' ye on yer first morning. Away up and see the boss. Tell'm if he gives ye the post, ah'll train ye.'

My thoughts race ahead. Could I do it?

'Go on,' says Andy, 'dae ye want tae be a kitchen porter aw' yer life? Nuthin' ventured, nuthin' gained.'

'Right!' I run my hands under the tap, dry them, then hang my rubber apron up. I turn round just as I'm about to leave the kitchen. 'He'll probably laugh me oot o'the office.'

Andy shakes his head. 'Ah bet ye he doesn't. He's sick of havin' tae get up early every morning. He'll welcome ye wi' open arms. You'll see.'

I stride along the plush carpet of the long, hushed corridor. I've hardly seen the hotel since that first day. I just come to work every day via the kitchen entrance. Normally, there's no reason for me to be out here. I wonder what the rooms are like? Anyway, I'll find out someday – when I come back as a guest. When I think about it, I've hardly seen the boss since I started. It's a rare event for him to appear in the kitchen. Under Chef Gallagher and his team everything runs smoothly. A good chef, in his fiefdom, is Master Of All He Surveys. Andy says that if a hotel has a well-run kitchen a sensible manager keeps well away. It's a sign of respect.

*   *   *

I knock on the door. 'HOTEL MANAGER' it says, on a brass plate. At the same time I'm trying to manufacture a wee bit of saliva in my rapidly drying mouth.

'COME IN!' Oh, Jeez! I wish I hadn't bothered. I open the door.

'Eh, could ah have a word wi' ye, Mr Cartwright?' As expected, he's seated at his desk, looking very grand. From somewhere, the thought comes into my head he was probably sitting there having a good read at the *Wizard*, and he's had to slip it into a drawer. I wish I wouldn't have thoughts like that.

'Yes, what is it?' He doesn't sound quite as superior as he did that first day.

'Eh, I wonder if it's possible for me tae be considered for the position of breakfast cook? Ah believe you're looking for one.'

He lifts his fountain pen and sits back. 'If I thought you could do it, I would consider you for the position. Have you any experience?' Once more my mind takes over; I feel like saying 'Oh, ah've ett stacks of breakfasts!' Jeez! Gonny stop daein' that! If ye laugh you'll probably get your jotters (cards). 'Well, what it is, Mr Cartwright. Chef Sandilands says he'll train me up on it. He thinks I'd learn it nae bother. And, if ah get the job, he'll come intae the kitchen with me on ma first morning tae keep me right.'

The boss holds his pen at the slim end and taps his lips, thoughtfully, with the cap. 'Okay, I don't see why you shouldn't get a chance.' I feel a surge of excitement. 'As you probably know, you'll have to come in early as breakfast cook. Once you've finished the breakfasts I'll expect you to put the rest of your shift in, doing what you do now, basically kitchen portering. Is that understood?'

'Oh, yeah. That's fine. I'm quite happy to still do my normal job after the breakfasts are done.'

'Right, we'll give you a try. Tell Mr Sandilands to start training you.'

'Thanks, Mr Cartwright.' I leave the office walking on air. Jeez! Breakfast cook. This is a proper, recognised job in the hotel business. 'Me? Oh, ah'm breakfast cook at the Portpatrick Hotel.' ZippedyDoodah! I just hope I can manage it.

Andy is a good teacher. First of all he puts me at my ease . . . 'Now, think aboot it. Breakfasts don't vary. You can have a fairly large selection of dishes on a luncheon or dinner menu. But there's only so many items on a breakfast one – and they don't change. Once you've learned how tae dae them, that's it.' He lists them. 'There's the full English – or Scottish – of bacon, eggs, sausage, fried bread, tomato and black pudding. Some folk like that, but with scrambled eggs instead o' fried. Some want poached eggs on toast, or muffins. Others like kippers. Before they have their cooked breakfast ye give them the choice of fruit juice, cereal or porridge. With their meal there's tea or coffee. That's just about it.'

'Sounds a lot tae me, Andy. Ah'll never remember aw' that.'

'Aye, ye will. When ye come in tae work in the mornin' bring a wee notebook with ye. Write in it what the breakfast menu consists of, what preparations ye can dae in advance, and what's yer routine in the mornings. Within a couple o' weeks you'll find you'll no' even be looking at yer notebook anymore.' He taps his forehead. 'It'll aw' be in here. You'll manage nae bother.'

And I do. Next morning, armed with a newly-purchased note-book, I come in just after five a.m. I lift off the three circular covers on the stove, stir up the sleeping coke, then pour in some more. On go some pans of water to start their slow journey to boiling, and I lay out the various dishes and implements that I'll need – Andy primed me the night before.

I go downstairs to the less than plush corridor of the basement staff quarters and find Andy's room. I quietly open the door. Jeez! There's a smell like a Bombay taxi-driver's hernia support! Holding my breath, I enter. Andy's lying on his back, mouth open, snoring. I give his shoulder a shake. 'Andy! It's half five.' I shake him again. Nothing. Then, on the third shake, he stirs. 'Fuck off!' I give him a final shake. 'Andy!'

'Andy, ye said ye'd keep me right.'

Without any bodily movement and, as far as I can see, without moving his lips, he makes an attempt at communication. 'Wishah'dneversaidah'dcum in wi' ye. Fuckinhatemoarnins!' This major effort seems to leave him momentarily exhausted.

'Aw c'mon, Andy. Ye said ye'd come in ma first morning.'

'Ahknow, wishahudnae.' There's a pause, then at great personal sacrifice he forces himself into a sitting position. I try not to laugh. He's just wearing a short semmet. He tiredly rubs his face with both hands, then sits, his face cupped in them, for all the world like a large, pissed-off garden gnome. 'Whit time did ye say it wiz?'

'Jist gone half past five.'

'Should be a law against huvin' tae get up at this fuckin' time.'

Ten minutes later Andy enters the kitchen, fully dressed in his whites but still bleary-eyed. 'Tea! Strong! Sweet!' He points to the simmering kettle on one of the hobs. Halfway through his mug of tea he finally swings into action, and for the next hour I receive a master class on being a breakfast cook. I soon find that all the things I watched Ma do over the years isn't how it's done in a hotel kitchen. It's very much 'tricks of the trade'. Scrambled eggs are cooked in a small pan which is placed inside a larger pan of simmering water. This indirect heat ensures the eggs won't burn or stick. Poached eggs are cooked in a pan containing water which is just off the boil, to which has been added salt and a little vinegar. Kippers are poached in an enamel ashet (rectangular dish). Eggs are fried slowly, so as not to crisp the edges, in a frying pan containing a goodly amount of best beef dripping. The egg doesn't get flipped over the way Ma would've done. Instead, you flick hot fat onto it until the top is cooked. I watch carefully, learn quickly and next morning succesfully produce nine or ten breakfasts alone. Less than a week later, as Andy forecast, I have no further need of my notebook.

I soon get used to rising at five a.m. and I really enjoy the brisk walk to work. It's as if the mornings belong to me, all the houses are dark and no one stirs. I feel real pleasure as I come into the silent, half-lit hotel; guests and staff are still abed. For thirty minutes or more it becomes 'my' hotel. I get the stove fired up and begin my preparations. The first batch of customers are usually the golfers, keen to make an early start on the links. The first member of staff to appear is usually Harry. To serve breakfasts he wears black trousers, white shirt and ordinary tie. This is as near to casual as Harry gets. He alternates with Maisie to cover the mornings. If we have a busy weekend both will serve. I always have coffee ready for Harry's arrival.

'Andy?'

'Whit?'

'Now that ah'm daeing breakfast cook, shouldn't ah have had a rise in wages? How much do ye think the job should pay?'

'Somewhere between eight and ten pounds a week ah would think.'

I look at my pay slip. 'Ah'm just getting the same as always.'

'You'd better have a word wi' the boss. He's mibbe forgot.'

Forty minutes later I've finished washing-up. I make my way to the office, knock, and I'm instructed to enter. 'Eh, Mr Cartwright. As ye know, ah've been doing breakfasts for over a fortnight. But ah'm still gettin' the same wages as always.'

'Well, that's all I can afford to pay you. After all, you're not *really* a breakfast cook, are you?'

I'm a bit taken aback. 'But ah'm doing the job. And ah'm still doing kitchen porter as well. Surely if ah'm doing breakfast cook ah should get paid for it?'

He sits there looking smug. He knows jobs are hard to come by in the village. 'Well, I'm afraid it's a case of take it or leave it!'

My mind races. He thinks I'll just put up with this. I like the job and I don't want to lose it. I'm now doing two jobs for this little bastard yet he's trying to see if he can get away with paying me just one wage – the lowest. I feel myself getting angry at the way he thinks he can treat me. I've been doing a bloody good job for him. A good two jobs. I know what Ma would tell me to do . . . 'Well, if ah'm no' gonny get paid for it, ah'm not gonny do the job, Mr Cartwright.'

That supercilious look never leaves his face. 'That's your decision. You can revert to your kitchen porter duties. I'll start doing breakfasts again until I get a proper breakfast cook.'

It's the 'proper' that does it. He's speaking to me just like he did on the day I first met him. I feel the hair tingle on the back of my neck. My reaction is spontaneous, knee-jerk. 'Ach! Ah don't think ah want tae work here anymair. You can take a week's notice, Mr Cartwright.'

THAT'S got the wee bastard! He tries to keep the smile on his face, but it's now rigid, forced. He's now short a kitchen porter and a breakfast cook. He didn't expect that. It's obvious he won't try and persuade me to stay. Superior people can't show that a minion has just fucked up their day. Probably their week. He tries to salvage something. 'Don't bother with a week's notice. You can finish now.'

I shrug my shoulders. 'Yeah, that's fine.' I turn to leave, then remember something. 'What about my week's "lying time?"'

'I have your address, I'll send it together with your National Insurance card. Goodbye.' He pretends that there's something important amongst the papers on his desk and he's got no more time for me. He's a bit red in the face.

'Cheerio.' I leave the office. I've just packed my job in, but for the moment I feel good. I think I just shaded that one on points.

I come into the kitchen. Andy and John are both busy. Andy looks up. 'Whit did he say?'

I tell him the tale. 'Aw, Jesus! Ah feel as if it's ma fault.'

'Don't be daft. How's it your fault? I intended tae ask him aboot ma wages, anyway. So it was bound tae happen. He thinks he can get away wi' it 'cause jobs are short roond here. Fuck him!'

'If ye wait 'til Chef comes in he might be able tae make him see how unfair that is.'

I give it a bit of thought. 'Naw. Ah don't want tae work for somebody who tried tae treat me like that. Ah thought ah was daeing a good job . . .'

Andy interrupts me, 'You were daeing a good job. Two good jobs. There's not been a single complaint aboot a breakfast. You're spot on wi' the washing-up.'

I'm surprised at how strongly I feel about what's just happened. 'Well, even though it means ah'm oot o' a job, ah'm not gonny let maself be shit on. Anywye. There's nae good wasting anymair time on it. Ah'm away boys. Say cheerio tae everybody for me, will ye, Andy.'

I'd like to say how much I liked working with them, and that I enjoyed the job. But I don't have the words, the confidence. I'd almost certainly start crying.

'Ah'm really sorry, son. You're a good grafter. I've enjoyed working wi' ye. Aw the best.'

As I leave the kitchen I turn and give them a quick wave. My last picture of Andy is of him leaning on his outstretched hands on the butcher's block, watching me go.

As I walk back up to the house my mind is full of it. Well, even though I'm out of a job, at least I wiped the smile off the little bastard's face for a while. Fuck him! I hope it's months before he gets a breakfast cook. I wonder how many mornings, as he's dragging himself out of bed, he'll think, 'Just another couple of pounds!' It's some consolation.

Of Trams and Tenements

It's nearly midnight. A couple of days now since I left the hotel. I'm lying in bed, in the dark, listening to *Late Date* on AFN (American Forces Network) from Frankfurt, Germany. Biff's sleeping, so I have it on low. Jeez. Americans really know how to present radio programmes. The DJ is some US Air Force sergeant. I like *Late Date*. They always play loads of Big Band stuff, or cool jazz. What they're playing suits my mood. I've got the blues. Bad. When you're American it's okay to say that. If you're British it somehow sounds phoney. We get pissed off. Or fed up. Either way, I'm depressed. I really liked that job. All the way from south Germany comes the strings of the Nelson Riddle Orchestra with the intro . . . then it's Sinatra with 'I'm Walking Behind You'. Instantly there's a direct connection from that far away studio, the needle on the record, the soft glow of this Bakelite radio's dial and Sinatra singing to me. Personally. Its just like he says, I don't want to be walking behind her when she marries someone else. When Nancy marries someone else. Oh man! Now I really have the blues. Sinatra knows exactly how I feel. I'm gonny write to her tomorrow. Tell her I still think about her. I'll have to. As the record ends, the DJ, low-voiced, smoothly cuts in. I begin to doze. I suddenly come wide awake. I know! I'm gonny go back to Glasgow!

It's a week later. The bus wends its way back up the rugged coast. All of a sudden there's a lot to look forward to. I've written to Nancy, told her how I feel, and she's quite happy for us to start seeing each other again. Yes, she promises there'll be no more of that stupid game of hers. But its not just that. After two and a half years I'm going to be back living in Glasgow! Those two facts make me feel so good, I'm not in the least concerned that I haven't got a job – and I don't know where I'll be sleeping tonight. I've also got just over seven pounds in my pocket. That's about enough for two weeks' digs. If I don't eat. There was no way I was going to ask my father for a loan. I don't want to owe him anything.

As the single-decker twists and turns its slow way north, I've plenty time to sit and think. I'd enjoyed my few months in Portpatrick. My curiosity as to what my father's new wife was like has been satisfied. His relationship with me has changed. Probably because I'm too big to bully now. Anyway, I sometimes felt quite guilty living with them, as though I was letting Ma down. I have no affection for him whatsoever. I never will. As far as I'm concerned, the wrong one died of cancer.

At long last the bus enters the Glasgow suburbs. My excitement grows. As usual I can't take my eyes off the trams and buses with their familiar Corporation livery of green, cream and orange. We enter the city centre with its fine buildings, all covered with the grime of a century or more of smoke and soot from a hundred thousand coal fires. Folk throng the pavements as they go about their business; I feel like knocking the window and calling, 'I'm back!'

En route I've been working out what to do to make the money spin out. I'll have to get cheap digs until I get a job. The going rate is usually at least three pounds a week for bed and breakfast. That'll leave me with just over a pound for a fortnight's grub. About enough to feed a cat. I'll also need money for fares if I'm job-hunting. There's only one place to go if it's cheap accommodation you're looking for – the Model Lodging House. I know from hearsay there are two in the city. Somewhere down the city centre is 'The Model', known in Glasgow rhyming slang as 'The Deedle Doddle'. This is the last refuge for the city's drunks and down-and-outs. Most of the accommodation is in dormitories, and stories are legion of newcomers waking in the morning to find valuables and clothing have been stolen in the night. To keep shoes safe it's usually recommended that you lift the end of your bed up and place a shoe under each leg at one end. Next up the ladder, by a very short rung, is The Great Eastern Hotel in Duke Street. A model in all but name. This is classified as 'a working man's hotel' – its residents are supposed to have a job. This rule doesn't seem to be strictly enforced. When I used to come in to Glasgow on the bus from West Lothian, it passed the Great Eastern. Often quite a few of the residents would be loitering outside, looking like an identity parade on a tea break. Little did I think that less than twelve months later I'd be joining them. Customers in The Model book their bed one night at a time. I've been told the accommodation

Tramcars and cobbled setts. When I returned
in 1957 it was still 'my' Glasgow.

in the Great Eastern is in cubicles and you pay on a weekly basis.
I decide, sight unseen, that the Great Eastern offers the best
chance of me spinning out my seven pounds – and hanging onto
my shoes.

The Great Eastern is a large, solid building with many rows of
smallish windows. It looks as though it really belongs in the
Bronx, or wherever Skid Row is located. As usual, there's a few
middle-aged men hanging about outside, trying to figure out how
they got here. I climb the broad stairs at its entrance, walk into
the unlit foyer and approach 'Reception'. A man in shirt sleeves,
copper collar-studs shining, sits behind the counter reading the
Daily Record. The paper-seller must have sold out of the *New
York Daily News*. Absorbed in the sports pages he doesn't see me
at first. I'm used to that. There's a noise coming from behind the
half-open office door. I lean forward a bit, certain I'll catch sight
of Edward G. Robinson – he's bound to be the manager. My
slight movement catches the eye of the clerk. He looks up. 'Aye?'

He must have recently transferred from The Dorchester.

'Eh, how much is a room per week?'

He folds the paper. 'Well, there's cubicles, and there's rooms.
There's nae difference in size, but the cubicles have nae windaes.
The rooms are really jist cubicles – wi' windaes. The cubicles are
thirty bob a week [one pound fifty pence], the rooms are thirty-
five bob a week [one pound seventy-five pence].' He stands
looking at me. If he was American he'd definitely be called Artie.
I have to make a decision; I'm only here for, hopefully, two
weeks. Who needs a window? It'll save ten bob.

'Eh, ah'll have a cubicle, please.'

'Ah'll gie ye a look at it. Some folk change their minds when they
see it.' Obviously he's majored in public relations. He selects a key,
then makes for the lift. I follow. The lift's well worn and has a
musty smell. So did the foyer. We rise to the third floor, the door
slides open and we enter a dark, wood-panelled corridor. We make
a few turns along the narrow, maze-like runs. There's a door every

eight feet or so. He stops at one, turns the key and pushes the door open. He reaches in and turns on the light; I never knew it was possible to get 20 watt bulbs. I look into the small, cell-like room. Maybe I should ask for one with a window. Then I think of the ten bob I'll save. There is a bed, small bedside table, chair and a narrow wardrobe. Should I ask for a look at the penthouse?

'Will this dae?' The Maitre d'Model scratches his neck.

'Aye, this'll be aw'right.'

'Right, 'mon ah'll show ye where the washroom is.'

He shows me. It's a fair sized, white-tiled room with a line of eight or nine hand basins under a large discoloured mirror. He points to the few baths, which are in cubicles. As we walk back out to the corridor he gives me the rest of the house rules. It's delivered in a monotone as though this is the 624th time he's delivered it. 'Every Thursday moarning ye put oot wan pillow-case and wan sheet also yer towel nae drunkeness allowed nae

*The Great Eastern Hotel. Once you were
in here, the only way left was up.*

noise that'll disturb yer fellow guests and the ootside doors is loaked jist efter eleven-thirty.' He stops to draw breath. I can smell drink on it. He continues, 'There's a canteen where ye can get cheap eats any other queries there's alwiz somebody oan the desk we need a week in advance if ye need a knock in the moarnin' jist leave yer cubicle number at the desk and state whit time.' He looks at me. I assume that means he's finished.

'Right, that aw' sounds fine.' I can hardly remember any of it, especially the arrangements for changing the bedding. Anyway, I can always ask again. 'Ah'll just came back doon tae reception wi'ye. Ah'll actually gie ye two weeks in advance.'

I come back up to the landing and enter my cubicle. I look around, then tap the 'wall'. As I suspected, it's just thin slats of wood. I look up. Jeez! There's no ceiling. The cubicles are made up of ten-feet-high partitions. The actual ceiling of the large 'floor' is four feet or so higher. Somebody who's fit enough could easily climb over into any of the cubicles. With the walls being so thin AND as there's no ceiling, I can hear most of what's going on around me. There are at least two folk snoring; a conversation going on a few doors away. I can hear it all. Och, well. Beggars can't be choosers. I look at my watch; just after half three. I know, I'll away up tae Maryhill, see who I can see. That thought cheers me up. I won't have to go far for a tram. The number 23 runs along Duke Street and on up to Maryhill. That's handy.

The 'new' tram glides to a halt at our stop on the Maryhill Road. I'm just a few steps from Sammy's close, but I'll wait 'til later. Sammy'll be at work. There they are! My eyes drink in the double pleasure of Cocozza's Café and the Blythswood Cinema. Always there. Permanent, reliable, a constant reminder of happier times. Great! My spirits lift – I can start going to the Blythsie again. As I walk along Trossachs Street I decide to call in to the little shop halfway along to say 'hello' to Mr and Mrs Barlow, the owners.

As I enter, the Barlows are behind the counter. 'Hiyah!' They look up.

'Oh, hello Robert. Haven't seen you for a wee while. How's life treating you?'

It must be the best part of a year since I last saw them, when I came into the city on a day trip from West Lothian. I give them a brief resumé of the last twelve months. 'So ah've decided tae come back tae Glesga. Next thing on the agenda is tae get maself a job before the money runs oot.'

Mrs Barlow looks at me. Like many Glasgow women 'in business', she's wearing a hat.

'You're looking for a job, are you?'

'Aye. The sooner the better.'

'Mmmm, I might be able to help you. Until I married Jimmy I was secretary to the manager of the Clyde Navigation Trust. Would you like me to ring him and see if there are any jobs going?'

I've never heard of it. But the name has a good solid ring. 'Oh, aye. Please. That would be great. Thanks very much.'

'Right. If you call in tomorrow afternoon I should have been in touch with him.' She gives me a mock searching look 'I'll be telling him you're a good, reliable lad. You won't let me down, will you?'

'Ah definitely won't. Ah can guarantee ye that.'

I chat for another few minutes, then decide it's time to do the rest of my rounds. 'Ah'll away and see if I can catch some of my pals. Ah'll see ye tomorrow. Thanks again, Mrs Barlow.'

As I walk round to Doncaster Street for my usual dose of pleasure and sadness, I'm feeling a lot cheerier. I'm glad I decided to call in on the Barlows. I'm pleased they didn't ask me where I'm staying. To mention the Great Eastern would give a bad impression. It's always associated with being down and out.

As I pass 60 Trossachs Street I decide to nip up to the top landing and see if my other good pal, John Purden, is in. Just before I knock I look at the brown-painted wall to the left of their door. One day I'd been waiting on the landing for him while he finished his dinner. I'd used the blade of my penknife to scratch into the flakey plaster, 'JOHN PURDEN-ROBERT DOUGLAS 1953'. A long four years ago.

Phemie, one of his sisters, answers the door. As I expected, she doesn't recognise me. 'Hello, Phemie. It's Robert Douglas. Does John happen tae be in?'

She laughs. 'John disnae live here anymore, Robert. He's married and living doon in Shamrock Street. Number 21. They're expecting their first bairn any day now.'

I haven't seen John for over two years. Even though, at twenty, he's two years older than me, it's still a surprise to find he's married – and about to be a father!

'Oh, Jeez, ah did'nae know that. Ah've been livin' oot o' Glesga this last couple o'years. Anywye, will ye tell him ah'm back livin' in the city again, and when ah'm settled ah'll take a wee run doon one evening tae see him.'

'Aye, ah'll tell him.'

'Right. See you around. Cheerio.'

'Aye, cheerio Robert. Nice tae see ye again.'

I go back down the stairs, my mind full of how quickly things are changing. Have changed. Jeez, it's no time at all since John and I were going to the pictures a couple of nights a week, sitting in the stalls; splitting five Woodbines between us; stuffing ourselves with sweeties. It's funny how I always went out with Sammy and John separately. They didn't know each other. I grew up with John. Sammy I met at secondary school. Now John's married and they're expecting a bairn.

I turn the corner into Doncaster Street. My street. As I do on every visit, I go up and stand at the entrance to my close. Once more I try to get the feeling that I still live there. That all I have to do is walk into the back close and the door will be dark brown; the brass nameplate with R.J. Douglas will still be there. And I

KNOW, right at this moment, Ma's in there. As long as I stay at the close-mouth and don't put it to the test, it's all true.

Even though my cousin Ada will probably be in, I decide I won't call in today. I've kept the best 'til last. It's time to go round to Sammy's. See Lottie and Frank. Jeez, I hope I'm not gonny find out Sammy's married and the father of twins!

Once more I climb the stairs at 375 Maryhill Road and stand a moment at their door. The plastic nameplate is still there. It never changes. I wonder if Sammy knows how lucky he is. The familiar sound as I ring the bell leads, as ever, to Sally running along the lobby, barking. 'Sally! Sally!' I then make my usual chirping sound. She stops barking, starts snuffling at the bottom of the door to try and get my scent. Now she gives excited little whines. I'm pleased that she never forgets me. There's a voice. 'Come oot the buggerin' road!' Lottie must have been on a dog-handling course. I hear the Yale lock turn, then Sally's out and round my feet.

'Hello, Lottie!'

'Fuck me!' She sniffs and turns at the same time, sets off back along the long lobby. 'C'mon then, if yer coming.' I shut the door behind me, then follow the wraparound peenie into the living room. That was probably much the same welcome Frank would have got in 1945 after four years on Russian convoys. I breathe in; the house has the same lived-in, cooking, dog and cat, Woodbine smell like always.

'So how are ye, Lottie?'

'Ach! Jist hinging oan.'

'Frank at work?' Frank is a male nurse at Ruchill.

'Aye, he's still battling away. Ah'll put the kettle oan.'

'Whit aboot Sammy?'

'He's workin' at some building site doon the toon at the minute. He should be hame shortly.' Sammy's a joiner.

We settle down on either side of the fireplace with our tea. 'Dae ye want a sandwich?'

'Ah wid'nae mind.'

She starts to struggle back out of her chair. 'Awkward bugger! Ye might huv said before ah sat doon.'

I can't help laughing. 'Ye did'nae ask me before. Ah did'nae know ye were gonny offer me a sanny.'

'Ah should'nae need tae ask. If ye wanted a sanny ye should huv said. You're at yer Aunty Lottie's. Anywye, whit dae ye want oan it?' She rummages about in the green and white kitchen cabinet. 'There's Spam,' one or two things fall out and land on the floor, 'and there's mair Spam!'

'Ah'll huv corned beef!'

'You'll huv Spam and fuckin' like it!' Jeez, how I love being up here.

We hear a key in the door and Sally, barking, rushes into the lobby. Toby, the black and white cat, wakens, gives her a dirty look, stretches, then gets comfortable again.

'This'll be buggerlugs,' says Lottie through a cloud of Cumulus Woodbinus.

Sammy comes into the room. 'Stone me! How're ye gettin' on, Robert?' He puts his toolbag down in the corner then steps back into the lobby to hang his jacket on the hallstand. He comes back in and gives Toby's head a vigorous ruffling with his fingers. He also gets a dirty look. The cat rises, turns, then settles down with its back to the assembled company.

We sit and blether for a few minutes, then the door opens slowly and old Sam comes in. As on my last visit, I hadn't liked to ask how he was in case he'd maybe died while I'd been away. I'm sitting in his chair, so I rise. 'Hello Sam, here's your chair. How are ye?'

'Och, not so bad.'

'He's jist came back tae live in Glesga,' says Lottie.

Sam shakes his head. 'Aye, that's good. Are ye fixed up wi' a job and digs?'

'Aye. Ah've got maself digs, and ah think ah might be gettin' a job wi' the Clyde Navigation Trust.' I tell them about my conversation with Mrs Barlow, but make no mention of the Great Eastern.

At around half eight I reluctantly decide it's time I headed back down town to spend my first night in the Deedle Doddle. As the day has worn on, the thought has become less and less inviting. Frank is on late shift, so I won't see him. As I leave, Sammy comes out to the door with me and we stand talking on the landing at the head of the stairs.

'Now that I'm back in the city, dae ye want tae get back intae the auld routine, going tae the pictures and things like that? Unless you're mibbe daeing a bit o' winching' (courting).

'Naw, that'll be great. Ah'm no winching at the minute. Been oot wi' the odd lassie, but nuthin' steady. Since you left ah've been stoating aboot noo and again wi' Tom Buchanan, the undertaker's son. But he's been winching strong this last wee while, so ah've no seen much o' him.'

'Right. So will we have a night oot later this week?'

'What aboot the day after the morra?' says Sammy. 'Come up for me aboot half seven and we'll have a wee donner oot.'

'That'll be great,' I say, 'be jist like auld times. Ah'll see ye.'

'Aye, cheerio. See yah, Robert.'

As I come out onto the Maryhill Road I decide I'll treat myself to one of Bundoni's fish suppers before I catch my tram. I'll take the long way round, via Hinshaw Street.

From 20 yards or more the smell of fish and chips goes round my heart. I begin to salivate. Under bright lights bouncing off white tiles, I join the queue. As we slowly move along I look around. It may be more than two years since I was last in, but once again, nothing's changed. Mrs Bundoni, her son and two daughters, are dressed in their immaculate whites and hard at work at the fryer. As the shop is busy I won't bother making myself known to

them. They'd probably remember me, but Mrs B would definitely remember my father. When he returned from Italy in 1945,
he'd spent the last eighteen months in the port of Bari in the
south. In a Royal Engineers' 'Docks Operating Company', he'd
been working every day with Italian labourers and, on his return,
spoke almost fluent southern Italian. Mrs Bundoni's Italian.
Whenever he appeared – usually a Saturday night – he and
Mrs B would move along to the far end of the counter and have a
'rerr auld parliamo' to themselves.

I walk down the Maryhill Road until I finish my feast, then catch
a 23 back to Duke Street. As I'm transported once more through
the streets of my city, I think what a long day this has been. I was
still in Portpatrick this morning. It seems more like two days ago.
The Great Eastern, and the 'room' that awaits me, keeps popping
into my head. I realise I've been putting off going there for as
long as possible. Anyway, I've no option. I try to think of other
things to cheer myself up. You'll be seeing Nancy soon. You're
gonny have a night out with Sammy a couple of nights from now.
I can go to the Blythsie one night this week, then over to
Cocozza's when I come out – if I have the money. Jeez! Things
haven't changed, Ma. Remember how we often had money for
the pictures, but not enough for the café. Huh! So what else is
new?

I make my way through the lobby of the hotel. Under the lights
it's even more dingy. The lift doors open at the third floor. Jesus
wept! It's gloomier than ever. There are just a few lights at the
ends of the narrow corridors. They rely on the overspill from the
low-wattage bulbs above each cubicle. God! If you weren't
depressed when you came in here, the place would make you
depressed. I unlock my door and step into my drab . . . cell. You
can't call it a room. Switching on the bulb has somehow made it
seem darker. I stand for a moment just looking at where I am.
The pleasures of the day evaporate. They can't compete with

this. C'mon! It's only until you start your new job. It's temporary. You'll really only be sleeping here. I take my thin, well-used towel and toilet articles and make for the washroom. It's empty. From what I've seen of my fellow residents I don't think I'll ever have to queue for a sink. I have a good wash, clean my teeth, then return to 'cell block twenty'.

I lie in bed reading *The Latter Days at Colditz*. It's hard to concentrate, what with new room, hard bed, and all the noises coming from every direction. The light is so poor I have to hold the book at an angle. The similarity between this dingy cell and Colditz isn't lost on me. Then there's the noise. Being unable to get away from other people. In all the escape stories I've read, there are frequent references to guys suffering from depression simply because they couldn't get away from other prisoners. A longing to be on their own in a quiet place.

Eventually the adventures of these persistent escapers takes me out of it, and I begin to get sleepy. As there's no bedside lamp, I have to get up to switch off at the wall. The faint light from other cubicles, bouncing off the dirty ceiling, leaves me in a grey twilight. Voices, mostly old, come from all over. Some drunk, some depressed, many angry . . .

'Will youse fuckin' shut up! Thurr's folk trying tae sleep.'

'It's no' half ten yet so you fuckin' shut up!'

'Blethering every fuckin' night. Ye want tae gie people a brekk.'

Another voice joins in. 'Why don't YOU stoap comfuckin' plaining? You make mair noise than they dae wi' aw' yer moaning.'

This little conflagration dies down, but there's a continual symphony of mutterings, coughing, farting, occasional shouts, things being dropped, groaning, snoring until, around ten forty-five one of the caretakers makes his nightly round, knocking on the doors of those still with their light on, telling them to put it out. Everyone seems to comply. There's no decrease in noise.

Feeling a bit down, I lie in the dark listening to all the ramblings going on around me. What a bloody place! Jeez, I hope Ma doesn't know where I am. If ye do, it's jist temporary, Ma. Honest.

Catch Twenty-one and a Half

The offices of the Clyde Navigation Trust are as late Victorian as the name would lead you to expect. The manager, Mr Bryce – Mrs Barlow's old boss – also suits the premises, but appears none the worse for that. Around fifty, wearing a dark blue pinstripe and sporting a well-trimmed moustache, he could have been supplied by central casting. The interview is so short I hardly have time to blush. In no time at all he's saying, 'I'm prepared to offer you a job with one of our maintenance squads. The starting wage is nine pounds fifteen shillings a week. The post is fully superannuated and, if that is acceptable to you—' he stops to consult his desk calendar, 'You can start on the first Monday in August. Is that all right?'

'That's fine, sir. But, eh, is it possible to start before then? I'm running a wee bit short of money.' This is the second week in July.

He smiles. 'I think you must have forgotten. We close down on Friday for the Fair Fortnight.' The Fair Fortnight is the annual 'trades holiday' when most big employers shut down while their staff have their two weeks off.

'Oh, Jeez! I clean forgot all about that. Anyway, I'll just have to manage.'

'On the Monday you're due to start, just make your way to Prince's Dock in Govan and report to Mr Alec McKechnie, the ganger, at eight a.m. He'll be easy to find. All the maintenance gangs take a wooden hut, a bothy, with them and erect it where they're working. As a matter of interest, do you know what the Clyde Trust do?'

'No, sir.' I've no problem calling this man 'sir'. What a difference from that jumped-up little get at the Portpatrick Hotel. I hope he's still looking for a breakfast cook!

'We are responsible for the general maintenance of the docks, quays and wharves on the river. We also dredge the river and keep it navigable for the many ships coming in and out. The ferries that criss-cross the Clyde from the city out to as far as Renfrew are also run by us.'

'Gee, I didn't know it was such a big organisation, sir.'

'Not many people do.' He rises and offers me his hand. 'I hope you'll enjoy working for us.'

'Thank you very much.'

As I leave the head office I'm pleased at landing a job so quickly. But not being able to start until after the Fair Fortnight is a problem. I hadn't intended going to the Buroo to claim unemployment pay if I'd been able to start next Monday. But's it's now more than two weeks until the holiday's over AND I'll have to work a week's lying-on. Jeez! It'll be the second week in August before I lift my first pay packet. I've got just over four pounds in cash. I've paid two weeks in advance at the Ritz. I'll have to pay another three weeks before I get my first wage. I've got to feed myself, I'll need tram fares. I'm going to have to sign on as unemployed until I start work, there's nothing else for it.

I approach the concierge at the reception desk in the Great Eastern. It's the same guy that was on when I arrived. It's late morning, so he's getting tore in to the *Daily Record*. I explain about me getting a job, and why I'll have to sign on for a couple of weeks . . . 'So what labour exchange deals wi' folk living in here?'

He holds the newspaper between his open knees. 'It's Bridgeton. Mind, if ye get any money doon therr it'll be a fuckin' miracle. They're as tight as a duck's arse – and that's watertight!'

'Is it as bad as that?'

Head Office of the Clyde Navigation Trust, on the Broomielaw.

'Aw the lads in here that have been, and that's maist o' them, say they're murder polis! They would'nae piss on ye if ye were oan fire!'

'Jeez! Dis'nae sound hopeful.'

I make my way to Bridgeton, an old district in the heart of the city, and find the Buroo. After a wait of forty minutes or so I'm called to the desk of a middle-aged woman. She gives me a smile like a step-mother's breath and motions me to sit down. 'Yes?'

'Hello.' I give her a nice smile. 'I just came back to Glasgow last week. I've been living in Wigtonshire for the last three months. I've been for an interview this morning and I've landed a job wi' the Clyde Trust – but I can't start until after the Fair Fortnight. I'm staying in the Great Eastern, the cheapest place I could find, to make my money spin out. But I've only got four pounds odd tae last me 'til ah get my first week's wage, so ah'm gonny have tae sign on for a week or two 'til I get my first wages.' I finish with a smile and hope she'll be impressed at how quickly

I've got myself fixed up with a job, and how short and to the point my summary has been.

'Right.' She reaches for a form. 'Where were you working last?'

'The Portpatrick Hotel, Portpatrick, Wigtonshire.'

'Under what circumstances did you leave that employment?'

I explain about going from kitchen porter to breakfast cook but not being paid for it . . . 'So I packed the job in and decided to return to Glasgow.' Her pen skids to a halt on the paper and I think I detect the trace of a smile. 'So you made yourself unemployed?'

'Well, ah suppose ah did, but only 'cause the manager was trying to exploit me. I'd finished up doing two jobs for him – but he was wanting to pay me for the cheapest.'

'Nevertheless, you made yourself unemployed?'

'Well, yes. But it was either that, or carry on doing breakfast cook AND kitchen porter for the lesser wage. Surely I'm not expected to put up with that situation?'

'The fact remains *you* terminated your employment, therefore you're not entitled to unemployment pay. If you'd been sacked or made redundant then we could give you money. But not if you left of your own accord.'

I run this over in my mind. 'So, if I'd been a poor worker or been sacked for misbehaviour, you'd give me money. But because I stood up for myself and wouldn't let the hotel manager do me out of what I was entitled to, you're not gonny give me enough money to live on until I start work. At a job I've found for myself,' I add.

'I'm afraid the rules are quite clear.'

I look at her unhelpful face and realise I'm about to bang my head against the proverbial brick wall. 'Okay. Ah've got just over four pounds. That isn't enough tae last nearly four weeks until I start earning. Ah'm gonny need six pounds to cover ma room at the Great Eastern plus, of course, ah'll have tae eat during this time. If it hadn't been for the Fair Fortnight I had no intention of coming here. But I can't start work 'til the first Monday in August. So, am I to be just thrown out the Great Eastern in a couple of weeks time? Have ah tae go hungry? Surely I can get some money from somewhere?'

'You'll have to go to the social security department. They may be able to give you something.'

'Where's that?'

She tells me. As I've nothing to thank her for, I leave without a word.

The social security representative has obviously attended the same charm school as his opposite number at the Buroo. Once more I'm given the impression I'm strongly suspected of trying to perpetrate a massive fraud on the social security system of Great Britain. At last, late into the afternoon, there's a breakthrough. My inquisitor looks up. 'We can give you two pounds and five shillings a week until you start work.'

Although I'm eighteen and normally of a placid nature, as the morning has turned to afternoon I've become increasingly frustrated at the unhelpful attitude of the two people who've dealt with me. I'm beginning to feel I could easily lose my temper. I clear my throat 'Could ah point out, ah need thirty shillings a week for my accommodation – the cheapest I could find – so that'll only leave me fifteen shillings a week to live on.'

'You've told me you have just over four pounds in cash. Between that and the fifteen shillings left over after you pay your rent, I calculate you should have enough to live on.'

I swallow hard. Occasionally, standing at the corner of Doncaster Street outside Lizzie's shop, I'd listened to tales from older lads telling of how they'd been at the Buroo and of somebody 'losing the heid' and throwing chairs about or assaulting staff. No fucking wonder. What an unhelpful lot of bastards. I'm going from one job to another. Unfortunately the Fair Fortnight intervenes, yet I'm being treated like I'm a work-shy layabout. I've never really lost my temper in my life. I'm getting pretty near to it; I draw myself back from the brink. 'Right. If that's all I can get, it'll have to do.' I can hear my voice sounds funny as I try to keep calm. I wonder if he – and his female counterpart – have a clipboard where they keep a list of victories and put a tick every time they do somebody down?

As I leave the office of the social security department I make a promise to myself that the only time I'll ever darken their door again is if I'm in imminent danger of sleeping in the street or starving to death. Like now, come to think of it.

For the next few weeks, I literally live on the breadline. I also realise, with hindsight, that I shouldn't have been honest and told them I had four pounds odd. They, of course, took that into account. I should have said I was just about broke. So much for telling the truth – you go hungry!

I have this stupid idea that I don't want folk to know how hard up I am. I keep it to myself. My first priority is to pay my rent. Even if I go hungry, at least I'll have a bed to sleep in. I buy the cheapest eats I can find, pies, bridies, sausage rolls. Occasionally, usually when I've just drawn my social security money, I might go into some working-man's café and have a fried breakfast and a mug of tea. Wonderful! At least once a week I go up to Bundoni's for a fish supper. Sometimes, much against my will, I'll have a greasy meal in the Great Eastern's canteen. Though I must admit, their soup's good. To supplement my money, a couple of evenings a week I go up to Sammy's or to my cousin Ada's. I always get there, accidentally on purpose, around six o'clock. Dinner time. They nearly always say, 'We're jist gonny have oor dinner, would ye like something?'

'Oh, ah wid'nae mind. Thanks very much.' Who knows, maybe they've guessed I'm skint? To help eke out the money I often don't buy anything for supper. I go to bed in my cubicle with my stomach rumbling like Mount Etna.

It's the Wednesday of the second week of the Fair Fortnight. The longest two weeks I've ever known. I'm due to start work next

Monday. It's tomorrow that I can draw my money from the social. As usual I'm hanging about up in Maryhill. It's as good a place to be skint in as any. It's late afternoon, I've had nothing to eat since a fried egg on a roll and a mug of tea this morning. My stomach feels hollow. It churns, sometimes seems to move. I wonder if your stomach will eventually start eating itself? I have Ma's wedding ring on my finger. I could easily go up to the pawn on Garscube Road and get at least ten bob. Once I start work I can redeem it. Ma wouldn't mind, she always pawned it to get food. Trouble is, I keep thinking back to the day after she died and I got it out the pawn. As I stood at the bottom of the stairs I'd promised Ma, and myself, it wouldn't see the inside of a pawn-shop again. I put my hand in my pocket. Just pretend you haven't got it, you haven't got anything worth pawning. Ma! It's NOT going in the pawn again!

I stand in Trossachs Street wondering where or how I can get something to eat. I've already been to Lottie's and cousin Ada's this week. I haven't the brass neck to go back so soon. A once familiar face turns the corner and comes along the street toward me. The red hair is the clincher. Jeez! Ian Orr. I haven't seen him since we left school. I know he lives further up Maryhill, somewhere around Rolland Street. Unusual for him to be in this neck of the woods. We'd started NKS – the 'big' school – on the same day, in the same class. At age eleven we'd both learned to swim within minutes of one another. Mr McGaughey used to take the class up to Maryhill Baths for our weekly swimming lesson. Ian and I had spent all our time in the shallow end trying to pluck up the courage to lift our feet off the bottom. Finally, he did it. Spurred on by that, minutes later so did I. Enthused by our new-found skill, for the next two weeks we plagued our mothers for money and met up almost every evening after school. Slowly but surely we increased the distance we could swim with our mixture of breaststroke and panic. By the end of the first week we could swim a width at the shallow end, without putting our feet down once. By the second week, starting from the deep end and keeping close to the side, we managed a length!

'Hello Ian. How are ye doing?'

'Robert! Imagine that! Ah have'nae seen you since we left the school. Hey, dae ye remember the day we started swimming at the same time?'

'That wiz the first thing that came intae ma mind when ye turned the corner.'

'So, how're ye getting on?'

'Huh!' I give him a short history of Robert Douglas since we left school, and finish by telling him of the helpfulness of the social security . . . 'Anywye, thank God, ah start work oan Monday. But at the moment, I'm "pink lint" (skint).' I take a deep breath, feel my face go red. 'Ah wonder if ye could dae me a favour, Ian? Ah hate havin' tae ask, but ah'm bloody starving. Ah've had nothing tae eat since an egg roll this morning. Could ye lend me a couple of bob for a fish supper?'

'Jeez, of course. You only have tae ask. Anywye, it's no' a lend, ye can have it.' He brings some change out of his pocket. 'Here,' he gives me half a crown, 'is that enough?' He proffers another one. I could do with it. Get me breakfast in the morning. But I don't like to take it.

'Naw, this is fine, Ian. Ah get ma social money the morra. Thanks a lot. Ma stomach thinks ma throat's cut!'

We stand talking about our schooldays. Ian brings up the swimming again. 'It was funny, the two of us getting away at the same time.'

I laugh. 'Mind, we'd maybe have got away quicker if we'd had a gym teacher that actually came in the watter with ye. Ah'll bet auld McGauchey wiz the only PT teacher that taught swimming fae the side o' the pool wi' a three-piece suit and a trilby.' We go into fits at the memory.

'He was the same in the gym, if ye remember,' says Ian, 'yon hat wiz never off his heid.'

We blether on for another few minutes with Ian telling me

what's been happening to some of our former classmates. He looks at his watch. 'Well, nice seeing ye again, Robert. You'll be all right once yer working, have some money in yer pocket.'

'Och, aye. Well, ah'm pleased ah bumped intae ye. It's great seeing ye again, and thanks for the half-croon. At least ah'll no' go tae bed hungry the night.'

'Aye, cheerio Robert. All the best.'

I wonder if Ma sent Ian along. It's just after three in the afternoon. Although I'm ready for something to eat, I know that if I have it now I'll be starving again by bedtime. I look along to Cocozza's corner. George Porter and George Gracie are in their usual places, standing at the lamp standard and junction box. I'll go and have a blether with them, take my mind off my raging stomach. I hope they can't hear it. Och, the sound of the traffic will drown it out.

As I approach them I glance at the green junction box. Every time I see it the memory of my adored Uncle George, and the last time I saw him, comes into my mind. I was fourteen. So it would have been 1953. He'd turned up out of the blue; his marriage broken up, drinking heavily. Two nights he'd stayed with us. Dying for a drink, he'd borrowed my last half-crown. With a penknife he'd scratched on the top of the green-painted junction box, 'IOU 2/6d – GEORGE.' That was the last time I saw him. I was sleeping when he came back from the pub. Next day, while I was at school, he left. I've never seen him since.

I look at the two men standing at the corner. George Porter; George Gracie. I've just been given a much-needed half-crown, feet away from where I gave Uncle George one when he was dying for a drink. Some coincidence.

In Full Employment

At long, long last the Fair Fortnight draws to a close. I'm starting work on Monday. I can hardly wait. Not just because I'll be earning money, but to be employed, to be working, have somewhere to go every day. I've known guys who are work-shy, who are quite happy lying in their beds in the morning, standing on the corner most of the day. But the last three weeks have bored me to tears. That's the longest spell I've been idle since I left school.

I've arranged for an early call on Monday morning. In great anticipation I begin my preparations the evening before. I've managed to hang on to enough money, and borrowed ten bob from Sammy, so I've now got sufficient to feed myself and buy that essential bit of working man's equipment – a sixpenny tea and sugar tin, though I won't need the sugar side of it. I've recently stopped taking sugar in my tea. I read in the *Sunday Post* that too much sweet stuff is bad for your acne. Haven't had much success cutting down on sweeties, though. I seem to eat as many as ever, when I have the money, but a lot of the pleasure is now spoiled for me. I feel guilty as I guzzle them.

I shave and get to bed by ten o'clock – I'll be as fresh as a daisy in the morning. At midnight I'm still wide awake. Eventually, sometime after one a.m., I begin to nod. Half an hour later, so it seems, there's a persistent, distant knocking . . .

'C'mon, son. It's five thirty.'

'Mmmm?'

'It's half five. Ye wanted an early knock.'

'Oh, aye. Aye!' I clear my throat. 'Aye, thanks very much. Ah'm up.' I sit on the edge of the bed while I try to shake off the tiredness. I listen to the man's soft footfalls fade away. All around is the lovely sound of steady breathing and the occasional snore. I look at my pillow in the semi-darkness. Maybe there is a lot to be said for being a lazy bastard. I could just do with another five minutes. I've only had about four hours sleep. I need at least eight. Preferably ten. Ah'm definitely going to bed early tonight. C'mon, give yourself a shake. I look at my watch; five thirty-five. Right! I get up, reach for the switch and flood the room with dimness.

It's just gone six when I step out into a deserted Duke Street. I make for a nearby dairy. As I push open the door the bell above it dings a couple of times; the smell of fresh morning rolls, newly sliced ham, corned beef, tongue and Spam mingles with tobacco, firelighters, and cheese, and all assail my nose. For a moment I'm entering Mrs Symington's in Cameron Street. I'll bet every wee dairy in Glasgow smells the same – and they all got their bells from The Dairy Bell Co. Ltd.

'Morning. Could ah have four rolls, well done, and two slices of tongue and two of corned beef.' I look at the glass display case. 'An' two Abernethy biscuits, please. Oh, and a pint of milk and one of them wee pats of Irish butter. Ah! And a quarter of Typhoo Tea, please. I think that's it.' Right. That's me got my rations. I walk further down Duke Street then call in at a newsagent to buy a *Daily Record*. Everything goes into my old army haversack which I've had since I worked at Polkemmet. Wide awake now, I step out at a good pace along the quiet road. Now and again a tram or bus passes me and I catch a glimpse of passengers reading their papers or staring, unseeing, out of the window. Glasgow folk on their way to work. At last, I'm one of you!

* * *

I walk to Buchanan Street then take the subway from there to Cessnock on the south side of the city. A short hike takes me to Prince's Dock. In many ways I'm a stranger to Glasgow. When I was growing up I rarely left Maryhill. Until the age of eleven I was seldom away from the few streets that made up 'my bit.' I could almost have been living in a village. Now and again Ma and I would take a tram down to the city centre, but somehow that didn't count. I always had the feeling 'doon the toon' belonged to everybody. Visting another district was different, then I was in other folks' territory. These trips were usually undertaken if Ma was going to see some childhood friend. As we travelled, on trams with strange numbers, I never paid any attention to where we were going. Ma did all that. On leaving school at fifteen, my first, job at NB Loco, was in Springburn, a district fairly near to Maryhill. That's the limit of my knowledge of Glasgow. Now I'm working for the Trust I'll be called on to travel to all the docks on the Clyde, north and south of the river, by tram, subway or on foot. I seldom take a bus. I'll have to undertake expeditions to the far-flung plains and minarets of exotic places like Partick, Govan and Shieldhall. I fully expect to bump into Dr Livingstone.

It's ten past seven when I find the Clyde trust bothy. At least I've judged my travelling time fairly accurately; I don't start until eight. The hut door lies open. The old 'watchie' is asleep. He sits by the pot-bellied stove, arms folded, legs stretched out, head on chest, sending up a non-stop stream of zzzzzzzs.

'Morning,' I give a tentative 'chap' on the door, hoping he doesn't have a weak ticker.

'Harummmpf!' He looks up. 'Hello?'

'Is this Mr McKechnie's hut? Ah'm a new start this morning.'

'Aye, this is it. In ye come. You're a bit sharp are ye no'?'

'Aye. Ah thought ah'd get here a bit early and huv ma breakfast, then make ma piece up.'

There's a large aluminium kettle singing softly on the stove.

'Jeez! Ah was getting everything ready yesterday, trying to be ahead of the game. Ah've just realised, ah hav'nae got a mug.'

'Ach, yer aw'right.' He rises from the bench. 'Ye can use mine the day.' He washes it out in a bucket of water, then rinses it in a second.

'Thanks very much. Ah'll go up tae the shops at piece-time and get maself one.' I empty my haversack. It seems like an old friend. Everything around me is new at the moment. As I make my breakfast sannies – and two for my piece – the watchie and me sit and blether. I find out there are ten men in the squad, that Alec McKechnie is a good ganger – as long as you give him 'his place' (respect) – and that the Clyde Trust is a good company to work for. There's never any short time, always jobs to be done.

As we talk, I eat my two rolls; one corned beef, the other tongue. All my walking has sharpened my appetite. They're washed down with a mug of unsweetened tea. Already I'm used to it and have discovered tea is a better drink, more refreshing, when you can actually taste the tea. I also find out from the watchie that it's possible to get a 'sub', an advance, on my wages. Things are looking up! I was beginning to wonder how I'd get by for money next week.

I'm in the middle of making a second mug of tea when, around twenty to eight, the first of the squad arrives. 'G' morning, John.'

'Morning, Peter,' says the watchie.

Peter looks at me. 'You'll be the new lad?'

'Aye, that's me.' He offers his hand.

'Right!' says the watchie, 'ah'll get maself away, Peter.'

'Aye, aye.' Peter's busy making a brew of tea.'

During the next fifteen minutes the squad turn up in ones and twos. Peter takes it on himself to introduce me to each of them.

'Did anybody tell ye a new lad huz tae buy everybody a cream cake oan his first day?' says one.

'Pay nae attention tae that fat, lying bugger,' says another.

'Here! Less o' the fat.'

I laugh. 'You're out of luck, boys. Ah'm skint. The first thing ah'll be asking the gaffer for is a sub.'

'Oh, jeez. He's no gonny be much use tae the card school.'

'Ah, once ah huv some money ah will,' I assure them. 'Ah like a game o'cards.'

'Och well, all is not lost then.'

At eight on the dot a figure wearing a belted tweed coat and cloth bunnet frames himself in the door. 'Good morning, lads.' This'll be the ganger. 'Is everybody here?'

'Paddy Herity's no' here yet.'

'She'll be lying oan his shirt tail again,' says a voice. There is general laughter. 'Oor new lad's here, Alec,' someone says.

'Aye, ah see that.' He gives me a smile. 'Ah'll have a word wi' ye in a minute, son.'

As everyone looks at me I feel myself colour up; I clear my throat. 'Aye fine.'

'Right, lads. Let's be havin' you.' There's a mass swallowing of last mouthfuls of tea and final draws on cigarettes as they all rise, me included. I stay standing as they leave the hut. A new face appears at the door. 'Ah'm here, Alec. Sorry ah'm late.' Presumably Paddy Herity.

'Aye, you're okay, Pat.' Alec gives one or two instructions before they leave, and I watch as they go off in teams of two or three to different parts of the dock. Obviously to sites where they've previously been working. The ganger watches them for a couple of minutes as they collect their tools and any materials. He turns. 'So,' he offers me his hand, 'I'm pleased to meet you, Robert. Do you get called Robert?'

'Pleased tae meet you. Aye, ah do.'

'Come and sit down for five minutes and I'll give you a wee idea of the job.'

As we sit and talk, I look at him. He's a heavy-set man with steely, gray hair and a strong blue jowl which makes him look as if he needs a shave. When he laughs, which is often, he shakes with mirth and makes a 'yumff, yumff, contented sort of sound. He's worked for many years with the Trust, on squads such as this, and has eventually made ganger. He's probably pushing fifty. He tells me that we're one of three such squads whose job is to keep the docks and wharves in good order and repair. We rarely stay in one place for long. Perhaps three or four days in one dock, then disassemble the bothy and move it, and our tools, to another one. After three or four weeks, if we're lucky, it's 'up sticks' and off on the wander again . . . 'In some ways it's quite good. You don't get bored working in the same place all the time.' When he finishes giving me my brief talk, he rises. 'Right, I'll show you who ah want you tae work with. Have you anything you'd like tae ask me?'

'I'm afraid there is. Ah hope ah'm no' being a nuisance, Mr McKechnie, but ah need some money for ma digs and food. Ah've been told it's possible tae ask for what's called a "sub"?'

'Och, that's not a problem. Nothing tae be ashamed of, being a bit short of cash. Happens to us all at some time in our lives. How much do ye think you'll need?'

'Ah think ah'd manage if ah had aboot four pounds. Ah hope that's not too much.'

'No, no, I can get you that. You know that'll be nearly half your take-home pay?'

'Aye, ah've worked it out. If ah have half a wage one week and half the next, I should be able to live on that all right.'

'Okay, I'll fix that up. I'll get it for you this afternoon. And listen,' even though there's no one around he lowers his voice, 'if either this week or next you find you're a wee bit short, just let me know. I can always let you have ten bob or a pound, and you can wait 'til you're drawing full wages afore ye let me have it back.'

'Jeez, that's very good of you, Mr McKechnie. Thanks a lot.' I feel quite touched at this unexpected gesture.

* * *

We approach a couple of the squad who are down in a trench. They stop, lean on their shovels and look up at Alec. He regards them in silence, then turns to me. 'I'm probably making a bad mistake, but I'm going to put you with this pair o' reprobates, yumff, yumff, yumff!'

The two middle-aged men look at each other then shake their heads. 'Zat slander?' enquires one.

'If ah knew what reprobate meant ah might be able to tell ye,' says the other. 'Anyway, are you gonna set the new lad away with us, Alec?'

Alec turns to me. 'I'll put you with George and Willie, here. They'll keep you right.'

'Yeah, just leave him with us, Alec. We'll look after 'im.'

'Good lads. See you later, Robert.' Alec wanders off.

One of them points in the direction of a large box. 'Gan ower tiv that chest, young 'un, and get tha'sen a shovel.'

Well he's definitely not Scots. I run my memory over all the accents I heard in the RAF. I bet he's a Geordie.

I return holding a shovel and jump down into the hole to join them. 'Right! Just tell me what ye want me tae dae.'

'Jist huv a blaw. Alec's oot the road, there's nae good killing yerself. Ye huv tae pace yerself.

'In't that right, Willie?'

Willie blows out his cheeks, shaking his head at the same time. 'Ye get nowt for being hasty.'

We all laugh. 'You'll have to remind me of your names, again. There was too many names being thrown at me this morning for me to remember.'

'Well ah'm George Finlay, and this is Willie Lilley.'

'Okay.' I repeat the names, then turn to Willie. 'And that sounds like a Geordie accent?'

Willie's leaning on his shovel. 'Aye. Newcastle born and bred.'

* * *

As the morning wears on we work, chat, and I get to know them a little. Both are in their fifties. George is a Govan man, married with four kids. He says he just comes to work to get a bit of peace and quiet. Willie was a regular soldier from the thirties until the end of the war. He met his 'Glasgow Lass' and they married in 1945. They live in Partick. Much to their regret they've never had children. Willie and I take a liking to one another quite quickly. He boxed for the army and, like me, is a boxing fan. As the months go by and we become friendly we regularly have a mock spar with one another. We'll be kidding each other on and I'll say 'Watch it ya auld Geordie bugger!' He'll always drop his shovel or pick and come over to me, shaping up for a fight. Standing toe to toe, our heads almost touching, hands half clenched, we work in close, pummelling and gently cuffing one another from all angles. Willie often runs the inside of his wrist up the side of my face, a throwback to his boxing days when, wearing gloves, he would 'lace' an opponent. All the time we are 'mixing it', as he calls it, Willie giggles and laughs, thoroughly enjoying himself. For a few moments he's a young man again. I also love to get him talking about fighting in the Boxing Booths. In the thirties, almost every travelling fair sported a Booth. Four or five 'boxers' would stand on the small platform outside the large tent, dressing gowns draped over their shoulders, already gloved-up, while the 'barker' would try and coax some of the local lads to take one of them on over – if it lasted so long – three rounds. To go the three rounds would earn the challenger two pounds. If, as rarely happened, the challenger knocked out the resident boxer, this would earn him the princely sum of five pounds! A good week's wage. There was also the chance of a bonus. Should a young lad put up a good fight, even if he loses, to show their appreciation the audience would throw coins into the ring; 'nobbins', they were called. These were a bonus, and an incentive for likely lads to try their best. Whenever the fairgrounds set up near where he was stationed, Willie, a young army boxer, always in training, would set off for the fair on a Saturday night with a few of his mates, all wearing civvies . . .

'By about ten o'clock on the Saturday, after the pubs had came out, you'd have a big crowd outside the tent. There was allus local lads, usually big, hefty built boys, gettin' geed-up by their mates to 'ave a go. 'Course, they'd all 'ad a skinful of beer, hadn't they. Mostly farmer's lads. So one or two volunteers would be up on the stage beside the boxers, then they'd all vanish into the tent and the barker'd be saying "Roll up! roll up! C'mon now, folks. See how your local boys do against my best lads." And the crowd would be paying their tanners (sixpences) to get in, an' next thing the tent'd be full to the gunnels.'

'So when did you and your mates step up?'

'Ah!' says Willie, eyes glistening as he lives it all again, 'You divn't want to be too hasty. We'd let the first couple of scraps run their course, they rarely lasted more than a round. These big lads would be rushing in, throwing haymakers, missing by a mile. They was easy meat for the Booth's lads.' As he's telling me his tale, Willie's bobbing and weaving, throwing haymakers, re-enacting the bouts. 'By this time, the crowd's got its blood up. So he's calling for more challengers. No bother at all, there's another three or four lads come forward, can't wait 'til get into the fricking ring. So, half an hour later, they're all finished. Might be one managed to gan the three rounds, might even have got some nobbins. The barker's walking round the ring again, ain't he, "C'mon boys, let your missis or your girlfriend see what a stout lad she's got!" Me mates and me look at each other, "Now?" we says. "Yeah, let's go! Here y'are!" we shouts. And the crowd's all givin' us big cheers as we strip tiv the waist, you just kept your trousers on, no shorts. And the barker's lookin' at us, and the boxers are lookin' at us, we're all lean and fit, short army haircuts, they know there's a fuckin' rabbit off.' Willie's eyes glisten, he chuckles to himself. 'But they can't do anything, can they? After all, says outside in big letters: "We Take On All Comers." Though mind, they used to try and give themselves the edge. Ah was boxing at lightweight in them days, under ten stone, so he puts me in wiv one of his lads who was at least middleweight! So ah'm givin' this bugger about two and a half stone, ain't ah! The only thing going for me is ah'm fit. The Booth's boxers were never really fit, most o' them were washed-up pros who'd never been more than preliminary fighters, ye kna', well doon the bill.' As he speaks, Willie's throwing left jabs, the occasional right hook. He's not standing in a trench in a Glasgow dock, it's a Saturday night and he's in the ring at a fairground in Shrewsbury. 'Ah gets on me bike, divn't ah. For two rounds I'm jabbing the head off him, in and out, in and out, an' he's gettin' real pissed off – and tired. We comes oot for the third and ah can hear 'is boss saying, "Now get that fucker put down!" Ah starts off on the bike again, by the middle o' the round he's ready for a lie-doon, knackered! Eh, it were easy, kid. Ah comes off the bike and just stands toe to toe, poor sod could 'ardly lift 'is arms, knocked him out. Cold! Crowd's going mad, ah'd tiv watch ah didn't get hurt there was that much nobbins flying intiv ring, tanners, shillings, the odd two bob bit! The Barker gives me me fiver. "Ah don't want to see you come into this booth again, you little fucker!" he says, 'is teeth gritted. Eh, it was great, lad! Went back tiv camp that night with seven quid in me pocket. Jack the fuckin' lad!'

Within a couple of weeks I've settled into the squad. They range in age from twenties to almost sixty and get on well with one another, and I get on with them. Like all Glasgow guys they believe that if you HAVE to go to work, you might as well have a laugh while you're there! Whether in the bothy or out on a site, kidding and geeing one another up is the order of the day. Every day. We have an hour for lunch and I always look forward to it. As we sit in the bothy, the banter and the patter are great. Half the squad, mostly the older men, sit and read their papers. The other half play cards for small stakes, usually Pontoon or Brag. Most days I join them. The sessions are accompanied by a never-ending slanging match! If someone wins a 'big pot', his parentage is immediately called into question. There are also continual aspersions cast on the skill – or lack of it – of those losing.

'Twist!'

The dealer tosses a card, face-up, in front of Eddie. 'Fuck me!' Eddie throws his hand in.

'Not while there's dogs in the street,' says Andy.

Paddy asks for a card. Charlie lays it in front of him. Paddy gives him a withering look. 'Ah've been here five years. Not wance huz that man ever twisted me a card withoot burstin' me!'

With a pained look reminiscent of Jack Benny, Charlie slowly looks round the assembled players. 'Perchance a slight exaggeration, therr.'

'Twist me,' requests Andy. He looks at the new card, then sadly places his hand in front of Charlie. He turns to Paddy. 'You've got him pegged dead right. Worst fuckin' dealer God ever put oan this Earth.'

If I can't afford to play I still sit at the table to enjoy the crack. Provided you're not a son of the manse it's a scream to listen to the inventive dog's abuse they hurl at one another. Nobody ever takes offence.

I'd enjoyed the company at the Portpatrick Hotel. Now I very much like being a part of this squad. I look forward to coming to work. All the walking and physical labour has made me very fit. I'm part of a small, close-knit group. I've got a job, I see Sammy regularly, and though I only go out to Seafield every second weekend, Nancy and I are better than we've ever been. And it's great not to have to go to bed hungry.

Back in the Old Routine

Nancy and I had been writing regularly since just before I'd left Portpatrick. Once I realised I was going to be short of cash until I was getting a steady wage, I'd told her it would be a few weeks before I came out to West Lothian. She'd offered to send me some money, or give me a loan, but I'd refused. She'd then offered to 'go Dutch'. I'd refused that too; not my style. Anyway, I couldn't even afford to go Dutch.

At last the big day is here. I got my first full week's wage from the Trust and I'm out to Seafield for the weekend. It's around four months since I last saw Nancy. I can hardly wait. At last we're going to be together again. According to her letters, things will be different. The double-decker chugs up the hill, past The Regal – I spot *Pal Joey* with Frank Sinatra is on; I fancy seeing that – we head into the centre of Bathgate. I anxiously scan the Saturday crowd milling on the pavement. THERE SHE IS! I'm upstairs, sitting at the front window. She sees me and waves. I dash downstairs and off the bus just before it comes to a halt. We greet each other with big smiles and, at first, a shy kiss. Public kissing, especially in the way I want to kiss her, is frowned upon. We don't want someone walking past and saying, 'For God's sake, will somebody throw a bucket o' watter ower them twa!'

'Will we go intae the cafe for a blether?' I suggest.

'Aye, that'll be nice.'

I take her hand as we walk the few yards to the Bathgate Café. Doesn't quite have the same ring as 'Rick's Bar'. We seat ourselves at one of the Formica-topped tables. The Everly Brothers are belting out 'Wake Up, Little Susie' from the jukebox.

'Ah like these two.'

'Me tae,' she says.

'What would ye like tae drink?'

'They've got an espresso machine now.'

'Jeez! Bathgate's certainly moving wi' the times since ah've been away.' I order two frothy coffees. 'It's really nice to see ye again. Ah haven't half been looking forward tae this day.'

She blushes. 'Me too.'

I decide to try and get things off on the right track. 'Do ye think we could mibbe start going oot wi' one another again, without regularly having rows?'

'Ah hope so.'

'And can we establish just ONE rule?'

'Aye, okay.' She blushes again.

'Anywye, let's get oan tae other things. Is it aw'right wi' yer ma and da for me to stay Saturday nights when ah come out tae see ye?'

'Aye, it's nae bother.'

'It won't be every weekend. Dae ye think it'll be okay, say, every second weekend?'

'Ah would think so. We'll ask them the night.'

'Now and again you can come intae Glesga for the day.'

'Oh, that's a good idea. We can go roon' the shops.'

We sit together in a comfortable silence. But all the while my mind's working. At some time or other I'm going to have to tell her I'm even younger than she thinks. Maybe best do it now. If she decides the gap between our ages is too much, well, best to pack it in now rather than later. It'll have to be done sometime. 'Nancy?' She looks across the table at me. I lean closer so's I won't have to speak too loud. I can feel myself start to blush. 'Listen, ah've got something tae tell ye. One of these stupid things that, when you've said it, you sort of have to keep it going.' I can see by her face she's probably thinking, 'God! Whatever is it he's about to tell me?' My mouth's going dry; I take a swig of almost cold coffee, clear my throat. 'Well, remember when ah first started taking ye oot and eventually we got talking aboot ages?'

'Uh huh!'

'Well, ah think ah told ye ah was twenty. Ah was really jist seventeen at the time. Ah'm eighteen and a half now. People always think ah'm older than ah look, everybody takes me for twenty-one, twenty-two. Is that aw'right wi' you?' God! I hope she says 'Aye'.

She looks at me, she has an almost embarrassed smile on her face, takes a draw on her cigarette. 'Ah'm twenty-five – and you're jist eighteen!'

'Yeah, but naebody ever takes me for eighteen. You quite accepted ah was the age ah told ye. If ah hadn't said anything you'd still think ah was twenty-one at the minute. Wouldn't ye? Anywye, what do ye think, are ye still gonny go oot wi' me?'

'Oh, aye. It won't make any difference. But maybe we should jist keep it tae oorselves, do ye think?'

'Aye, that's a good idea. Ye know whit folk are like for taking the mick. We'll jist let them carry on thinking ah'm twenty-one.'

'Ah'm no' gonny tell ma mother and faither, either. My faither would'nae bother but my ma would be saying, "He's far too young for ye, it's too big a gap."

'Well, you and me know it isn't really. But that's what we'll do, keep it tae oorselves.' I sit back, relieved. 'Ah'm glad that's out, it's been on my mind for ages, even before I went down to Portpatrick. Anywye, where should we go tonight?'

'Either tae the Palais, or the pictures. There's quite good films on at both the Regal and the Pavilion.'

I reach over and place a hand on top of hers. 'Mmmm, ah think the dancin' would be nice. Ah hav'nae been since I left here,' I smile. 'It'll be a good excuse for putting my arms around ye – and maybe sneak a wee kiss noo and again!' This brings more blushes from her.

* * *

Nancy and I courting.
Seafield, late 1958.

After a wander round Bathgate, which takes all of thirty minutes, we catch the bus and get off in Blackburn so as I can have a quick visit with Jim, Jenny and my assorted cousins who now include the new arrival, Alec. We later catch the bus to Seafield. I feel almost as apprehensive about seeing Auld Sanny and Beenie as I did the first time I met them. I know Sanny won't be any help, he loves tormenting the life out of me. Jeez, when I tell him where I'm lodging he'll have a field day.

'You're staying where? Yah bugger! Dae ye hear that, Ma? Livin' in the workhoose . . .'

Although I'm laughing, I manage to interject. 'It's no' the WORKHOOSE! It's a Model Lodging Hoose.'

He tries to look serious. The twinkle in his eye always gives him away. 'Same difference. Have ye ever heard sich a cheek, staying in the doss-hoose and taking oot ma dochter. Are ye listening, Ma?'

'Leave the poor laddie alane. Did ye want him tae sleep in the street?' She puts an extra couple of potatoes on my plate. 'Pay nae attention tae him,' she says. But Sannie's in his favourite place for expounding – seated at the kitchen table. 'If this gets roond Seafield ah'll no' be able tae show ma face in the village!'

'That'll be a blessing,' says Nancy.

I'm still trying, vainly, to get a word of explanation in. 'Noo that ah'm working ah'll be getting maself proper digs. Honest. It was jist 'cause ah was short o' money.'

'Short o' money! You'll no be taking ma dochter tae live in the doss-hoose, mind,' he's trying his best not to laugh. He looks at Nancy. 'Is that right, hen?'

'Yes, Faither,' she doesn't look up. 'Jist let it go in wan ear and oot the other.'

Sannie pretends to be hurt. He looks at his wife. 'Ah'm gettin' nae respect here. Are you no' gonny say something?'

'Aye. Eat yer dinner yah silly auld fool!'

Nancy and I dance cheek to cheek as the glitterball spins slowly above the dancers, showering us with slivers of light. The Palais is always crowded on a Saturday night. We've smooched the last hour or so away, hardly moving, oblivious as to whether it's been quickstep, jive or foxtrot. It's gone eleven-thirty when we get back to Seafield. Her ma has left a couple of sandwiches under a plate, for our supper. Just after midnight we stand in the kitchen, in the dark, keeping one ear on the alert in case Beenie decides on a surprise raid. As we kiss and cuddle and begin to cross the border into heavy petting, I'm becoming more and more aroused. Nancy, as usual, tries to keep my hands under control. Then, 'C'mon you two, time youse were in yer beds!' We know if we don't move, she'll be down. Some things haven't changed.

A City Boy

I think I love the mornings best. As my squad is allocated to different docks, I have to travel through various parts of the city to get there. I sometimes wonder why I never take the bus. Is it because I've just about mastered the trams and don't want to complicate things by starting to memorise bus numbers and routes? Partly. But really I just love being on the trams. Always have. Now that I've only myself to rely on for getting up and going to work, I find I don't have too much of a problem dragging myself out of bed. Ma would have been pleased to hear that.

How much travelling time I need affects what time I arrange for my early knock. I also have to allow for stopping off at some wee dairy to pick up something for breakfast – and my piece. My getting-up time varies between five-thirty and six a.m. I'm pretty much used to living in the Great Eastern now. Most of the noise just washes over me. Once I'm asleep I'm out of it all, nothing disturbs me, yet often the slippered feet of the night porter as he approaches my door, is enough to waken me . . . 'Jist gone half five, son.'

I exit the washroom and head back to my cubicle. The smell, which I never notice when I first wake, now hits me. It's a fetid, unwashed bodies, urine, bad ventilation kind of smell. I suppose I should really be making a move toward finding proper digs. But it's cheap. I really only use it for sleeping in. Nobody bothers me. It'll do for another week or two. You said that last time!

*   *   *

It's about ten past six when I come out into Duke Street. We're working at Yorkhill Quay at the minute. I so love having the streets to myself. It's not quite light, the street lamps still burn atop their green-painted columns. I take some deep breaths before the traffic starts polluting the air. The last month or so of hard physical labour and all the miles I've walked have made me really fit, there's hardly an ounce of fat on me. I sometimes feel I'm bursting with energy. Being back in the city also makes me feel good. And being back with Nancy. Often, as I make my way to work, just stepping out at a brisk pace isn't enough. Even though I'm not late I sometimes trot a hundred, walk a hundred, just for the exercise.

I come off the tram in the less fashionable part of Argyle Street, just before the Kelvin Hall, and make my way through the maze of streets toward the quay. There's a dairy in Kelvinhaugh Street. There's a dairy everywhere in Glasgow. All these little dairies-cum-grocers-cum-'Johnny aw' things'. Every few blocks there's one. Same with newsagents. I go into the Kelvinhaugh Street shop. I wonder if it was still a dairy when Ma was a wee lassie. She was brought up round here. I order my usual four well done rolls, slices of cold meat and a couple of snasters (Ma's name for sweetmeats) for afters. I've already picked up a *Daily Express* on the way. I've started buying it recently and find I like it. As I step out on the last part of my journey, I pass the bottom of Sandyford Street. I stop for a minute. This is where Ma was born. I look up the short, sloping street. I try to imagine Ma and her three brothers, James, Bill and George playing round here. Being near the river, where the city started, these are old tenements. They've been slums for half a century. Our tenement block in Maryhill was built thirty years or more after these. Ours were modern slums!

'Morning, John.'

'G' morning, Robert.' The watchie's always pleased to see me. It's just after seven. Now I'm an established member of the gang it means he can get away. Nobody comes in as early as I do. 'Ah've got the kettle bileing for ye, son. Ah'll huv a wee glance at yer paper while yer mashing yer tea and making yer piece.' I wish folk wouldn't ask for my paper before I've read it. I'm quite happy to give it away when I'm finished, but I hate someone reading it before me, especially if they hand the bugger back all creased and badly folded. I pass him the *Express*. Like most Glasgow working men he immediately turns to the sports pages. Except to check out a fight result, they're the last pages I turn to. Football doesn't interest me.

I carefully tear open the paper bag my rolls were in and use it like a plate to prepare my breakfast and piece-time sannies. Next, a brew of strong tea is made. I'm always ready for breakfast after my hike to work.

'Right, here's yer paper, son. Well, if it's aw'right wi' you ah'll make tracks.'

'Aye, away ye go. Ah'll be here 'til the boys come.' As I speak I'm pointedly tidying up my paper and trying to restore it to a reasonable facsimile of how it was when I handed it to him. Auld John's paying no attention whatsoever. He puts on his grimy mac and slings his ex-army haversack over his head with the strap running diagonally across his chest, the way a schoolboy wears his satchel. 'Right, ah'll see ye in the mornin'. If we're spared.'

'Aye. Cheerio, John.'

With the bothy to myself I have a leisurely breakfast and a thorough read at the paper. Peter comes in at quarter to eight then the rest begin to arrive, and the banter begins . . .

'Bugger me! Dae you sleep here?' Paddy Herity sits down beside me.

'Naw, ah like tae get in nice and early. Ah huv ma breakfast here.'

'Would ye no' rather huv yer breakfast before ye leave the hoose?'

'I laugh. 'Well, actually naw. Ah just rent a room. Ah live in digs.' I haven't told anyone at work where I stay.

I can tell Paddy would like to know why I'm in lodgings, but doesn't want to ask.

One of the great pleasures of the job is the access it gives to the docks area of the city, much of which is restricted to the public. Maryhill is in the north-west of Glasgow, so I grew up knowing nothing of the riverside. Only rarely, from the top deck of a tram, would I catch the occasional glimpse of river or ships. Now, on a daily basis, I work along the quays and wharves where freighters and coasters load and unload cargoes from literally all over the world. Often, two or three cargo ships are tied up in a line, stevedores swarming all over them, tall dockside cranes trundling along their rails to take up post beside them and swing bulky cargo nets on and off, full of produce from five continents.

*Princes Dock. Like all Glasgow's
docks in the 1950s, always busy.*

Warehouses run parallel with the rails for the entire length of the dock and are soon filled with these cargoes. Over the next few days, fleets of lorries will be arriving constantly to load up and take the goods to their eventual destination. Often we're working a few yards away, doing some pointing or relaying granite setts. I spend a lot of time watching the activity on board these large freighters as ship's officers stroll about, high up on the super-structure and crew members come ashore to spend a few hours in the city – often returning, sometimes rather tipsy, carrying boxes or parcels containing gifts for their families. I love to read the Port of Registration on the curved tails of the vessels; London, Oslo, Hamburg, New York, Singapore, Monrovia – wherever that is. Many have Lascar (Asian) seamen on board, usually quartered at the rear. The smell of curry drifts out of open portholes and fills the air, adding to the sense of the exotic which these large ships already give me.

Dockers, or stevedores, are employed on a casual labour basis. When a ship is due in, forty or fifty men gather outside the dock gate. Perhaps only thirty are needed. Two or three gangers will stand outside with their backs to the gates and hand pick the number of men they need. Those not chosen make their way back home and sign on the Buroo for another few days, or longer. This unsatisfactory way of employing men saves the stevedore com-panies from having full-time employees, and paying them when there are no ships in. It is also open to abuse. The favoured few are always chosen, along with those willing to 'kick back' a few pounds to the ganger.

If the weather is good I often resist the delights of the bothy and sit myself near the open river to have my sandwiches. From some of the quays there are magnificent views along the Clyde. With blue skies and the ever-present breeze coming off the water, I sit as though in the middle of some real-life CinemaScope movie. There are ships of all sizes tied up on both banks. Across the way, two new freighters are under construction on the stocks of John Brown's Shipyard. There is the occasional twinkling of welders' torches, then the 'rrrrrrr' of the riveter's gun. A large cargo ship comes down-river, heading for the open sea. The Swedish flag flutters at her mast. There are always one or two crew leaning on the rails, taking their leave of Glasgow. They look across at me, I give a wave. As expected, they casually wave back. It's a nice feeling.

Over this panorama of ships and yards men move about like ants, seemingly insignificant. But it's men who've built all this. I think back to my first job at NB Loco. The City of Glasgow builds ships and locomotives and sends them all over the world. Industries like these made her the 'Second City of Empire.' Yet just five years later, NB Loco will close, and ship building start to go into a decline. One by one almost all of these yards will be dismantled, supposedly because they're being undercut by yards in the Far East. Whatever the reason, men who've served their apprenticeships and worked most of their lives for world-famous companies will be out of a job.

The Call of Lotisha

Michael 'Mick' Quinn joins the Trust a few months after me and is allocated to our squad. Around twenty years old, there's no doubting Mick is of Irish blood. The curly hair and snub nose surrounded by freckles gives him the 'look of the Irish'. Only his strong Glasgow accent shows he's a generation or two removed from the Emerald Isle. He lives in Govan with his widowed mother and his brother.

He and I hit it off straight away and team up as a pair most of the time. Mick is pale, and a little frail. If we're shovelling sand or gravel onto a lorry I usually finish up shifting most of it. Mick tries his best, but tires easily and frequently has to 'have a blaw'. This doesn't bother me, I just keep shovelling away and blethering to him at the same time. I look on it as good exercise.

It's piece-time and, as usual, Mick sits smoking a roll-up, drinking his tea, and studying the 'Runners and Riders' in the *Daily Record*'s racing section.

'Cummin' a walk up tae Dumbarton Road wi' me? Ah think ah'll huv a wee bet. There's a couple o' good things running at Haydock.'

I shake my head in mock sorrow. 'Again? Whit happened tae yesterday's two certs?'

'Don't ask.'

Five minutes later we're elbowing our way through the smoke-filled atmosphere of the crowded betting shop. Although not yet legal – the bill to do so is going through Parliament – the police have tended to leave betting shops alone this last few months. Street bookmakers have all but vanished. Bookies shops are like pubs without beer. They have all the atmosphere of a Glasgow bar: almost exclusively male, everybody's smoking, bare tables and chairs, men smelling strongly of drink – they've just nipped in from the nearby pub (there's always a nearby pub) – all conversations are peppered with the F-word and everybody seems to be delighted to be on premises where fresh air is strictly barred.

'Whit sort of bet are ye puttin' oan?'

'Three cross sixpenny doubles and a thrupenny treble.'

Instantly I'm transported back to Doncaster Street. I'm walking through the Mulholland's close and Davey the Bookie and a punter are muttering incantations and casting spells in the shadows. 'First three favourites across the card, and if there's anything tae come ah'll huv these three oan a Yankee . . .' I look at Mick. 'Aye, sounds good.'

He smiles. 'Ye huv'nae a fuckin' clue whit it means!'

'Ah know, but ah like the sound of it. Anywye, better get a move on, Mick, or we'll huv Alec efter us. It's nearly wan o' clock.'

'Right!' I watch him wend his way to the counter. I sometimes feel he's too frail for all this.

As the months go past Mick tells me about himself. At fourteen he went through major surgery to remove a brain tumour. It wasn't fully taken away and there's a chance it'll maybe recur when he's around twenty-one. He's now twenty. Since leaving school he's only worked intermittently, as a succession of illnesses have plagued him. The wish to contribute more than sickness benefit to help his widowed mother means he's always trying to hold down jobs for as long as possible.

Like me, he enjoys a laugh and a joke, but makes it plain he wants no part of any rough and tumble in case he bumps his head. Occasionally I think up something he can be a party to – usually playing practical jokes on Willie.

It's coming up for piece-time. 'Mick, when we get the shout tae knock off, ah want ye tae stand at the compressor wi' yer back tae the row of taps. Kid on you're reading the racing page in the *Record*. When auld Willie comes past, call him ower tae look at something in the paper. Make sure ye get him tae stand wi' his back tae the taps.' Mick begins to laugh in anticipation.

'He'll kill ye, mind.'

'Ach, he's alwiz gonny kill me. It's already been three times this week. He loves it really, the auld Geordie ratbag.'

Minutes later comes the shout from the bothy that it's break time. It all goes like clockwork. I go behind the noisy diesel compressor and switch it off. Quiet descends. There is still, of course, plenty of highly compressed air in the tank. I stay, head down, out of sight behind the machine. Willie makes his way up from where he's been working. Mick casually unfolds his paper and stands holding it opened wide, his back less than a foot from the row of taps.

'Ah'll tell ye what, Willie, there's wan or two good things at Newbury the day. Have a look.'

Ever on the quest for the 'Mother Lode', Willie stands shoulder to shoulder with Mick, perusing the day's runners and riders. 'What's caught yer eye, then, mate?'

'Here, take a haud o' the paper,' says Mick, 'Ah'll point them oot tae ye.' With both hands he passes the fully open *Record* to Willie, who obligingly takes it in both his hands – after placing the roll-up he's smoking between his lips. 'What races?' enquires the unsuspecting Willie. This is my cue. While they've been speaking I've sneaked up closer to them. I glance up at the bothy. They've all seen what's going on and are quietly craning their necks to look out of door and window. I throw open the tap closest to Willie; with an ear-splitting roar, compressed air, under many pounds per square inch of pressure, blasts out the tap, whisks the roll-up straight out of his mouth and snatches the paper from his fingers – giving him the fright of his life at the same time! There's a roar of laughter from the bothy as the separating pages of the paper fly up in the air, then gently begin to waft down over a wide area. Convulsed with laughter, I appear from behind the machine, running off like a startled rabbit.

'Yah Scotch bastard!' He sets off in pursuit. I can easily outpace Willie, but, as usual I have the giggles and he starts overhauling me, laughing and chuntering away to himself as he does. After a few yards I stop, helpless. He collars me and we finish up, as Willie loves, standing toe to toe, heads on each other's shoulders, 'mixing it' for a couple of minutes until, honour satisfied and both out of breath, we head for the bothy where we sit together and eat our piece. Every now and again Mick and I spontaneously start to laugh, which causes Willie to take his bunnet off and give me a few swipes.

It's shortly after six o'clock on a weekday evening. I've come in from work, washed and changed, and decided to eat in the Great Eastern's canteen. From the table d'hôte menu I've selected mince and tatties. The mince is always a bit greasy for my taste – being the cheapest money can buy has something to do with it – so I always mash it into the tatties. Sitting at the table with me is Dieter. He's a melancholy soul. Taken prisoner during the war, and unwilling to return to his home, which is now in East Germany, Dieter has a job sweeping up in factory and has lived in the Great Eastern for years. He is a dead ringer for Chalky, the schoolteacher created by the *Daily Express* cartoonist, Giles. With his skull-like head, Dieter, when helmeted and uniformed during the war would have been everyone's idea of the typical Kraut! In reality he is a kind-hearted soul who, instead of turning to drink because of his lonely life, has turned to religion. I sometimes wonder if he made the right choice. From our previous chats I've come to the conclusion that Dieter would be a lot happier if he had a lady friend. Sadly, I imagine the last time Dieter 'pulled' it was the pin out of a grenade. His unprepossessing looks, alas, are against him. In his strong German accent he's for ever trying to 'bring God' to those around him. His conversations regularly feature 'oor Gott' in a mixture of colloquial Glaswegian and German. I, just as fervently, try to get him to tell me of his war service on the 'other side'. An infantryman, he saw action in Russia until, early in 1944, his division was transferred to France to prepare for the anticipated Allied invasion.

I raise another fork full of mince and tatties to my mouth. 'Yon Russian winters must have been really cauld, Dieter?'

'Oh, murder polizei! Many times ve haf more casualty from der kalt than die Russkies. Unbeliefable kalt. Many times 20 oder 30 degrees unter freezing.' He holds a finger up. 'But Gott is goot, oont I survive.' He blesses himself.

'Aye, he must have been looking after ye. Ah'll bet you and yer mates were glad tae get tae France, eh?'

'Oh, yah. Ve think all oor birthdays are coming at the once. Anyvay, vat about this, Robert, maybe vun Sontag you like komm to oor kirk? It is yoost off St Fincent Street. Not far to valk. Ve haf goot minister.'

'Naw, ah'm afraid you've got the wrong man, Dieter. Ah'm not a one for the church.'

'Ven you let Gott intae your life you vill immer be happy. Beliefe me, I know.'

I think to myself, 'If that's you happy, Dieter, I wouldn't like to see you sad.' I'm about to try and prise more war stories out of him when one of the relief porters comes to the table. 'There's somebody in the lobby asking for ye.' He's looking at me.

'For me?'

'Aye. Robert Douglas.'

'Jeez, that's a surprise. There's no' that many folk know ah'm here.' I rise and make for the lobby. It's Sammy! 'What's the matter?' I hope he's not down to tell me his ma or da has taken ill – or worse.

He looks embarrassed. 'Well, whit it is. Ah've went and let slip that you're living here. Ah forgot for a second ah wiz'nae supposed tae say.'

'Och, it's aw'right. There's nae harm done. Ye didn't have tae come aw' the way doon here tae tell—'

He interrupts me,

'Ah, well. When ma ma heard where ye were living she played hell wi' me for no' telling her. She said "Ah'm no' huving him livin' in that place. His poor mother wid be spinning in her grave if she knew!"' He clears his throat. 'So she's sent me doon tae tell ye you've tae leave this minute and come up and stay wi' us 'til ye get yerself proper digs.' He shrugs his shoulders. 'She says ah'm no' tae come back withoot ye!'

There's a lump in my throat. I swallow hard. 'Well, that's it, in't it? Lottie has spoken. We don't even get the option o' a fine.' We laugh. 'Ah'll away upstairs and pack ma stuff. Ah'll no' be long.'

As I gather my belongings together I'm glad in a way. I'm beginning to get too used to it in here. It's cheap, and now I'm into a routine I can't be bothered to go looking for real digs.

Ten minutes later, we catch a 23. Thirty minutes after that, Sammy opens the door with his key. I brace myself as I walk into the living room, Sally's jumping round my legs.

'Whit ur you daeing livin' in the Model and no' letting oan tae anybody?' Madam looks at me.

'Sammy knew.'

'He's as daft as you,' says Lottie, 'so that's nae fuckin' help! Anywye, ye can stay here 'til ye get yerself proper digs – or until ye get oan ma tits and ah throw ye oot!' She takes a draw on the ever present Woodbine.

'There was nae need for ye tae stay doon there, Robert,' says Frank.

Lottie points at the two brown paper carrier bags I hold. 'Zat aw' you've got?'

I raise them up in the air. 'Aye.'

'No' be taking up much room in the wardrobe, then.'

I give a rueful smile. 'Naw.' What a pity Ma and Lottie never knew one another. With us not being brought up round the same streets, our parents never met. Sammy's family only ever saw my father once. Briefly. Late on the evening my mother died he found out where I was and came up to collect me.

'Right!' I do an about turn. 'Ah'll away and unpack, then.'

'Are ye hungry?'

'Well, ah was eating when Sammy came for me, but ah left half of it. It was awfy greasy.'

'So will ye manage bacon and eggs?'

'Oh, aye. That wid be lovely.'

'Frank! Put the kettle oan and get the frying pan oot.'

Frank has been sitting at the table. He sighs, then looks at me. 'Ah'm jist in fae ma work.' He turns and looks at Lottie. 'Can ah no' huv a minute tae maself?'

'Yer arse in parsley!' she says. From behind the smokescreen she's busy laying down.

In Absentia

Life's pretty good. Nancy and I are together again and I'm more in love than ever. I really like my job and my workmates. I'm living in Glasgow and staying with Lottie and Frank – which means a laugh a minute – and Sammy and I are out two or three times a week. Things couldn't be better. Then . . .

It's one of those things where, when you realise your mistake, you think, 'how stupid!' I know I still have my two years' National Service to do. When I left the Boys' Service they'd told me, 'This nine months doesn't count. You'll be called up when you're of age.' So that was it. I expected that eventually I'd literally get a letter through the post to tell me I'm 'called up'. Wrong! While I was living in West Lothian, and later Portpatrick, I didn't really give it much thought. But now I've turned nineteen I sometimes wonder when I'll hear from them.

It was around nine months after my return to Glasgow when I spotted the first poster. The tram stops at the lights. Nearby is a row of advertising hoardings sporting a colourful line-up of the usual suspects; 'Heinz 57 Varieties,' 'Milanda Bakeries,' 'Persil Washes Whiter' and so on. Then I spot it. 'National Service Act: If you were born between 1 January and 31 March 1940, you should register for National Service at your nearest labour exchange NOW! Failure to do so is AN OFFENCE, making you liable to imprisonment.'

When I look at the dates I think, 'Oh, won't be long until

they're down to me'. I was born in February 1939. I make a mental note to keep an eye open for future posters. I've already resolved that when my time comes I'll do it with a good will. Unlike when I was in the RAF. For some reason, stupidity probably, I believe that they are working their way down to my birth year group. In reality, they've already passed me by.

So, as far as I know, things are going really well. Especially my acne, which is positively flourishing. I stay at Sammy's for about six weeks, until Lottie drops a subtle hint one evening.

'Z'it no about time you wur looking for permanent digs, eegit features?'

'Oh! Aye, right Lottie. Ah was jist waiting for you tae say the word.'

'Ah'm saying it!' comes a voice from behind a bank of low cloud.

A brief study of the postcards stuck in the windows of local newsagent's turns up an address just round the corner. Number 158 Wilton Street. In a way, I look on it as a kind of advancement. As a kid I regularly raked their middens. Folk in these houses threw out better things than we ever had! The building is one of the red sandstone tenements with 'wally closes' (Art Noveau tiled entrances), just a few hundred yards from where I was brought up. The landlady is a Mrs Milne, a widow woman in her mid-seventies. The 'house' is a large, four-bedroom downstairs flat and is pretty much how I always imagined these houses would be – dark varnished, wooden doors, richly-patterned wallpaper, ornate ceiling roses and coving. It is self-contained, with kitchen, bathroom and toilet. The furniture and decor mostly date from the 1920s and 30s. The bathroom delights me; a large wash basin with china 'hot' and 'cold' discs on the taps. The toilet bowl is a beautiful, blue and white patterned Edwardian one – if it was mine I'd take it out and have it sitting on the mantlepiece.

* * *

I'd enjoyed my spell as 'Lottie's ludger' and it had been a wrench to move out of 375 Maryhill Road. But better that than outstaying my welcome.

'Dae ye fancy going doon tae the Pavilion one night?' suggests Sammy.

'The theatre! Why, what's on?'

'Tae see the Lex McLean Show. Ma mother and faither have started going quite regular, they reckon he's a scream. The place is always full.'

'Aye, no harm in giving it a try. It'll be a wee change from the pictures. Anywye, what's happened wi' Lottie going tae the wrestling ower at Govan Town Hall? Ah thought she was mad aboot the wrestling?'

Sammy shakes his head. 'She's been barred! She loves that Bert Royal, so every time he threw his opponents oot the ring Lottie wiz laying into them wi' her bag. She's been warned aff! The last night she wiz there it hud been raining. Bert threw the Emperor Chang oot the ring, and Lottie broke her umbrella ower his heid!'

So starts an enjoyable few months as Sammy and I quickly become Lex McLean fans and join the weekly pilgrimage. Lex has built up a great following at the Glasgow Pavilion, when he appears for his three months stint. A mixture of comedy and variety, the main core of the shows are Lex and his regular team who put on a series of short comedy sketches. These are interspersed with supporting acts; typical music hall 'turns' – a singer, a tap dancing duo, a magician. At the start of every evening, Lex always comes out 'front of curtain' to do a ten-minute spiel. This is always topical, very Glasgow, and becomes a favourite of mine.

The sketches are also so Glaswegian, often set during the war or in the late forties. All the essential ingredients are there . . . Ration books, husbands arriving home on leave unexpectedly,

On my return to Glasgow in 1957 Sammy and I soon became fans of 'Sexy Lexy'!

Pavilion Theatre

The Lex McLean Show

PROGRAMME 6d.

amorous lodgers, Germans etc. There are gales of laughter as the audience are reminded of their recent past.

By the late 1950s, Lex McLean is the hottest act in Scotland. During this period, with television growing fast, he receives many offers to go on TV, or take his act 'down south'. He resists them all. At a time when many theatres are finding it hard to survive the onslaught of TV – 'the haunted fish tank', – Lex bucks the trend. Year in, year out, he takes his show to the same three cities, Glasgow, Dundee and Aberdeen. He does three months in each, then has three months off – during which time next season's sketches are written. He won't go south of the border, simply because he is very much a Glasgow act. As for TV, Lex knows it eats up – and spits out – comedians at an alarming rate. He can perform a fifteen minute 'spot' on television, and that routine can't be used again. The same material can be used, on stage, every evening for nine months in three different cities. He's quite happy to remain a big fish in a little pond.

*　　*　　*

During this settled period Nancy and I are into a regular routine. I usually go through to Seafield every second weekend, stay the Saturday night, and travel back to Glasgow on the Sunday. Now and again Nancy will come into Glasgow on a Saturday, just for the day.

I also decide that, at four pounds a week, my Wilton Street lodgings are a bit too dear. A search through the small ads in the *Evening Times* turns up a room to rent for thirty-five shillings a week, at 32 Granville Street, down near Charing Cross. This is 'accomodation only'. I'll have to arrange my own meals and laundry. There's one good thing about being able to fit all my goods and chattels into two carrier bags – flittings are relatively painless!

It's shortly before I leave Wilton Street that I discover I should have read the National Service posters with a bit more care . . .

I take a quick walk up to Dumbarton Road to get a couple of mutton pies and two custard tarts from the City Bakeries. On the way I pass some hoardings. Up amongst the adverts is the latest National Service poster. I read it in passing. I'm about to lose my appetite . . . 'If you were born between 1 April and 30 June 1940 . . .' That's funny, it's moving AWAY from my birth date. The last one had been for those born between 1 January and 31 Mar . . . Mammy Daddy! I should have bloody registered twelve months ago! I'm probably a deserter or something!

I hurry back down to the bothy, all thoughts of mutton pies banished for the moment.

'Mick, come here a minute.' I take him to one side. 'Ah've jist been lookin' at yon govermment posters, the National Service wans. Ah've jist realised, ah should huv registered twelve fuckin' months ago. In fact longer, nearly fifteen months. Ah got maself mixed up wi' the dates. Ah'll bet ye the buggers'll no'believe me, especially wi' me regularly changing ma address. They'll think ah've been trying tae put them aff the scent. They'll probably clap me in the jail!'

Mick tries to keep a straight face. 'Well ah don't believe ye. So you've got nae chance wi' them! Huv ye thought o' the French Foreign Legion?'

'Eh?'

'They let ye join up under another name. It's either that or Barlinnie! No registering is jist the same as deserting.' Finally, he can't keep it up any longer and dissolves into laughter.

'Fuckin' hell, Mick. It's nae laughing matter, ye had me worried therr. Ah'd better have a word wi' Alec, see if ah can get away early and nip up tae the Buroo.'

'Well, if ah wiz behind the coonter and ye came in wi' that story, ah don't think ah'd believe a word of it. Ah'd jist send for the polis!'

'Thanks a lot, EX-pal.'

Just before four p.m. I tentatively enter the labour exchange on Garrioch Road, Maryhill. Shortly afterwards I sit facing one of the staff and try to simplify my tale of their posters, me moving around the country, regularly changing digs, and thinking they were working their way down to me. My story is so stupid, thank God he actually believes me.

I'm now registered for National Service. During this period I move from Mrs Milne's in Wilton Street to my new digs. One of my first acts is to let the authorities know my new address. A week or two later I go for my medical and this is duly followed by a brown official postcard addressed to 'Robert Douglas, c/o Irvine, 32 Granville Street', popping through the door. It informs me I'm classed as 'Grade 1'. I suppose that's nice to know.

Numbered Days

That's what it feels like, now I've registered. I haven't got a date yet for my call-up, so I might as well enjoy myself until that envelope arrives. But there's one thing for certain. My days are numbered.

'Did ye know this bugger worked for the Germans during the war?' Joe nods in the direction of Dave, who just laughs and keeps on eating his sannie. We're sitting round the table in the bothy. I know Dave isn't yet thirty, so he'd be too young to be a POW. Unless . . .

'Did ye join up underage and get taken prisoner?'

Dave's mouth is full, he shakes his head 'no'.

'How auld are ye at the minute?'

He takes a big mouthful of tea. 'Ah'm twenty-nine.'

'Right. That means you'd jist be sixteen in 1945.' I try to think of some other option. 'Are ye serious? Did ye really work for the Germans?'

'Yeah. From 1943 'til the end o' the war.'

I look at him. 'Ah give in. You're gonny huv tae tell me.'

He takes another long drink of tea. 'Ah wiz a cabin boy oan a merchant ship. It wiz ma first trip, ah was fourteen, and we were sneaking along the south coast at night when some German E-boats attacked us and we got torpedoed. Me and three others were in a raft for nearly two days. When the first morning came it wiz foggy. We could hear oor planes flying aboot, looking for survivors, but they could'nae see us. So we spent aw' day and another night adrift, floating toward the French coast aw' the

217

time. We could'nae dae anything aboot it, we'd lost the fuckin' paddles. Next morning we got picked up – by the Jerries!'

'Were ye frightened?'

He laughs. 'Not a bit of it. Ah wiz jist a daft boy, ah thought it wiz dead exciting. Ma three shipmates weren'y ower happy about it. They were aw' married men, so they were pretty pissed off. It wiz another E-boat that picked us up, full o' these German sailors in their smart uniforms,' he laughs again. 'Ah thought it wiz great. Anywye, they landed us at Brest oan the French coast. Stacks o' German sodjers aw running about wi' their "coal scuttle" helmets an' field-grey uniforms . . .'

'C'mon, let's get the cards started,' Paddy Herity begins to clear the table. I move along and sit next to Dave. 'So whit happened next?'

'Well, 'cause ah wiz so young, and ah wasn't a sodjer, ah finished up being interned for a while in this camp near Tours. Then they asked me if ah wanted tae work, so ah said "Aye". He finishes off his tea. 'Anything tae get oot o' that camp. Ah finished up working for the Todt Organisation. It wiz aw' forced labour, maistly French, Belgians, Dutch. It wiz really interesting working wi' aw' these people. We were all over France and Belgium from '43 intae '44, building factories and roads, defence works. We used to dae a lot of sabotage. Putting sugar intae the cement mixers – makes it weak – stuff like that . . .'

Joe joins us at the table. 'Are we gonny be playing cards the day?'

'Aw, jist let me hear the end o' Dave's story. This is really interesting. Go on, Dave.'

'Anywye, efter D-Day in '44, they kept moving us back nearer and nearer tae Germany. By this time maist o' the work we were daeing wiz repairing bomb damage tae railways, roads, that sort of thing.'

'How did the Germans treat ye?'

'Ah never had any bother wi' them. With me being sae young, and the fact ah wiz Scots – they like the Jocks so they dae. Ah got oan aw'right wi' them.'

Pat begins dealing out the cards. I'm anxious to hear the end of Dave's story. 'Where did ye finish up at the end of the war?'

'Somewhere tae the east of Dusseldorf. Mind, it wiz beginning tae get a bit hairy by then. Especially if ye were anywhere near a big town. We were bombing seven bells o' shite oot o' their cities, the Yanks by day and the RAF at night. Then, all of a sudden, it wiz all over. Toward the end of March we wiz liberated, oor troops overran the area we were camped in. And that wiz it.'

'Did ye get intae trouble for working for them?'

'Well, if ah'd been an adult ah probably would've. But they jist put it doon tae me being a daft boy. Ah telt them ah did it tae get oot the camp, and get better food.' He smiles. 'So they gave me a telling-off, and telt me no' tae dae it again!'

We pick up our cards and begin to sort them out. Dave leans toward me. 'It's always good for a laugh whenever ah've went for a job interview. When they ask, "Where have you worked previously?" And ah say, "Well, ah started working for the Todt Organisation, then he got killed in a plane crash – and ah finished up working for Albert Speer!" Dis'nae half get their attention!'

Mick's been off sick now for nearly a fortnight. Joe Cahill is his uncle, and also works for the Trust, operating a large, diesel cement mixer. He knows Mick and I have become good mates. It's September '58 and we're back at Yorkhill Quay again.

'Robert!' Joe motions me to come over. He's busy swilling out his mixer; we've been using it this morning. 'Ah suppose ye know about that big op Mick had when he was a laddie, tae remove that tumour?'

'Aye. Mick told me about it himself.'

'Ah'm afraid he'll no be coming back tae work, son. They said it would return when he was about twenty-one. This is it starting again.'

'Fuckin' hell, Joe! Is there nothing they can dae?'

'Naw. It's too dangerous tae operate.'

'Ah know for the last few weeks, before he went off, he was

taking some terrible headaches. He had to go hame early a few times.'

'He's deteriorating rapidly. There's times his mother has tae stop him banging his head off the wall.' I can see Joe's eyes moisten. 'The doctors give him, at most, three months. Probably less.'

'Jeez oh! Ah wish ye had'nae telt me, Joe. Ah'd rather have not known for as long as possible.'

Joe sighs. He still keeps wiping down the mixer, though it's already dry. 'Well, ah wasn't sure whit tae dae, son. Ah know you and Mick had sort of teamed up together.'

'Yeah, ah suppose so, Joe. Ah was beginning tae wonder why he'd been off for so long.'

I have my piece and resist invites to play cards. I walk down to the edge of the quay and stand looking up-, sometimes down-river. Poor Mick. As usual there are freighters and coasters spread along the wharves being loaded and unloaded. A squat tug hurries up-river, pushing a large bow wave in front of herself. Tugs seem too powerful and muscly to be called 'she'. The faint sound of riveters at work in the yard opposite drifts across the water: 'Rrrrrrrr'. In the distance the Govan ferry makes another crossing. All this industry and bustle and life. Mick won't see much more of this if Joe, and the doctors, are right.

And I thought my days were numbered.

Spoken For

'Would ye like to get engaged?' I blush to my kneecaps. There, it's out. The glitterball is giving us its usual Saturday night bombardment as we glide round the Palais floor. I decided the dancing would be quite a romantic place to propose. I've been working myself up to it for the last hour. For the last month. We still keep dancing cheek to cheek. Is it not about time she answered? Jeez, maybe she's gonny say 'no'.

'Aye. That would be nice.'

I turn my head slightly and give her a succession of little kisses along her cheek until I find her lips. Yah bugger! I'm glad that's over. It's early November, 1958. We've been courting just over two years. On and off.

It's nearly a year and a half since I came back to Glasgow. During all this time there's never ever been the thought of anyone else but Nancy. When I'm in Glasgow it's just a case of going to work and, until recently, going out with Sammy. A few months ago he was called up for his two years. He asked for, and got, the RAMC (the Medical Corps). With Frank having been a Chief Petty Officer sick berth attendant during the war – and now a nurse – it must run in the blood. I still go up to Lottie and Frank's a couple of nights a week.

The following weekend Nancy comes through to Glasgow and we head for the Argyll Arcade, just off Buchanan Street. Glasgow's jewellery centre. Three out of every four shops are high class jewellers. We've looked in half a dozen windows or so, then we come to the premises of Atholl J. Crabbe Ltd – there's a grand name to go to church with!

'Oh! Ah like the look o' that yin.'

I follow her finger. 'The one at £24/19/11d?' That's more than two weeks' wages.

'Aye. Ah'd like tae try that one on.'

'Ah've only got aboot sixteen pounds, Nancy.'

As we speak, she hasn't once taken her eyes off her selection. 'That's okay. If ah decide that's the one ah want, ah'll give ye the extra. It's nae bother.' Nancy has recently been promoted from supervisor on a production line to overall supervisor at Manclarks, the Edinburgh clothing company where she works. She earns double what I make, maybe more. She's also something I've never been – a good saver. Not that I've had much to save.

'Well, ah was thinking it would be nice if ah bought the ring.'

'You still can. Look at it this way. Ah really fancy that one. Remember, this is something ah'll have for the rest of my life. Do ye want me tae wear a ring ah really don't fancy, just because it costs under sixteen pounds?'

'Well, ah suppose . . . no'.'

'Jist let me chip in for the minute. At some time in the future, if you're flush, you can pay me back – then that'll be jist as if you paid for it yourself. Won't it?'

I begin to feel better about it. 'Okay, that's what we'll do. Right, let's go in.'

The tray is brought from the window and the object of desire placed in Nancy's palm. The assistant goes into his pitch, though it's hardly needed. 'It's 9 carat gold, with platinum shoulders holding a single, quarter carat diamond.' Huh, no wonder it's so dear.

Five minutes later we walk out into the brightly lit arcade. The ring sparkles on Nancy's finger and her eyes sparkle too. We both spend the rest of the day glancing at it whenever we can.

* * *

'Shall we go straight back tae Seafield and let them see we're engaged? I never told them why ah was coming tae Glesgay the day.'

I shake my head. 'It's no' "Glesgay". It's Glesga! Anywye, ah suppose we might as well. Get it over with, eh?'

'Aye.'

Two hours later, with more than a little trepidation on my part, we're walking down the steps at 38 Cousland Crescent. I swallow hard as I brace myself for a mega-blushing session. As we enter the living room, Auld Sanny wakens up underneath the *West Lothian Courier*. Nancy's ma comes out of the kitchen as she hears the front door close and room door open,

'Whit are youse yins daeing here say early?' she looks at Nancy. 'Ah thocht youse were gonny spend the day in Glesgay?'

In reply, Nancy holds out her left hand, fingers splayed. 'We've decided tae get engaged! Do ye like ma ring?'

Sniff! 'Well, ye might have told folks.' She pauses, probably recovering. 'Oh well, if that's what youse want. Youse are auld enough tae make up your ain minds.'

Sanny sits up in the armchair, the *Courier* scrunched up on his knees. He's still half asleep. This, allied with his increasing hearing problem, means he hasn't really heard what's been said. 'Whit's going oan?' He turns his head to the side, favouring his 'good ear'.

Beenie speaks louder. 'It's these twa. They've been intae Glesgay and got thursels engaged.'

'Bugger me!' He's quiet for a few seconds, then starts chuckling. 'Och well, it had tae come.'

He straightens out the vandalised *Courier*, sits back, and begins to read. Nancy and I look at one another and smile. That's that done. We're engaged.

I return to work on the Monday, walking on air. We're out at George Fifth Dock at Shieldhall. I tell all the lads on the squad, and have to put up with the statutory ribbing . . .

'You'd get a wee bit jig-a-jig oan Setterday night, then.'

'Nane o'yer business, nosey gits!'

As it happened, I hadn't. I'm nineteen years of age – and still a virgin.

It's the third week in December when the brown envelope with OHMS on it arrives! A flight of butterflies take wing in my stomach. During the interview, after my medical, I'd stated a preference for the Royal Navy. I knew the odds were against me. When you're called up you can *say* where you'd like to serve; navy, army or air force. There's very little likelihood you'll get it. It's only regulars, folk who are signing on, who do get their choice. National Servicemen are placed where they're needed, which is mostly in the army. I'd been told at my interview that the Royal Navy only take around 10 per cent of conscripts, 'So don't hold your breath!'

I'd quite fancied myself as a 'Jolly Jack Tar' or should that be 'Jock Tar'? Well, I'll soon find out. I reach in to the envelope and pull out the contents. C'mon, say 'Royal Navy', I really suit blue. The letter is headed 'Enlistment Notice'. I get a twinge in my stomach, this is it! My eyes skip over the preliminaries . . . 'You are required to present yourself on 8 January 1959 at No.3 Training Battalion, RAOC, Hilsea Barracks, Portsmouth. A railway warrant is enclosed and a postal order for four shillings and sixpence as subsistence for your journey . . .' In my mind's eye an aircraft carrier sails off into the distance. I ain't on it. 'Huh! It's the fuckin' army for you, boy.' I carefully fold the letter and postal order and replace them in the now ragged envelope. Jeez, that ain't much notice. I sit down on the bed in my small room. That's me got just over three weeks left. I think back to my nine months in the RAF. I feel that should give me a head start on the other recruits; I know all about foot and rifle drill, bulling kit, making bed packs and laying out kit for the weekly inspections. I also recall the promise I'd made myself as I'd left – to do my best when, eventually, I got my call-up. That's still my

NATIONAL SERVICE ACTS, 1948 to 1955

ENLISTMENT NOTICE

MINISTRY OF LABOUR AND NATIONAL SERVICE REGIONAL OFFICE

MILITARY RECRUITING DEPARTMENT,
92 UNION STREET,
GLASGOW, C.2.

(Date)

1 7 DEC 1958

MR. *Robert DouGLAS*
c/o Irvine
32 Grenville Street
GLASGOW C3

Registration No. *MCK 24942*

DEAR SIR,

In accordance with the National Service Acts, 1948 to 1955, you are called up for service in the Regular Army and are required to present yourself on.............THURSDAY............day
......- 8 JAN 1959.................(date), between **9 a.m.** and **4 p.m.** to:—

No. 3 TRAINING BATTALION,
ROYAL ARMY ORDNANCE CORPS,
HILSEA BARRACKS,
PORTSMOUTH, HANTS.

PORTSMOUTH & SOUTHSEA (nearest railway station)

*A Travelling Warrant for your journey is enclosed. Before starting your journey you must exchange the warrant for a ticket at the booking office named on the warrant. If possible, this should be done a day or two before you are due to travel. If your warrant is made out to travel from London you may obtain a railway ticket at, and travel from, the most convenient station to your address.

A Postal Order for 4s., representing an advance of service pay, is also enclosed.

Immediately on receipt of this notice, you should inform your employer of the date upon which you are required to report for service.

Yours faithfully,

YOU SHOULD READ CAREFULLY THE NOTES OVERLEAF

G. S. BOLLING
for Regional Controller.

* *Delete if not applicable*

[P.T.O.

N.S.12A   J.369 Wt.50266/14001 50m 10/57 FAC

The letter every young man dreaded. Report for basic training.

intention. I'd had to be awkward in the Boys' Service so's I'd get thrown out. This is different. I want to prove to myself I can do my two years with the right attitude. Become a good soldier.

There's one thing to be done before I leave Glasgow. Mick's been on the sick more than a month, now. Joe says he's really going downhill. We were good pals. Even though I know all about his illness it's still hard to take in. He's just twenty-one and he's going to die. That's really hard. I always admired the way Mick would try his best even though, physically, he wasn't so strong. We had such good laughs. I don't really want to go, but I hate the thought of Mick thinking, 'I thought Robert would've come to see me.'

'Joe, how's Mick?'

The answer's in his face. 'He's not very good, son.'

'Ah've had ma call-up papers for the army. Ah'm away in jist over a fortnight. Ah'd like tae go and see him before ah leave. Can ye give me his address?'

'Aye, of course. But mind,' he looks me in the eye, 'you'll huv tae prepare yourself for a shock. He's in a bad way. Lost a lot of weight. And he's gone blind.'

'For God's sake!'

'It's a terrible ordeal he's going through, and the family.' He stops speaking. I try to ease things for him.

'Right. If ye give me their address, Joe, ah'll take a wee run up the night. Ah don't want him thinking ah've forgot about him.'

Sometime after seven I make my way over to Govan and find the address. God, ah'm not looking forward to this. I climb the stairs and find the door with the nameplate 'Quinn' on it. The red-headed woman who answers is obviously Mrs Quinn.

'Hello. Ah'm Robert Douglas, ah work wi' Mick at the Clyde Trust. Ah'm away intae the army in a few weeks, so ah thought ah'd come and see him.' She opens the door wide.

'Och aye, come away in. He's often talked about ye this last year and aw' the things the pair o' you get up tae.' We both smile.

We step into the room on the right. There's already two or three folk in, including Mick's younger brother. One of the visitors is the priest. Mrs Quinn introduces me. They smile. I say 'Hello, Father.' I wonder if he'll think I'm Catholic? I look over to my left. Mick is lying in a low, single bed. 'C'mon over,' says his mother. 'Mick, it's your pal from work, Robert Douglas, to see ye.'

He turns his head, not quite looking in the right direction. 'Hello Robert. Huv ye no' got yerself married yet?'

I try to hide the shock of seeing how ill he is. 'Naw, we've got engaged since ah saw ye last. Anywye, ah've jist got ma call-up papers for the army. Ah'm away in a fortnight or so, eighth of January.'

'Hah-hah! That'll sort ye oot.'

I'm about to reply, but suddenly he goes into a fit. He twitches and squirms and almost kicks off the single blanket that covers him. He's naked under it. His mother tries to cover him. 'He takes these wee fits every twenty minutes or so. It's the pressure. He's very warm, that's why he's got no pyjamas on.'

I touch her arm. 'It's okay, Mrs Quinn.' A couple of minutes later, Mick has recovered enough to continue our conversation. I try hard to talk just the way we would at work. 'Ah think auld Willie Lilley is missing the two of us, Mick. You'll huv tae get yerself back so's we can carry on tormentin' the life oot o' him.'

'Aye, ah'll try ma best. Remember when we turned the jet of air on him?' We both laugh at the memory. I make small talk for another five minutes or so. It's the sightless eyes I find so sad.

'Well, ah think ah'd better away, Mick. Ah'm liable tae get lost in the middle of Govan.' I stand up, reach forward, take his hand in mine and squeeze it. He squeezes back. 'Cheerio, Mick.' I have a job to keep my voice steady.

'Cheerio, Robert. Aw' the best when ye get married. And good luck in the army.'

I look down at the thin, white figure. I can't say anything else. I know I'll never see him again.

I say my goodbyes to his brother and the other visitors. His mother accompanies me to the door. We stand for a moment under the single bulb in this typical tenement lobby. Just like all the others in Glasgow, coats hang on a row of hooks. I'm near to tears at the sadness of it all. I manage to say, 'He's not very well, is he?'

'No. We've always known this day would come. Of course, you pray it won't.'

'I'm really sorry, Mrs Quinn. Him and I were good pals. Worked together every day. He really is a good lad, always tried to pull his weight.' I realise I'm speaking about him as if he were already dead.

'Yes. Well, he's in the Lord's hands. Thanks for coming to see him.'

'Aye, with me going intae the army soon, I didn't want to go without . . .' my voice trails off.

'Anyway, cheerio son. God bless.'

'Yeah, bye. Ah hope everything goes all right.' I step out onto the landing and the door closes softly behind me. I set off down the stairs. I know I'll never forget my last sight of Mick.

All of a sudden the thought of two years in the army doesn't seem such a bad prospect.

Soldier of the Queen

I step out of the close at 32 Granville Street for the last time. For just a moment I stand on the pavement. On my left the bulk of the Mitchell Library looms dark and silent, closed for the night.

It's late on a winter's evening, 7 January 1959. I'm nineteen years old and about to set off for England once more. Jeez, since Ma died I always seem to be going somewhere. Never settled. Just short of four years ago it was the RAF. Now it's the army. I take a deep breath, then set off for the Central Station to catch my train.

I don't know it, but this is the last time I'll live in Glasgow. There's also no way I can know, or even dream, that just over forty years later I'll return to the Mitchell Library to launch my book!

It's a long journey to Portsmouth, and it includes changing at Crewe. From childhood I've regularly heard those magic words, 'change at Crewe'. In 1959 Britain is still criss-crossed with a spider's web of railway lines. From the days when the railways were run by the great private companies, LMS, LNER, GWR et al, many of their lines met at Crewe. It was there that passengers had to disembark and catch the train of another company. As I grew up, I'd regularly hear the mantra 'change at Crewe' in films and on radio. During the war, various uncles in uniform, wearing their full kit and carrying their rifle – this was part of a soldier's kit during the war – would call in to see Ma for an hour or two. Almost without fail, when taking their leave, I'd hear those mysterious words, 'Ah huv tae change at Crewe.' It couldn't have been anymore intriguing if they'd said, 'Ah'm gonny be taking the Silk Route tae China,' or 'Ah'd better be going, ah'm catching the Orient Express at ten.' Well, at last, it's now my turn.

Come next month, February, it'll be four years since I left the Central to travel down to RAF Cosford to start, as far as I was concerned, a twelve year sentence. Now, with a strong feeling of *déjà vu*, I'm once more walking along a cold, shadowy platform, the taste of steam and cinders in my mouth from the locomotive which will soon take me away from Glasgow. As before, the train isn't busy and I get a compartment to myself for my overnight journey.

Just as I did four years ago, I look at my reflection in the window. God, how depressed I was then. I'm not exactly turning somersaults now, but things are a lot better. I'm engaged. I'm only going away for two years in the army – not twelve in the RAF. I'm almost twenty, not sixteen. Nobody cared about me back then. Now I've got Nancy. We'll be writing three or four times a week, I'll be spending all my leaves at Seafield. Yeah, things are better. A LOT better.

We've left the city behind, there's nothing but impenetrable blackness outside the window. I stare into it for long periods. Thinking. A trail of steam from the engine floats past. Sometimes, way in the distance, a single light will burn. As we make our way through the night, the lamp appears to move slowly from left to right. I watch until it vanishes, try and figure out what it is. An isolated farm? There'll be another one along shortly. There always is. Now and again I look at myself in the window. I remember doing that often as I travelled to Cosford, trying to figure out why I'd been given all that misery.

'Ach!' I get the carrier down from the rack. I'll have a read. Just make myself depressed if I think too much about Ma and me. I'm reading *Hatter's Castle*. Four years ago it was Desmond Young's biography of Rommel. I'm enjoying this book. Writes a good story, does A.J. Cronin. Good characters. Draws you in to their world. There's a list of other books he's had published, I think I'll keep an eye open for them and read some more of his stuff. I find my place and soon I'm far removed from this night train as Cronin works his magic. Jeez, no wonder they cast Robert Newton as James Brodie when they filmed this back in the forties. A dour, dominating character with a heavy, blue jowl. You couldn't cast anyone else BUT Robert Newton. Well, you could. My father would've been a natural.

I stretch out on the long bench seat, my rolled-up gabardine mac as a pillow. I begin to feel sleepy. Better get some kip, tomorrow will be a busy day. It'll be another 'chased from arsehole to breakfast time' day. That's for certain. I reach up and switch the compartment lights to 'dim' and place the book on the floor. I get as comfortable as is possible. Well, it all starts tomorrow, boy. I remember when I got chucked out the RAF. This is different. Every lad does his two years. That's the main thing to remember, it's just two years. I want to prove to myself I can knuckle down. Show willing. My thoughts wander on. Jeez, I'm gonny miss my job with the Trust, and all the guys in the squad. I loved going round all the docks, being amongst the ships, feeling I was part – I know it was a small part – of one of the world's major ports. I wonder if any of the guys ever thought like that? Trouble is, you can't ask. They'd take the piss out of you for evermore. I bet some of them did think like that – but they'd only admit it under torture! I wonder if I'll finish up anywhere near Sammy. He's just been posted to Wheatley Hospital, at Oxford. I couldn't go into the Medical Corps. I'd be spewing up all over the place. And John Purden. Now he's married and a dad I never see him. Got a daughter AND a son now. Things aren't half changing.

* * *

I sleep fitfully as I'm carried away from Glasgow through a winter's night. Now and again I waken, realise where I am – and where I'm going – then lie staring at the dimmed lights, my thoughts taking me in all directions until, once more, I doze off. Sometimes I think about the whole idea of National Service. In some ways I'm looking forward to 'doing my bit', then, at other times I think, 'what a fucking imposition!' There's no war on, yet 'they' are saying, 'Right, pack your job in and come and give us two of the prime years of your life – for which we'll pay you washers.' If you think of it like that, it's a bit of a liberty, really. Then, you never know, what if them Russian gits start while I'm doing my two years? The Yanks have the right idea; have three or four times as many H-bombs and rockets as they've got. They know it ain't worth their while to start anything. There'd be no winner. It also splits Nancy and me up for most of the next two years. What if she finds somebody else? Ach, it's all too fucking complicated . . .

The train slowing is enough to wake me. This should be Crewe. At last, the famous Crewe. I'm too tired to feel enthusiastic. I sit up and look out the window. At first there's nothing to see, then we enter the outskirts of a town. There's no sign of minarets or marble palaces; maybe it's not as exotic as I thought. We slow even more, then glide into a poorly-lit station.

I step onto the platform. I shiver, as much from tiredness as from cold. Another five or six folk have also got off. They'll also be able to bore the tits off their grandkids with, 'I changed at Crewe!' It's coming up for three a.m. I've got half an hour or so to wait. I look around. Bit disappointing. There's nothing remarkable about it. Just another mid-Victorian railway station. Draughty, dingy – and in the middle of a January night, freezing! I head for the tearoom.

British Rail refreshment facilities have long been the butt of comedians' humour. I open the door and find out why. In spades!

Chilly room, well-worn chairs and tables and a half dozen or so customers sitting well apart. A few ageing travel posters hang framed on the wall and try to look cheery . . . 'See You At Scarborough!'; 'Skegness Is So Bracing!' A tired looking woman, pushing sixty, leans on the other side of the counter. As our little influx of new customers enter, she looks aggrieved. Her lips move, as though counting us. One of our fellows is foreign; he has the nerve to approach her. 'Do I sit at table and you come?'

'Noooh, we don't do table-service, love.' To show that's final, she gives the counter a wipe. I walk over to her. When she realises her annoyed look isn't going to deter me, she moves to Plan B. 'Yes?'

I look at the large glass dome on the counter which contains some 'stage prop' sandwiches. I don't have to ask what's in them; the top slices obligingly curl back. 'A mug of tea and a corned beef sandwich, please.' I point to the dome which protects the public from the cakes. 'Eh, and two custard tarts, please.'

As she goes about her business I've nothing to do but look at her. She wears the old-fashioned linen 'tiara' on the front of her hair. At first glance there appears to be two balls of steel wool attached to it. Closer inspection reveals them as hair. She emerges from the clouds of steam issuing from a large, gasometer-like boiler and places my mug of tea on the counter. Some of it slops over onto the surface. She feigns not to notice. There's a distinct 'clunk' as my sandwich hits the plate; the custard tarts emit a note from higher up the tonic scale.

'One and tenpence, love.'

Holding the still-dripping mug in front of me, I carry my iron rations over to a remote table. I can be as British as anyone else when I want to. I'm too tired to risk conversation. To make certain, I pick up an abandoned *Sunday Pictorial*. I half-read it as I take bites of sandwich, quickly followed by mouthfuls of tea to soften the stiff bread. Well, I suppose it's a small price to pay to be able to say, 'I changed at Crewe!' I wonder if there's a club?

*　　　*　　　*

Sometime after eight a.m., I arrive in Portsmouth. As we draw in my resident butterflies take off. I take my bag down from the rack, place it on the seat, then stand looking out the window across the row of platforms. Amongst the many civilians are quite a few sailors in uniform. That's what I'd expect to see in 'Pompey', home of the Royal Navy. I wonder how the army managed to sneak in? I also feel it's a little ironic. I asked for the Navy. They've put me in the army – but sent me to Portsmouth!

I've hardly taken half a dozen steps from the carriage when an army corporal, one of four or five NCOs spread along the platform, homes in on me. 'You for Hilsea, lad?'

'Yes, corporal.'

There's another youth behind me. 'You for Hilsea, too?'

'Yes, mate.' I automatically grimace; I know what's coming.

The corporal bristles. 'I'm not your bloody mate!' He points. 'Join that lot over there.' I think to myself, 'that's your card marked, son.'

We make for the travel-weary, bedraggled group of lads standing aimlessly under the station clock. They watch without interest as we join them.

'Is this the queue for the short-back-and-sides?' I say.

Nobody answers, but a couple manage a smile.

'Right, Corporal Hardisty, you takes this lot,' instructs a sergeant; I'll later find out his name is Evans. The bespectacled corporal marches briskly toward us.

'C'mon then, form yourselves into threes.' Some of us know what he means, we guide the others. Eventually we're lined up in a reasonable fascimile of what's required and march off, badly out of step, to another platform. Here we catch the local train out to Hilsea. It sounds a real southern name to me, the sort of name I'd expect to find in *Swallows and Amazons*. Sunny beaches and blue sea, children paddling.

At Hilsea Station, just as at Cosford, Bedford 3-tonners wait to take us the short hop to the camp. I watch from under the canvas canopy as we drive through the gates and the sentry shuts them behind us. You're in the army now, pal!

How Nice to be Shouted At Again

Basic training, though seemingly crude, works. Raw civilians, who don't want to be in the forces, are conscripted, and for the next six weeks bawled at, bullied, brainwashed and badgered. At the end of this short period they will, along with a hundred others, respond as one when given orders, march in step, do complicated arms drill, and learn not to argue. Most, especially those who left sedentary jobs, will be fitter than they've ever been. This subservience to military discipline will have been brought about by that fearsome group of men known as D.I.s – Drill Instructors. The main requirement of a D.I. is to have a throat and lungs of leather. It is their 'stock in trade'. Most of their day is spent shouting. When they do talk, it is in a clipped, staccato manner which could be called 'army speak'. Whether southern English or northern Scot, eventually only traces of their origins will be heard. They have become D.I.s.

Every drill instructor, and the great majority of all other NCOs in the British Army, model themselves on the most famous Regimental Sergeant Major of them all, 'Tibby' Brittain – 'the loudest voice in the British Army'. RSM Brittain, Coldstream Guards, a tall burly man with a waxed moustache, was already a legend in the army when he appeared in the film *They Were Not Divided*, made towards the end of the Second World War. Although he only had a short cameo playing, of course, an RSM, he almost stole the film and his fame spread nationwide, as did his catchphrase, 'Never seen anything like it in all me life!' Overnight, all NCOs, from lance corporal upward, became clones of the great man. His influence and manner still resonates to this day amongst NCOs – though many will never have heard of him. He was the template.

As expected, our first day is a bewilderment of drawing kit, marching everywhere 'at the double', being allocated to a hut in the lines (wooden billets) with twenty or so other guys, and being shouted at at regular intervals to start us getting used to it. We have also been informed that sometime after the midday meal we will be going to the medical block for the mandatory FFI (Free From Infection) examination. This is to ensure you have no communicable diseases of a sexual nature, i.e. diseases of the willy. We are sitting and lying on our beds in the billet, one of the dozen or so similar wooden huts.

'CORPORAL PRESENT!' The lad nearest the door has seen him enter and, as we've all been instructed, has alerted the rest of us. Every time an NCO enters our hut, no matter how low in rank, we all have to stop what we're doing and leap to our feet as though he were God. During basic training, he IS God.

'AT EASE!' We relax. Most sit back on their beds. 'I want you outside, fully dressed, in threes, NOW!'

Fuck me! There's a mad scramble as we struggle into battle-dress jackets and cram berets on our heads . . .

'Can't get into me bastardin' boots!'

'Slacken the laces a bit more.'

'Where's ma fuckin' tie?'

'You should never take it off.'

'What, even when I'm in me jammies?'

'No, you daft bat.'

As we run about, getting in each other's way, dropping things, at the same time we're laughing at the antics of one another and the state the army's got us into already.

'NOW! NOW! NOW! Let's be 'aving you.' Corporal Hardisty has appeared on the scene, adding to the confusion with continually shouted exhortations.

After a fashion, we line up on the road outside the hut. 'C'MON! Fists clenched, thumbs down the seam of the trousers.' Hardisty physically moves some of the worst cases into a facsimile of 'standing to attention'. 'Right, I'm now going to march you over to to the medical block. The order, when it comes, will be "Quiiiick MARCH!"' Two or three guys attempt to start marching, they bump into their stationary neighbours. Another two or three, when they see the first lot starting to march, think they must have misheard the good corporal so *they* belatedly try to set away. All is confusion. Some of us get the giggles.

'AS YOU WERE! GOD'S STRUTH!' Hardisty looks heaven-wards. 'Why me?' He crunches his boots on the tarmac two or three times. 'Shambles doesn't cover it! How can I train those ejected from the Home For the Terminally Cretinous? I'm going to have to hand me stripes in!' He paces up and down in front of us a couple of times then does a smart 'halt' followed by an immaculate 'left turn' to face us. 'I will try again. SQUAD! SQUAD 'SHUN!' We come to attention at different speeds as can be heard by the staccato pitter-patter of our boots on the road. Hardisty shakes his head then mutters another imprecation to the God of D.I.s, 'Why do I ALWAYS get the worst fuckin' squad? Why can't you send me Girl Guides?'

Order is restored and we're marched, after a fashion, to the medical block, dismissed – some turn to the left instead of right – and led inside by a medical orderly with a clipboard. A Glasgow guy called George Maharg and I stand together. We've taken adjacent beds in the billet and have already teamed up.

'Pay attention!' says clipboard, 'I want you to form up in a long, straight line.' We do so.

'Now, drop your trousers to your ankles and be ready, when told, to lower your underpants.'

'Fahk me!' says a cockney voice, 'not gonna give us one up the jacksie, are they?'

'OFFICER PRESENT!' shouts the orderly. We stand to attention, trousers round our ankles, shirt tails flapping, feeling rather silly. There are one or two titters.

The young M.O., a lieutenant, strolls into the centre of the room and halts, facing us. 'I'm now going to give you what is known as an FFI. Free From Infection. I shall also check that none of you has a rupture. This necessitates me handling your private parts. I know we haven't been introduced and I haven't had the decency to take you out to dinner. But that's the army for you.' We watch as the M.O. and orderly put on rubber gloves. 'Drop your underpants,' says the orderly, 'and as soon as we pass you, get dressed again.'

They proceed along the line. Eventually they confront me; I obligingly lift up my shirt. The M.O. takes hold of my penis, looks at it, then lets go. He takes my testicles in his hand. 'Cough!' I cough. 'A bit stronger.' I oblige. They move on.

The remainder of the afternoon, with the exception of dinner in the mess, is spent in the billet sorting out kit and making a start on knocking the billet itself into shape. Corporal Hardisty and a couple of lance corporals are on hand to give advice, show us how. Now and again Sergeant Evans, who we first met at the railway station, graces us with his presence. By 'lights out' new uniforms have been pressed, a start made on 'bulling' boots, lessons given on how to make bedpacks, the dozen windows of the hut have been washed and polished, then the wooden floor swept, waxed and buffed up using heavy, long-handled 'bumpers'.

Since we have still not finished as the lights go out, candles – bought in the NAAFI – are lit and the bulling continues. As we sit there in the semi-dark, just isolated pools of light spread round the hut, guys are in groups of three or four sitting on other guys beds, working on their kit and finding out about one another. Within minutes of lights out, the 'duty bugler' begins Last Post.

As its beautiful melancholy fills the darkness, conversations stop or falter for the duration. We all know we are listening and that it's putting thoughts into our minds; thoughts of where we are, or of those at home. Finally, tired and weary, we get undressed, don our army issue blue and white striped pajamas and, in twos and threes, shivering with the cold – the pot-bellied stove devoured the miserly issue of coal hours ago – we flit back and forth to the bogs to wash hands, clean teeth, then topple into bed.

Sometime after midnight the last few candles are snuffed. Desultory conversations, interrupted by much yawning, continue in the dark for a while . . .

'I just can't get the mixture right to bull me boots.'

'Don't worry, ah'll show tha in t'morning.'

'Thanks mate.'

'Aw, man! I forgot to get a stamp out t'NAAFI for her letter. Ah'll miss first post.'

'I'll let you 'ave one. Ah's got a book.'

'Smashin'. Thanks pal.'

Forty-eight hours ago these lads hadn't clapped eyes on one another. The adversity of basic training, of being in the army, is bonding us. Nothing in civvy street has this effect. I think back to Cosford. Even though I hated every minute of it, I still loved to lie in the dark and listen to the Last Post echoing through the barrack block. Then I'd usually cry myself to sleep. I lie alone with my thoughts as the conversations begin to falter. I could be back in Cosford. I place my two hands behind my head and stare, unseeing, at the ceiling. I certainly won't be crying myself to sleep tonight, or any night. We are indeed being chased from 'arsehole to breakfast time', but already I know I can handle it. There's times I've laughed out loud today, in spite of all the hassle. Must try and get a letter off to Nancy tomorrow. I turn onto my side. Better get some shut-eye.

*   *   *

Where's that buggering bugle coming from? I'm jarred awake. All the lights are snapped on at once. I'm being pulled, VERY reluctantly, from a deep sleep. Where am I?

'C'MON, LET'S BE 'AVING YOU! RISE AND SHINE! YOU MAYBE BROKE YOUR MOTHER'S 'EART – YOU WON'T FUCKIN' BREAK MINE!'

'Awww,' I do know where I am. I close my heavy eyes. I'm in the fuckin' army!

The two lance corporals carry on making a din, pulling covers off guys, and doing anything else they can think of until we are all up. Everything is at the double, including washing, shaving and scoffing our breakfasts. Then we start to get busy. Before we leave the billet it has to be left 'ready for inspection'. I know how to do a bedpack. I give another couple of guys a demonstration. We rush outside, drill for an hour on the square, have a ten-minute NAAFI break, do some more drill, then PT, then return to our hut to find Corporal Hardisty and Sergeant Evans waiting.

'This 'ut is a fucking disgrace!' says the sergeant. Well, there's a surprise. We are all standing by our beds, at attention. Most of the bedpacks – not mine – have been shaken out and lie on the mattress. Other items of kit which haven't passed muster also lie scattered on the bed. The sergeant parades up and down the floor. 'This will NOT 'appen again! EVER!'

We double-away to the mess for lunch. I eat mine as fast as possible. With a bit of luck I might get as long as thirty precious minutes lying on my bed before we're hard at it again. I return to the billet. 'Ahhhh!' I lie on top of my firm, army bed. This must be the finest bed in all of Christendom. Beds in the Savoy or Dorchester couldn't compare with it. Within minutes I am deep in the embrace of Morpheus . . .

'C'MON! OUT OF IT! Never seen anything like it in all me bloody life!' I'm jarred awake, but even so, that much-needed kip has refreshed me.

'Let's be having you. Outside, in threes, NOW!' Once

again there's a mad scatter; less than two minutes later we're outside.

'SQUAD! Squad 'SHUN!' We come to attention almost together. Corporal Hardisty walks up and down the line, halts, and turns to face us. 'Now then. It's back to the medical block for you lot. Few jabs to get. Yes, you heard right. A few! Gets it all over and done with in one fell swoop.' He brings himself to attention. 'SQUAD! Right TURN!' 'Turn' is actually spat out as 'TAH!' The same applies to 'March!', which comes out as 'MAH!' Whenever he emits these operative words they are always ejected as a scream. This is the way of the D.I. He gives the order in a staccato manner, then, when he comes to the final word of command, he clenches his entire body, fists balled, jerks forward from the waist and projects that last word as though giving birth . . .

'By the LEFF, quick MAH! What a bloody shambles!'

We're dismissed outside the medical block yet again and file into the same room as yesterday. A Medical Corps corporal appears this time, carrying what looks like yesterday's clipboard.

'Strip to the waist, you lads. Leave your clothes on the floor where you can find them. Right, follow me.' He leads us along a corridor. At the end of it a queue of lads, also stripped to the waist, slowly move forward through a door. We join on. Geordie (George) Maharg and I are together. There's not much conversation going on. An air of quiet nervousness permeates the corridor. As the queue shuffles slowly forward we hear the occasional, 'OHYAH!' issue from the room. One of them is followed by, 'He's going! Catch the bugger!' This is accompanied by shuffling feet. Now and again there's a dull thump, signalling some 'bugger' hasn't been caught. I'm reminded of a childhood visit to Glasgow's Dental Hospital. I have the same feeling as I did then – something bad is happening in there. I also know there's nothing I can do about it. As we draw nearer to the door, Geordie and I stand on tiptoe to try and see exactly what is going on. A guy, two in front, gives a brief summary of what's happening in the room . . .

'Fuck me! Everybody's getting FOUR jabs!'

I turn to George. 'Ah bet ye the MPs could arrest him fur spreading alarm and despondency.'

I notice he's a trifle pale. He looks at me. 'Ah hate gettin' jags.'

'Me tae.' We both give forced laughs. 'Jeez, ah jist hope ah don't faint,' I say.

'So dae ah. Ah'll feel like a big lassie if ah pass oot in front of everybody.'

'Jist take some deep breaths when it's coming up for yer turn. That'll help.' I try to remember where I got those words of wisdom from. Probably the 'Doc's Page' in the *Sunday Post*.

The queue crawls forward. Soon the two of us are in the open doorway and can witness the full horror. We look at each other and give weak smiles as another guy has to be supported.

'Remember, deep breaths.' There I go again with the advice. Dr Douglas. As Geordie stands next to me I'm gratified to hear him taking big breaths.

'Next!'

'After you, Percy,' I say.

'No, after YOU, Claude,' says George.

'Yah big feartie!' I add.

'Aw, fuck it!' George walks forward and stands between two medical orderlies. One takes hold of his upper left arm. The other, his right. Each arm gets a wipe with a cotton wool swab. They pick up syringes then do that thing they're always doing in the movies; hold them in the air and squirt some liquid out of them. Quite a bit of liquid. It looks like half his jag has landed on the linoleum. Nervousness always makes me try to be funny. Should I say, 'Excuse me, half ma friend's dose has landed on the floor!' Simultaneously, the orderlies plunge the needles into his arms. I watch as he walks forward to sit at a table facing another two white-coated orderlies.

'Next!' I stop watching Geordie. The little bugger hasn't

flinched, never mind fainted. I'll have to do the same. I stand between the two medics. I remember my tip about the breathing. Jab! Jab! I grimace, but make no sound. I walk forward and sit facing the two at the table. 'Stretch your arms out, elbows on the table, palms up.' Should I say, 'Ma mammy says it's bad manners to put yer elbows on the table!'? Geordie passes me. That's him finished. He gives me a wink. There is a clatter behind me as another victim of needle phobia hits the floor. I watch in apprehension as each orderly takes hold of an arm, swabs the same spot on both forearms, then hold up syringes the size of small fire extinguishers. The natural instinct is to pull away. I'm just starting to break out in a cold sweat when they plunge them into me. Jeez, thank God that's over.

'Okay, get dressed now.'

'Ah'm bloody pleased we've got that behind us.'

'Me tae.' I look at Geordie. 'Well, at least we did'nae go doon.'

'Ah know. They were dropping like flies. Did ye notice, it was nearly aw' the big guys?'

We return to the room and get dressed. Just before we leave, the same M.O. from yesterday, accompanied by the same orderly, addresses us. 'One of the injections you've just had, the one in the left, upper arm, is called the T.A.B., Typhus A and B. When you waken in the morning you'll find you have a stiff and VERY painful upper arm. For the rest of today, and especially this evening, try and keep your arm busy. Don't nurse it. Clean your kit, bull your boots, keep it moving.' He turns to the orderly. 'Thank you, Hopkins.'

'SAH!' Hopkins comes smartly to attention. He doesn't salute. In the British Army you only salute when wearing a cap or beret. The officer is wearing his cap. He salutes.

Once more we're plunged into a day of non-stop activity. It's late afternoon when we're marched over to one of the huts belonging to the Army Education Corps. At last! A chance for a skive.

Around eighty of us file into a lecture room laid out with rows of wooden benches on either side of a central aisle. We sit shoulder to shoulder on the hard benches, facing a small stage. The transition from cold barrack square to warm, cosy hut is most welcome. One or two of us give involuntary shivers at first until our bodies adapt to the heat. I look over to the windows. Outside it's already becoming dark. A cold January wind scuffs the panes with snow flurries now and again, as if to remind us it's waiting.

Geordie rubs his hands briskly together in pleasure. 'Bloody great this, Robert. By the time we're finished in here we won't be back oot oan the square again the day.'

'ATTENSHUN!' An Education Corps sergeant appears. Most of us 'sit to attention' as is required. A dozen or more, who are still not into the swing of things, jump to their feet, realise their mistake, and sheepishly sit down again as the rest of us laugh. A young officer walks out onto the stage. 'Good afternoon, men. I'm now going to give you a talk, for the next forty-five minutes or so, on the laws of our country, Great Britain. About Common Law and Statute Law, how they came about, and the differences between them.

Geordie speaks out the corner of his mouth. 'Fuckin' great! Forty-five minutes in the warm. Jist look at it!' He inclines his head towards the windows. The snow flurries have graduated to hail. The blustery wind drives the hail against the hut at regular intervals with a 'sheush-sheush' sound, as though it's trying to get to us. The dark, winter afternoon makes the hut seem more cosy than ever. I incline my head toward Geordie. There's a strong feeling of being back in school as, to avoid being spotted, I also indulge in 'penitentiary-speak', just like James Cagney or George Raft do in the movies. I twist the corner of my mouth, 'How come they canny have OOR billets centrally-heated like this? It's the same kind of huts. Why do we huv tae put up wi' that stupid wee stove in the middle o' that big hut? If ye stand and get yer willy warm, yer arse is freezin''

'Ah know,' says Geordie. 'Bastards!'

* * *

The pair of us sit four or five rows from the front, at the left end of our bench. Within ten minutes everybody, including me, cannot keep their eyes open. The soporific heat, allied to the last few days' non-stop activity and the lack of sleep, is taking its toll. I nudge Geordie awake. 'Look!' The nine or ten guys along the rest of the bench are all dozing off at the same time. Tightly jammed shoulder to shoulder, they fight a losing battle to stay awake. In unison, heavy eyelids droop, heads slowly sink onto chests, then one guy begins to slowly topple forward. Because they are crammed together and mutually supporting, he also starts to take his semi-conscious neighbours on either side with him. This spreads along the whole row until a dozen or more guys, in an early form of the Mexican Wave, begin to undulate forward. I watch in fascination as they lean further and further out until some built-in gyroscope kicks in and, without waking up, the one furthest forward automatically goes into reverse, taking all his fellows back with him. I look around me. The 'Hilsea Wave' is going on on every bench. So fatigued are they, each guy thinks he's the only one dozing off. Very few realise what's going on. Sometimes, when they sit up, one or two will open their eyes and look around for a moment to see if anyone's spotted they almost dozed off there! Sixty seconds later, the Hilsea Wave is back in action. Minutes later, I join it.

As the lights are on in the classroom, the young officer must be able to see what's going on. Having almost certainly been a National Serviceman himself, he'll know what it was like to do basic training and be continually short of sleep. He obviously chooses to turn a blind eye. Forty-five minutes later we exit the hut, quite refreshed and none the wiser about the laws of Great Britain.

As 'lights out' approaches, our upper left arms, as forecast, are a little tender and slightly stiff.

'Well, if it dis'nae get any worse than this it'll be aw'right, George.'

'Aye, it's no' as bad as they said it would be. A good night's kip an' we'll be right as rain.'

We both lie in our beds, reading. I'm just about dropping off when the duty corporal opens the door. 'Right ya're, lads. Time to hit the hay.' Only about half the denizens of our billet are in bed. Some still fiddle with their kit, others bull boots, one or two write letters. Most of them are still dressed. It makes no difference. The corporal smiles, then clicks all the switches to off.

'Say goodnight, Gracie,' he says as he closes the door.

'Goodnight, Gracie!' say three or four in the dark.

Esprit de What?

We all lie deeply asleep in the dark, still hut. The bone-tired sleep that only recruits know. Outside the thin walls of the hut, January is trying, yet again, to prove what a bad month it can be. It is succeeding. Our watches lie on bedside cabinets or in drawers, ticking inexorably toward six a.m. The temperature inside the hut is maybe 5 degrees warmer than outside. No. That should be 5 degrees *less cold* than outside. The stove in the middle of the billet burned out hours ago. We're allowed one bucket of coal per evening. This should last from six p.m. until 'lights out'. It doesn't. It barely lasts half that time. The army knows that. Why don't they give us enough coal?

Every morning we are always tired. Dog tired. Every morning we swear blind, 'tonight we'll go to bed early. That's a promise!' It never happens. After the duty NCO puts the lights out, we lie and blether, tell jokes, play tricks on one another in the dark, hold World Championship Loudest Fart Competitions. For a scant few days I held the Scottish Title.

It's two minutes to six. If someone were awake they'd hear nothing but regular breathing. Gentle snoring. Now and again someone breaks wind with an effort that would see them crowned champion. It goes unrecorded. The Tannoy blares and at the same instant, all the lights come on. If we weren't so near death the shock would kill us!

'C'MON, LET'S BE 'AVING YOU! HANDS OFF COCKS AND ON WITH SOCKS!' Aw, man! I was fed up hearing that at Cosford. It's still not fuckin' funny. The two D.I.s walk briskly up and down the billet, boots crunching, shouting at the tops of their voices. One carries a stick which he rattles up and down inside the curved, metal bed-ends as though they were dinner gongs. I lie there, terminally tired. I make a solemn promise. I'm DEFINITELY going to bed early tonight. Already one or two, wearing just pajama bottoms, shiver their half-bent way to the ablutions. There seems to be a lot of moans, groans, even yelps this morning as guys rise. I'm too tired to figure out why. I know I should make an effort to get to the bogs and claim a sink. Just as at Cosford there aren't enough sinks for everybody and the hot water always runs out. Why do they do that to us? I would imagine our conditions are on a par with conscripts in the first World War, never mind the Second. To shave my plooky face in hot water is bad enough. To shave it in cold is an ordeal.

In spite of all the noise and activity I begin to doze off . . . 'THAT MAN!' I'm jerked awake as one of the corporals lifts the bottom of my bed a couple of times, letting it crash to the floor. The covers are whisked off me. I think it's time to get up. I put my hands on the mattress with the intention of pushing myself up into a sitting position. 'AHHHH!' An excrutiating pain fills my upper left arm; I look to see if there's a bread knife sticking out of it. I fall back onto the mattress. 'AHHHH! Ma arm!' It's too tender to even touch. I'm suddenly aware of more 'OOOYAHs!' and assorted 'Fuck mes!' from around the billet.

'Robert?' Geordie croaks from the next bed, 'Are you still alive?'

'Ah don't know.'

'Is yer arm the same as mine?'

'Fuckin' worse.'

'Could'nae be.'

'It's that bastardin' T.A.B. Jeez, they said it would be bad. Ah did'nae think it would be THIS bad. Ah feel bloody lousy as well. Whit aboot you?'

'Ah'm at death's door,' says George. 'Why can they no' jist let us lie in oor beds the day?'

'Don't be stupid. You're in the army.'

For the rest of the day, our painful, ultra-tender arms dominate everything. As we stand in the permanent long queue in the mess there are regular cries of, 'AHHH! Mind me bloody arm!' Now and again someone bumps against somebody else and their howl of pain is counterpointed by the sound of breaking china as nerveless fingers drop a mug. As ever, this immediately evokes a cheer from everyone else. On the parade ground we're excused arms' drill but are given plenty of marching – with arms swinging.

The adversity we face on a daily basis from the D.I.s bonds us into a self-supporting team – as it's meant to. If you can't get the hang of bulling boots, someone in the hut will show you. If you still can't manage, he'll finish up doing them for you. He'll moan and groan, curse you. But he'll do them because you're in the same squad. Each billet contains a squad. They all have their own full corporal and two lance corporals. The D.I.s compete with each other to see who'll produce the best squad at the end of basic training. We are continually exhorted not to let down our squad or our D.I.s. WE must finish up as No. 1. It is, of course, all army bullshit. Whilst we are trying our best for the squad, we are also becoming a disciplined body of men who, on command, will act as one. Meanwhile, all the other squads are being cajoled into doing the same. It's a prime example of the unofficial mantra of the British Army . . . 'Bullshit baffles brains.' It works.

To my surprise, I sometimes find myself taking on the role of devil's advocate. Two or three of the lads often find it hard not to lose their temper when being screamed at by some corporal or other. I try to make them see that it's not personal. This is the British Army. During basic training, NCOs often place their face inches in front of yours and cast aspidistras on your lineage, looks, and sexual orientation. 'Don't take it personal,' I tell them, 'Just say, "Yes, corporal, No corporal, Three bags full corporal!" It's all done to break you in to accepting discipline. At some time or other you'll see them doing it to everybody in the squad. Often more than once. So it's not directed just at you. Don't take it personal. It isn't.'

It seems to have worked. None of the hotheads have got themselves into trouble.

Getting it together! Square-bashing beginning to work.

As we near the end of our six weeks, we at last begin to become a unit. Repetition, especially on the barrack square, slowly but surely eliminates mistakes and we begin to move 'as one'. There is actual pleasure to be had when you finally begin to master arms' drill. As the D.I. barks his commands, 'Slope arms!' or 'Order arms!' it's a satisfying sound when twenty hands smack, in unison, against the wooden stocks of Lee Enfield ·303 rifles.

No longer are they the heavy, cumbersome objects of just a few weeks ago. We lift, swing and throw them about with practised ease. There is yet another skill that we begin to master. One of the first tasks we had to do after drawing our kit was to hammer 'segs' or 'tacks' into the soles of brand new boots. We presumed it was to save wearing them out. Wrong! To hear half a dozen squads drilling on the square at the same time is another, unique, army sound. As these separate units drill on different areas of the large square, the loud shouts of their NCOs bounce off nearby buildings. If three or four of the squads are marching slightly out of sync with one another, instead of sounding discordant, the crunch of studded boots and shouted commands begins to echo and re-echo in a unique military vibrato that sweeps across the parade ground in waves.

It is fascinating to listen to – and enjoyable to be a part of. As one squad comes to attention, another stands at ease. Perhaps three or four are marching. As each group obeys its word of command, boots rhythmically crunch on tarmac and palms smack on rifle butts 'as one'. The sounds ebb and flow across the large square, for all the world as though someone was turning the volume control up and down on a radio.

During our first six weeks we're not allowed to leave the camp. On arrival that first day we'd been supplied with brown paper and string to parcel up our civvies and send them home, at the army's expense. I've sent mine to Nancy's. After the passing out parade we'll be allowed our first weekend off – a forty-eight hour pass in army parlance. Wherever we choose to go, it will have to be in uniform.

Nancy and I have been writing to each other almost on a daily basis lately. When the Post Corporal enters the billet, just after lunchtime, it is always wonderful to hear, '404 Douglas!' and be handed the now familiar-looking pale blue, Basildon Bond envelope. I go over to my bed, sit on the edge, and hold the letter between two hands. This has come from Seafield. Nancy held this in her hands less than forty-eight hours ago. She licked that stamp. I hold it to my nose, pretending to see if it carries any scent. In reality, when no one's looking, I brush the stamp with my lips. A letter from your fiancé is a great boost to flagging morale. Once you've read it three or four times it has the same effect as a whiff of oxygen. Somebody loves me!

By the last week of training we're beginning to feel good about ourselves. We are becoming convinced that WE are the best squad. The army certainly knows what it's doing. Bullshit baffles brains. We are now so efficient at cleaning our equipment, laying out kit for inspection, pressing uniforms, polishing brasses, bulling boots, blancoing webbing, shining floors, washing windows, we can now get it done better than ever – and faster. This means there's now time to go along to the NAAFI for the last hour before 'lights out'. When the duty NCO arrives to switch off the lights, no longer are most of us still dressed, busy trying to get our kit done. Candles don't burn 'til near midnight anymore. Now we're in our jammies, reading books, writing letters.

Sometimes I lie on my bed and look around the billet. I remember my first glimpse of certain guys just five short weeks ago. Those who had office jobs or other sedentary employment now literally glow with health. If they were slim and weedy, never lifted anything heavier than a pencil, they've now filled out. If they arrived overweight and unfit, the circuit training, daily PT and marching has slimmed them down, toned their muscles, given them condition. Those who spent most of their time indoors in office or factory now have colour in their cheeks. Although I was fit from labouring and tanned from working outdoors, I had been lean from subsisting on cheap eats in cafés or canteens. My general fitness has been maintained and, thanks to the army's diet of steamed food, I find I've put on exactly 14 pounds since arrival.

*　　*　　*

George Maharg and I have become good mates during this period. There are other guys I've also become pals with; Billy Best from Nottingham, Jock Blackburn from Coatbridge, Percy Lewis, a diminutive Jamaican who arrived in Britain just in time to be called up, and Jim Kirkpatrick, another Scot. Jim has newly graduated from university and intends to become a teacher. His National Service was deferred while he took his degree. After basic training, because of this degree, he will be going to Officers' Training School to become an officer on what is called a 'Short Service Commission'. Jim is tall, over six feet, and is a good-natured, always smiling type of guy who is totally uncoordinated when it comes to marching or arms drill. When the order 'Quick MARCH' is given, he invariably sets off on the wrong foot – usually a second or two behind everyone else. When he does get started, he marches with left arm and leg going forward together, same with the right. To onlookers it appears we have this

Basic training, Hilsea Barracks, Portsmouth, February 1959. Cpl Hardisty, centre. Next on left, George Maharg. Back row extreme left, Jock Kirkpatrick – kept off Passing Out Parade as he's totally uncoordinated! I'm standing next to him.

demented, six-feet-tall marionette in our midst. When we're about to start rifle drill, there's a certain amount of jockeying for position by the squad as everyone tries to secure a place well away from him. Reason? When the order 'slope arms' is given, there's an even-money chance his rifle will come gaily flying over his shoulder. He regularly drops it – a mortal sin – and being anywhere near him is fraught with danger as it scythes through the air while he executes a turn to left or right. The D.I.s try their best, but to no avail. Because he's so tall, and marches to a different drum, he sticks out like a sore thumb. A decision has to be made . . .

It's just a couple of days to passing out. Corporal Hardisty comes into the billet. 'Kirkpatrick!'

'Corporal!' Jim has been lying on his bed. He now does his impression of a trained soldier leaping to attention. It's more akin to an egg-bound ostrich rising from its nest.

Hardisty gives a sigh. 'When the passing out parade takes place on Friday morning, it's been decided – on account of you being useless – that you won't be on it! If the brigadier was to see you in action he'd 'ave a blue fit. It's nothing personal, lad. But you know yourself you'll never get the 'ang of it as long as you've got an 'ole in your arse! So just stay in the billet an' read a book. Okay?'

'Very good, Corporal.' Jim looks relieved. He knows it's for the best. Hardisty departs. Jock Blackburn is sitting on his bed, bulling his boots for Friday. He looks at Jim and shakes his head. 'Fuckin' hell, Kirkpatrick. You're going away tae be an officer. You're no' even good enough tae be a private!' Jim laughs as heartily as the rest of us.

At last it's here. We pass out this morning! The billet has been bulled until you could eat your dinner off its highly-polished floor. Windows sparkle. There's not one speck of dust to be found on top of door, locker or window ledge. Our kit lies on top of beds, ready for inspection. Boots gleam, buttons shine, uniforms are pressed. The brigadier will inspect the billets, then, shortly thereafter, we'll parade on the square to be personally inspected. After that, the brigadier will mount the dais at the edge of the parade ground for the highlight – the passing out parade!

For the last fortnight all the squads have been practising marching together, as a single unit, behind the depot's bugle band. During this period I discover there's even more pleasure to be had from doing things in unison – but this time as a company. The crunch of boots hitting tarmac, hands smacking crisply on rifle butts, is even better when over a hundred men get it together. I then find that marching behind a bugle band adds a certain 'extra' – and then some! As we practice our routines, accompanied by the band, I think back six weeks to the disparate bunch of individuals who, reluctantly, came through those gates. Yeah, bullshit baffles brains.

Most of our preparations have been done last night. We rise at six on the dot, get ourselves ready, have a quick breakfast, now it's back to the billet to put the finishing touches to it, and ourselves. The families and friends of those passing out are invited to the parade. The best part of two hundred people have made the trip, mostly those who live in the south. They haven't seen their loved ones for six weeks. Many express almost open-mouthed astonishment at the transformation in sons, brothers and husbands as we march past them onto the square. Some have difficulty recognising their own kin. Ugly ducklings have blossomed into swans. Pale civilians now stand square-shouldered and solid. Podgy, out of condition mother's boys have lost a stone or more and glow with health. And pride.

The billet's been inspected, we've been inspected. Now it's the bit we've all been waiting for. Jeez, I wish Nancy was here. But it's just too far. The brigadier, all 'red-tabbed' and bemedalled, stands on his dais. Our company officers and, most important of all, our D.I.s, wait impatiently. It's them who've brought us to this moment. Will we do them justice? The civilian visitors line one side of the parade ground. The RSM gives the order . . . 'By the LEFT, QUI-ICK MARCH!' The side drums of the band start with a flourish. From our first step, the big bass drum beats out the pace. The hairs stand on the back of my neck, a tingle runs down my spine. I KNOW that everyone around me feels the same. I can feel it. Electricity. The RSM, smart as paint, pace-stick tucked under his arm and held with one hand, marches smartly round us, like a sheepdog ready to harry his flock if need-be. Sometimes he points the long pace-stick at someone. Other times he marches backwards alongside a particular squad, muttering imprecations to the sergeant in charge. Then the buglers come in. Once again the hair stands on my neck as the bugles play, the drums beat and we march – as one – in perfect time to them. I'm in the left-hand rank of our squad and can see the length of the long outside column. More than twenty men. The rows of arms swing back and forth – as one. Legs lift, reach out and crunch down onto the barrack square – as one. The bugles now begin to blow again, this time one of the well-known brass band marching tunes. Probably by Sousa. The RSM falls into step a few yards from me, but going backwards,

'C'MON!' he exhorts, 'Let's have some SWANK! You're in the BRITISH ARMY. Finest army in the world. SHOW IT!' My scalp, spine and just about everything else, tingles. I feel my eyes smart. I look along the line; arms swing higher than ever, we swagger with pride as we parade in front of these poor civilians and let them see what we've become in such a short time, what our D.I.s have achieved. We've gone to be soldiers!

All too soon it's over. Those with families present go to join them at the edge of the parade ground after we're dismissed. Jeez. If Nancy'd been here I'd probably have burst with pride. We drift back into the billet, take our berets off, unbuckle our belts and unbutton our battledress tunics. George and I sit on our beds, facing one another.

'Well, Geordie, ah don't mind saying it, but it was fuckin' great marching behind that band.'

'Ah know. Gies ye a real tingle, dizn't it?'

'Nae wonder them Germans are alwiz off tae war at the drop of a hat. They jist hear a military band strike up – an' ten minutes later they're knocking fuck oot o' Poland!'

We get our postings for 'trade training'. I'm off to Blackdown Camp near Aldershot for driver training, which I'm dead chuffed about. George has been allocated to the Central Ammunition Depot at Longtown, Carlisle. We're disappointed we're not going to the same place. We've barely mentioned it. I clear my throat. 'Well, it's a bit of a bind we're no' going tae the same place, Geordie. It would've been good if we could have stuck the gether.'

'Aye, it's a bit of a choker. And there's nothing we can dae aboot it. Anywye, are ye coming tae the fitba' the morra? Stoke City are doon here tae play Pompey. Ye know Stanley Matthews plays for Stoke? It'll be a chance tae see him.'

I'm not a big football fan. In fact, I'm not even a wee football fan, but I'd still like to be able to say I saw the great Matthews play. He must be very near to retirement. 'Aye, ah think ah will. Better take the chance tae see the great man while the going's good.'

Next day, half a dozen of us make the trip to Fratton Park, Portsmouth's ground. We are all there just to see the maestro play. We don't. Sadly, he's injured and not in the team. Never mind. For the first time in six weeks we're out of camp. We are all in uniform and feel very much Jack-the-lad as we swagger about, ogling every girl we pass. When we're out of earshot we tell each other what we'd like to do to them. I suspect that, like myself, the majority of us are still virgins. At least I'm now a soldier. Almost.

That night I lie in bed, in the dark, hands behind head, eyes open. We'll all be breaking up tomorrow. There's just a couple coming to Blackdown with me. It has maybe only lasted six weeks, but I know that already the hardest part of my two years is behind me. It's designed to break you in – or break you. There's now a couple of months' trade training, then I'll get my permanent posting. They don't hold any fears for me. It's just a case of knuckling down and keeping my nose clean. What a difference from how I felt at Cosford. Since I was a boy I've known I would have to do two years' National Service. Every lad knows that. As I grew up in Doncaster Street I saw, in turn, all the 'big boys' disappear for a few months, then, just as I was beginning to forget about them, they'd come walking up the street in uniform! Home for their first leave. Charlie Dickson, Billy Robertson and Robert Walker in the army. James Dinning in the navy. Jimmy Kennedy in the RAF. It's my turn now. I promised myself I'd have a real good go at it when my call-up came. My eyes begin to close. I turn onto my side. I'm off to a good start.

Keep Death Off the Roads

Jeez! I'm really excited about learning how to drive. Not that I'll ever be able to afford a car, only well-off folk have cars. But to have my licence will be smashing. I can always get a job driving a lorry or, like John Kinsella in our close, become a chauffeur for a company director.

At the end of February 1959 I arrive at Blackdown Camp for trade training. I just turned twenty a couple of weeks ago. I quite like being twenty. I'm finally out of my teens. Aldershot is known as the Home of the British Army, and Blackdown is one of many camps surrounding the town, such as Pirbright and Deepcut. There are vast areas of heathland, and other tracts containing rifle-ranges and places where tanks and infantry can train to their heart's content.

Shortly after my arrival I find myself billeted in a late Victorian barrack block with twenty or so new guys. One of them is Tommy Watters, a Glaswegian who hails from Partick. Under the Birds of a Feather Act, he and I soon pal up. He's also allocated to driver training.

The pace of life is considerably less frantic at Blackdown. Square-bashing is down to a couple of times a week, just to keep us up to scratch. Bulling and polishing everything in sight has also lessened. We spend most of our time wearing well-washed, pale green denims (boilersuits) and, of course, our berets. The first couple of days' driver training are spent in the classroom, finding out how the combustion engine works and cramming up on the Highway Code. At last the great day comes. I'm going to get behind a steering wheel today. My built-in butterflies start up their engines in advance as we march out to the vehicle park and line up opposite rows of khaki-painted lorries. The majority of the training vehicles are the ubiquitous Bedford 3-tonners, a mainstay of the British Army since the Second World War, but shortly to be phased out. They are quite compact, and their short, square-cut bonnet, with its bar across the front, is a familiar sight on Britain's roads. Since the end of hostilities in 1945 many thousands have been sold off as 'war surplus'. These Jacks of all trades were snapped up at bargain prices by builders, haulage companies and any other small business in need of a reliable, easily-maintained vehicle. They will remain a familiar sight on the roads right through the sixties and well into the seventies.

Around thirty of us stand at ease, waiting impatiently to get started. Over to the left an untidy heap of driving instructors, consisting mostly of National Servicemen, begins to gather. A sergeant appears, carrying the obligatory clipboard, and stands in front of us. He brings us to attention.

'Now then, there aren't enough Bedfords to go around, so some of you will 'ave to train on the four-and-a-half-ton Commers.' With his Biro he points in the direction of these behemoths. 'That's them big buggers over there.' They dwarf the petite Bedfords. Everything about them is BIG. They are taller, wider, longer and even have a higher clearance than the 3-tonners. And, of course, at four and a half tons they're half as heavy again. The cab looks to be about the same size as our single-end. The bonnet seems to go on for ever. I've seen smaller aircraft carriers. I begin to get that sinking feeling in my stomach. I know. I just fucking know, I'm going to be allocated to one of these monsters. When I was with the Clyde Trust I'd sometimes get a lift in one of the contractor's Bedfords. As I sat in the snug cab, I'd watch the driver change gear as we headed into town and I'd often think, 'I bet you these would be easy to drive.' I look again at the Commers. God? Are ye in? Gonny let me get one o' them Bedfords, eh?

The sergeant starts calling single names, followed by the name of an instructor.

'404 Douglas!'

'SAR'NT!' I come smartly to attention. He looks across his list.

'Corporal Trent.'

I make a smart right turn, fall out, and walk over to make the acquaintance of my instructor. He's already detatched himself from his group. He's an untidy sort of guy. Scruffy, really. I'm amazed to see he hasn't bothered to shave this morning. We fall into step, side by side.

We walk along the line of Bedfords. I pray silently for him to stop any second. He doesn't. We pass the last one, and a few vehicles later stop in front of a Commer. Fuck! I knew it.

'What's your first name?' he asks.

'Unlucky Bastard!' I'm tempted to say. 'Eh, Robert, Corporal.'

'Right, every time you're about to take a vehicle out, first thing you do is take a walk round it and make a visual inspection. Every time.' As we circumnavigate the beast, he gives each of the tyres a couple of kicks. He mustn't like Commers either.

'It's a pity there aren't enough Bedfords tae go around, Corporal.'

'Yeah. Drivers are supposed to train on 3-tonners. It's a lot easier than learning on these great gits.' My heart sinks.

The first forty minutes are spent sitting in the parked vehicle while he introduces me to the intricacies of gears, clutch, and something called 'double-declutching' which, seemingly, you only indulge in when you're wanting to go 'down the box'. Once more I'm back in 'Algebra Land'. Although the lance corporal is in no way as fearsome as Harry Forshaw, my former Maths teacher, he seems to have adopted the same teaching methods, i.e. addressing me in Serbo-Croat. Just like Harry, he's assuming I know what he's talking about. It all begins to blur.

'Eh, ah'm sorry, Corporal. But this is the first time I've ever sat behind the wheel of a car or a lorry. Ah just can't take in the things you're telling me.'

He looks aggrieved. 'Well, what we'll do is start you orf driving. A lot of the things I've been telling yah, you'll pick them up by doing them as you drive. That's the easiest way to learn.'

Jeez, I hope he's right.

Thirty minutes later I'm beginning to enjoy myself. After some early gear-crunching I seem to be getting the hang of it. I think I might be a natural. We approach the crest of a hill . . .

'Now, as you drive dahn this hill I want yah to change into a lower gear. Why? 'Cause the engine's the finest brake of all. When you're in a lower gear, the vehicle can't go above a certain speed. The lower the gear, the slower you go. In other words, it's acting like a brake. Don't forget, you 'ave to double-declutch when going down the box in this lorry.' He's beginning to lose me, but as we start to go down the hill faster and faster I try to follow the instructions he's reeling off. 'Right, clutch in, gear-stick into neutral, clutch out, give a rev, clutch back in and slip her into third. Now, feel how she's slowing because she's in lower gear?'

What he doesn't know is, I have the lorry in lower gear more by good luck than from following his instructions. The Commer still seems to be going pretty fast. The hill steepens at this point, gravity takes over, and it starts to go faster. As the speed increases, the more the engine – or is it the gearbox? – screams.

'I want you to change her down to second,' shouts the corporal, 'and you'll need a really big rev to make it go in.' The screaming gearbox, increasing speed, and the fact the hill's getting steeper are beginning to unnerve me. I have a feeling the

Photo machine, NAAFI Club. Aldershot, April 1959. Trying to get a good shot of my 'Tony Curtis'.

lorry's running away with me. Probably because it is. I try to remember the sequence for 'going down the box'. I recall the first two. Maybe. Somewhere in neutral I fail to give a big enough rev. Twice. We're now roaring down the hill with the clutch, and me, depressed. With neither lower gear nor brake impeding us we continue to accelerate. By now, every part of the four-and-a-half-ton leviathan is vibrating as it gains speed by the second, the corporal and me pinned to our seats. A scene from a movie flashes into my mind where Nigel Patrick is approaching the sound barrier and the plane's just about shaking itself to bits.

'Fahk me!' says my instructor, 'Let the bloody clutch up so's she'll slow!'

I've been slightly distracted, half-listening for the expected 'boom!' as we break Mach 1. 'Which one's that again?' I enquire.

'The one on the left, for Christ's sake,' he says.

I make sure I'm going straight, thus giving myself the opportunity to look down into the footwell and maybe spot it. It's dark down there so it takes a few seconds while my eyes adjust.

'You're going into the fuckin' side of the road!' My instructor's voice, like the engine's note, is getting higher. I look up and skilfully make the required correction. I've now let the clutch up, yet we continue to accelerate at a positively alarming rate.

'Eh, shouldn't it be in gear so's it can slow us, Corporal?'

His mouth falls open. 'Ain't we – HIT THE FAHKIN' BRAKES! HIT THE—'

With commendably fast reactions I slam my foot on the one in the middle. Hard! There are no seatbelts. The lance corporal flies forward, bumps his head on the windscreen and bounces back into his seat. His beret has came forward and almost covers his eyes. Luckily, I've had the steering wheel to brace myself against. From the corner of my eye I see him put a hand up to his mouth. 'Ni've bit me funkin' tongue!' he says.

The rest of the journey toward Woking is completed in silence – except for him making the occasional sucking noise. Eventually, 'Pull off into this car park,' he says, 'I'm needing a cuppa to calm me nerves.' The cinder-covered area belongs to a cafe-cum-lorry stop. As we enter the building, there are already quite a few instructors and pupils in residence. It's an hour before he's sufficiently restored to climb back into the cab. During the next few weeks we will spend a lot of time in this cafe and another one near Guildford. These are precious hours during which I could have been taught to do things correctly.

On the way back to the depot, after our failed attempt at the World Land Speed Record, I'm allowed to drive through Woking Town. While navigating its ancient narrow streets, for a moment I mount an even narrower pavement. As I come off the kerb and the beast drops into the gutter, because it is so well sprung the entire vehicle sways and the canvas hood catches the edge of a shop sign, bending it back until it's parallel with the wall. I glance in the mirror.

'Eh, ah think ah've maybe caught—'

'Just keep fahking driving, mate. Ignorance is 9 points of the law. Summat like that.'

Three weeks later I sit my test. The examiners are civilians. I have to do a hill start – but roll backwards – then reverse round a corner while being guided by hand signals from someone standing in front of me. I mount the pavement – my speciality.

If I'd been a regular soldier, I'd have been given more tuition and allowed to take another two or three tests. As a conscript I'm only allowed one. If only the test had consisted of questions such as, 'How many rounds of toast can your instructor polish off in a session?' and . . . 'How often does your instructor doze off and leave you to drive around aimlessly?' I'd have skated it!

It's now decided I'll be transferred onto the Fork-lift truck course. This is small consolation. The future vision of me taking wife and bairns on a trip to the seaside in my fork-lift truck is not an exciting one. I pick it up very quickly and I'm gratified to find I have the 'good eye' and delicate touch needed to make a better than average operator. It's not the same, though. I so wanted my driving licence.

At the end of our time in Blackdown we're allowed a forty-eight hour pass for our last weekend. When we return on Monday we'll get to know our permanent postings. Most of the English guys go home. Tommy Watters and I decide Scotland is too far for such a limited time.

Even if we took a railway warrant we'd be travelling for almost a third of the forty-eight hours. To hitch would take even longer. I'm so dying to see Nancy I'm tempted to go. But it would be a case of just popping in for a few hours, getting some much needed kip, then going back to Edinburgh to catch my train. It would be a waste of a precious warrant. Instead, Tommy and I decide to hitchhike down to London, a much shorter distance.

We've never been to the 'Big Smoke' as everyone – except Londoners – seem to call it.

Still in uniform – we won't get our civvies until we reach our permanent postings – we have no problem getting lifts to London and arrive on the Saturday afternoon. This is London in 1959. It hasn't been too long since Tommy Steele was discovered in the 'Two Eyes' coffee bar in Soho. We head down there to have a look at this notorious district, and take in the somewhat nondescript cafe. As evening draws in we watch, goggle-eyed, as prostitutes appear in almost every shop doorway. As we walk along, much to our delight, we're constantly accosted . . .

'Looking for a nice time, soldiers?' We look at each other and try not to giggle. After wandering aimlessly for hours we begin to tire. 'Jeez! What a bloody big place this is. Ma feet are killing me.' It's now beginning to get dark. And late.

'Where ur we gonny spend the night?'

'Waterloo,' says Tommy.

'The station?'

'We're a bit late for the battle!'

Sometime after eleven p.m. we kip down in the waiting room. There's quite a few waifs and strays already in residence. The police appear during the night on a couple of occasions and evict any itinerants or 'milestone inspectors' (as Willie Lilley calls tramps). We are assumed to be 'in transit' and are left alone. Even so, we have very little rest. The room is warm and our thick uniforms make us sweat. As the hours slowly tick by, the wooden benches become harder and harder. I sometimes manage an hour's unbroken sleep before my aching back wakens me. If I turn on my side, my arm and shoulder soon become cramped and painful. We've had enough by six-thirty in the morning and make our way to the toilets for a wash and brush up. We haven't brought shaving kit.

*   *   *

Sometime after seven a.m., bleary-eyed, we exit the station. A fried breakfast and two pots of tea restores our spirits, and we spend the rest of the morning and early afternoon 'doing the sights' – Piccadilly Circus, Trafalgar Square and anything in between. Later we stretch out in the sun in Regent's Park and catch up on some of our lost sleep. By late afternoon we are tired, fed up, and running out of money. We only get twenty-five shillings a week. We sit on a bench in some tree-lined square. 'It's too fuckin' big, London. How are we ever gonny get tae the outskirts and find the road going in the direction of Aldershot?'

I look at him. 'Tae be honest, ah don't fancy hitching back tae camp. Dae you?'

'Bloody sure ah don't. It's easy enough coming IN. But going back OOT again. Whit road dae we take? How will drivers know where we're going? It'll be a bloody nightmare! Ah wish we hud enough dosh for the train.' He leans forward, head in hands, exhausted at the thought of it. This is my cue. 'Wait 'til ye hear this. Somebody told me if ye go tae Horse Guards Parade, jist aff Whitehall, there's an RTO always oan duty. If ye gie him a sob story that you've lost yer tickets, he'll gie ye a railway warrant!'

This seems to energise Tommy. 'Fuckin' great! Whit's an RTO?'

'Regimental Transport Officer, something like that.'

An hour later, having popped in to have a look at Downing Street en route, we approach the imposing gates of Horse Guards Parade. There are usually two mounted Household Cavalry in each of the sentry positions. Instead, two cavalrymen stand, still fully booted and spurred, wearing shiny breastplates, cockaded helmets, and holding their swords in front of them.

'Ah thought they alwiz sat on hoarses?' says Tommy.

'Did ye no' read it in the paper? The hoarses are aw' doon wi' the equine flu.'

'Ah! Ah wiz wondering.'

There are perhaps three dozen or more tourists, from all over the world, taking photos and making home movies of these shining examples of the British Army. Tommy and I, scruffy and unshaved, feel at a disadvantage. Nobody seems to want shots of us. Maybe they don't realise we're in the same army! 'Ah'd better ask where the office is, eh?'

Tommy looks at me. 'They're no' allowed tae speak tae ye. Ah seen it oan Pathé Pictorial in the cinema wan time. They're jist supposed tae concentrate oan their duties.'

I glance at the nearest dismounted sentry. His breastplate and helmet gleam. I wonder how much Silvo he goes through in a week?

'Well, we're aw' fellow sodjers. He'll no' mind.'

A young Japanese girl skips over and stands next to the immaculate cavalryman. As she giggles uncontrollably, her equally giggly friend takes a photo. The sentry shows no emotion. As the girls skitter away I sidle up to him. The tourists stop clicking for the moment. He's like a Tussaud's waxwork. So still. I lean, confidentially, toward him

'Can ye tell me where the RTO office is, pal?'

The corner of his mouth moves imperceptibly, like a ventriloquist, 'Fuck orf!'

'Oh!' I oblige.

I eventually find it by other means.

Tommy and I get back to Blackdown just in time for dinner. We are starving.

The rather sceptical RTO, a captain, had reluctantly accepted our story and supplied us with two single railway warrants. Safely back in our billet, we regale our mates with tales from the Big Smoke and, long before Last Post, we're tucked up in our beds, sound asleep.

'Douglas!'

'SAH!' I come smartly to attention. We are lined up in threes. The officer looks along his list.

'Germany.'

I can hardly believe my good luck. 'SAH!' I say in affirmation. This is what I'd been hoping against hope for. I very much want to get to Germany for my remaining twenty-one months. It's my intention to take the army's language course when I get there. By the end of my time, after working with German civilians every day, I should be speaking good German.

Tommy has also been put on the same draft. We're ecstatic. The rest of the day is spent having excited conversations about what we'll do and where we'll go once we're stationed in the middle of Europe.

That evening I start a letter to Nancy, telling her all about it, suggesting that if I really like it out there, I might even sign on! That would mean, if we got married, I'd be entitled to married quarters. She could come out, too. With her dressmaking skills she wouldn't be short of work. A future of endless possibilities opens up before me. It's well after midnight before I finally fall asleep.

There are thirteen of us on the Germany draft. It proves to be an unlucky thirteen. Next morning we're told the draft has been cancelled. We're reallocated. I'm now going to Chilwell Depot, near Nottingham. Tommy's got Bicester. The unfinished letter is torn up and lands in the bin. As the sergeant leaves the billet after imparting the bad news, we slump down on our beds. I look at Tommy. 'Jist ma poxy fuckin' luck! Ah must be the unluckiest bastard in the world. How can they huv us oan a draft for Germany, then next morning we're no' needed, eh?'

'Ah know. Ah'm sick as a fuckin' chip. Ah wiz so looking forward tae it. Bastards!'

'Buggering Nottingham! Who wants tae go tae Nottingham? An' your no' coming tae Chilwell, are ye?'

'Naw. Scabby hooring Bicester!' Shattered dreams.

* * *

I stretch out on my bed. Look up at the ceiling. Does the army do this deliberately? George Maharg and me were just getting to be good mates – they split us up. Tommy and I are just getting to be good mates – so they do it again. Surely when I get to Chilwell – my permanent posting – I'll hook up with one or two guys and we'll get to be good mates, and NOT be split up? Jeez, I hope so.

My thoughts go back to all the excitement and daydreams of yesterday. That would have been a great posting. *Auf Wiedersehen*, Germany.

A Trained Soldier

It's our last evening together at Blackdown. Tomorrow we're all off to various corners of the UK. Some guys have got Cyprus. Tommy and I are still a bit depressed about Germany. I occasionally take little glances round the billet. Just as at Hilsea, it's all happening again. A bunch of guys thrown together for an intense few weeks, friendships made, now it's coming to an end. A few guys are doing as much packing as they can so as they'll save time in the morning – I belong to that school. Others don't give a monkey's. 'Ah, plenty of time in the morning!'

Billy Best comes bursting in. 'Here! Come over here and listen to this. You're never gonna believe it!' Nine or ten of us gather round, spread ourselves over three beds. 'You know that little guy Bennet in the next billet?' Some know right away who he means. Those who don't receive a graphic description . . . 'Little, skinny, weedy kid. Dark-headed, glasses, wouldn't say "boo!", to a goose. He's on the clerk's course.' We all recognise him.

'Oh, ah knows who you mean. Yeah, couldn't be anything else but a clerk.'

'That's what he is in civvy street,' says Billy, 'worked in an office.'

'So? What about him?' enquires someone who wants to get on with his packing.

'Duss tha know what posting he's got?'

There's a collective 'No.'

Billy pauses for dramatic effect. 'Naples!'

'Get to fuck!'

'Naples in Italy?'

Billy looks heavenward. 'No, Naples in fricking Lancashire, you doughnut!'

'What's oot there?' I ask.

'Load of Italians,' says some helpful soul.

'It's a NATO headquarters,' says Billy, 'there's all these small detachments of allied nations, Yanks, Brits, French, Belgian, whatever. He's got this posting as a clerk. BUT, there's no camp. You live in a flat, paid for by the army, and just go to work every day at the HQ.'

'Man! That's not a posting, that's a bloody extended holiday!'

'Ah, but that's not all. Because it's NATO, you don't wear the tailored horse blankets we 'ave to put up with. It's made to measure uniforms in Barathea, ain't it. AND, because he's "on detachment" he gets about eight pounds a week in Lira . . .'

'That'll be about sixteen trillion million Lira,' says a voice. Billy gives him a dirty look.

'On top of that,' says Billy, 'he gets expenses of another fifteen pounds or so for meals, etc.'

'That'll be ANOTHER twenty million billion!' says the same voice. Billy ignores it.

'But you'll never, EVER believe what I'm gonna tell yah!'

'Sophia Loren's gonna come round an' give him a good shagging twice a week!' In spite of wanting to know what Billy's about to disclose, we all fall about.

Billy pretends not to be concerned. 'Ah'm tellin' tha. You'll never believe it.'

He's got us. Silence descends. You could hear an ammo pouch drop. Billy looks around imperiously. For a second I'm back in Guthrie's the butcher with Ma, and Lena Robertson's about to lay an exclusive piece of gossip on the queue.

'He's refused it!' Billy sniffs. I'm surprised he doesn't adjust his bosom with a forearm.

There's a mass 'EH?!' 'Is he mental? Get out of here! Why?'

'He'd originally got Bicester before this NATO thing came up.

From Bicester he can get home every weekend to see his girl-friend. So he's refused it. Says he doesn't want to be separated from her for long periods. So they've given it to another guy.'

'Who the fuck's his girlfriend, Shirley Ann Field?'

We all rise from the beds, shaking our heads, unable to believe the folly of some guys.

The trip up to Nottingham – wearing all my webbing – is uneventful. On the day I'd arrived at Hilsea and drawn all my gear, a stamping kit had been passed round the billet. Every single item, from 'drawers cellular' to 'pack, webbing, large' had been stamped with my army number 23603404. Wherever I go, it has to go with me. All of it. It reminds me of being on jankers. Could've been worse, though. If it had been wartime I'd have been lugging a rifle as well!

Chilwell Depot, home of 6 Battalion, RAOC, is vast. It lies 5 miles from the City of Nottingham, between Beeston and Long Eaton. It is the main MT (Motor Transport) spares depot for the British Army. In stock are spare parts for every vehicle – from tanks to trucks – in use by the army. On a daily basis, everything from door handles to diesel engines are being posted or otherwise transported to camps all over the world, from Hull to Hong Kong. Chilwell is run by a staff of 600 officers and men, and nearly 3000 civilians. Within days of my arrival it's decided that as well as being a fork-lift driver, I'll also be trained up in the depot, as a 'storeman technical'. This means that any time I'm not needed to drive a truck I can double up as a storeman.

On the day I arrive in Nottingham I only get a brief glimpse of the city. Mostly from the carriage window as we enter the environs and make for the station. What I see, I like. Just as at Wolverhampton a few years earlier, there is street after street of red-brick terraces. I always find this so English. As we come nearer to the centre, this changes to mostly stone-built, late

Victorian buildings, offices, shops, large department stores. A typical English city. But not too big. Weighed down with my kit, I'm not in a position to do any sightseeing, but already I'm looking forward to my first evening 'on the town'. The railway station, as expected, is another Victorian creation. I make enquiries and am soon on the local train to Attenborough Halt, the station for the camp. A five-minute stroll from there and I'm approaching the main gates of the depot. I show my ID to the uniformed depot policeman on duty and he gives me directions to the Battalion office. As I take my first walk into the camp I immediately have a good feeling about the place. It is, of course, spotlessly clean. But it's not just that, there's an air about it. It feels right. As civvies and squaddies go about their business they exchange a few words in passing, sometimes a bit of banter, a laugh. The pace seems to be unhurried, yet somehow efficient. Lorries, Landrovers, the occasional staff car go by at the statutory 10 miles per hour. I'm going to like it here!

On arrival at Nottingham station I'd got a good taste of the local accent. Billy Best is a Nottingham lad, so I was slightly tuned in anyway. Asking what train I should take for the depot and then for directions from Attenborough Halt had on each occasion elicited friendly responses, delivered in the rich local dialect and ending with 'has tha got that, me duck?' and 'tha can't go wrong, me ode.' I'd always thought 'duck' was only addressed to the fairer sex. Not in Nottinghamshire, seemingly. As for 'me ode', who knows? Short for 'me *old* pal/mate'?

From the company office a 'runner' is detailed to show me my new billet, then help me draw bedding from the quartermaster's stores. As we turn a corner at the side of one of the large warehouses I look up a grassy slope and get first sight of my home for the next twenty-one months. The Sandhurst Building, a long, two-storey barrack block, perhaps 300 yards from end to end, dominates the scene. Built of pale red brick, with a flat roof, it is the essence of 1930s Art Deco and must be a full cousin to Fulton Block at RAF Cosford. Running parallel at the foot of the grassed bank are smaller barrack blocks in the same style. On the other side of the road stand some old-fashioned wooden huts, 'lines', which have been there since the First World War. They are identical to the huts I knew at both Cosford and Hilsea.

By dinner time I've stowed my kit into the metal locker and wooden bedside cabinet in my new billet. I note with pleasure that fitted to the wall above each bed is an individual reading lamp in a brown metal conch-shaped holder. At last! I'm beginning to catch up with the modern army. At about ten to five I'm trying to find other things to do when there's a clatter of boots and hubbub of voices from the long corridor as squaddies return from their day's labour in the depot. As the residents drift into the billet in twos and threes they all greet me. The room holds twenty but is running with around sixteen at the moment. Some blokes strip to the waist and head for the ablutions to freshen up. Others take their boots off and stretch out on their beds with indolent sighs.

'Have you come straight from Blackdown, Jock?'

'Aye.'

'Hurrah! Now I can say to somebody, "Get some in!"'

Amongst National Servicemen, great store is set on seniority. Mostly for fun. It doesn't matter if you're just two weeks senior to a guy. Being able to say, 'Get some in!' is the ultimate putdown. Two blokes may be having a difference of opinion about some matter, sport, history, sex, anything. If one is beginning to lose this verbal tussle, and he happens to be senior to the other guy, he can always play his Ace in the Hole . . .

'GEORDIE?' A guy whom I'll later find out is called Jim Cleaver, sits holding a magazine.

'What?' says the Geordie – later identified as Geordie Benson.

'Brummie' Cleaver holds up the magazine. 'Joost listen to this yow Geordie twatbag. Aston Villa hold the record for the grytest noomber of FA Cup wins.'

'So?' Geordie Benson lies on his bed, legs spread wide, reading the *Rover*.

'Yow said it were Newcastle. Ah told you it weren't, keed,' says Cleaver, who hails from West Bromwich and has a Black Country accent you could cut with a knife.

'So?' repeats Benson, still intent on his comic.

'So yow were bloody wrong, keed!'

'Ah'm trying to find out what's going to happen to Alf Tupper, The Tough of the Track,' says Benson, keeping his face straight with difficulty. 'Do you mind?'

'Never mind Alf fookin' Tupper,' says Cleaver, 'Yow was wrong-gah, keed. I was right.'

'Get some in!' says Benson. There are some laughs from the assembled roommates.

'Never mind "get some in",' splutters Cleaver, 'Yow were wrong-gah. DEAD wrong-gah!'

'Okay. FUCKIN' get some in!' There are even more laughs.

'Bullocks!' says Cleaver.

Benson tuts. 'No respect for seniority, Brummie, that's your trouble.'

Brummie gets his eating irons and mug from his locker. 'I'm off for me dinner, not gowing to waste anymore time on a Geordie cretin.'

'SENIOR cretin if you divn't mind.'

Exit Brummie Cleaver, fuming. As he passes me he says, 'I wouldn't care, he's onlyy two bloody weeks senior to me.'

Yeah. I think I'm going to like it in this billet.

During the next few weeks I quickly settle in to life at Central Ordnance Depot, Chilwell. Within a few days I'm issued with my permanent pass and security gate pass. This means that provided I'm not on guard duty (sentry duty), I can come in and out of camp at will, evenings or weekends. I can now send for my civvies. Within a few days Nancy posts me my somewhat worn blue suit, two shirts and (only) tie. The suit will have to do. I certainly can't afford a new one on army pay. Since arrival at Chilwell my pay's gone up to thirty-five shillings a week. Golly! Gee! Wow! On camp is a Garrison Cinema which only charges a shilling. Trouble is, it's mostly old movies they show. If I read a review of a new movie, and I want to see it, I have to take myself into Nottingham on the bus. It's handy if it's showing at the Essoldo, which lies in a suburb on the way into town so I don't have to go all the way to the centre.

Provided I don't spend too much on my Saturday night out with the lads, I'm usually left with enough for two NAAFI breaks a day when the van comes round AND to amble along to the NAAFI canteen in the evening for a cuppa and a 'wad' (sandwich) before bedtime. My only other luxuries are the *Daily Express* every day and the *Sunday Post*, bought from the civvy paper seller who brings his van into the depot every morning. A writing pad, envelopes and stamps are, of course, a necessity. It's not quite *La Dolce Vita*, but compared with my nine months in the RAF and my basic training at Hilsea, I'm living in luxury. I'm not cold or hungry anymore. The block has central heating and the food in the mess is good and plentiful, a big improvement on both Hilsea and Blackdown. Drill and bullshit is down to a minimum. We're here to work in the depot. If there's a group of us we have to be marched down to where we're working. Individually you can go on your own. Every Friday morning the billet is inspected, so Thursday evening is 'bull night'. We all know what to do by now. A couple of hours intensive cleaning, dusting, polishing and bumpering the floor brings the billet up to scratch. Last thing before we leave to go down the depot on Friday mornings, the billet gets its final finishing off. Very rarely do we fall foul of the inspecting officer and RSM. If we do, it just means it has to be done again for the Saturday morning. Nobody wants that. Especially the guys who usually head off home on Friday evening. Bullshit baffles brains! On the whole it's a fairly pleasant life. No more being chased from arsehole to breakfast time. I get lots of sleep, lovely sleep.

* * *

Within the next six weeks, another five guys will come into the billet who will form my main group of pals. Brian Gurney from Benson, Oxfordshire; Michael 'Butch' Palmer from Bilton, near Rugby; Stan Deakin of Warrington, Lancashire; Gordon Hinchcliffe from Leeds and Pete Smith of Swanley, Kent. To my delight I prove to be senior to them all – the Ace in the Hole is mine! Individually or en masse, I tell them to 'get some in' whenever the occasion warrants it. Or even when it doesn't.

I've not long turned twenty and I'm about to start what will prove to be one of the most contented periods of my life since losing Ma. I'm engaged to be married, enjoying the army, surrounded by good pals and I'm becoming more and more confident about my abilities. For the first time since Ma died, I'm not just finding my way. I'm finding me.

The Ninety-six-hour Pass

I can hardly wait. At last, after nearly four months, it's time for some leave. I'm going to see Nancy again. Be able to kiss her, touch her, just look at her. I've applied for a ninety-six-hour pass. Four days leave. As I don't want to use one of my limited number of free railway warrants – I want to keep them for longer spells of leave – I've decided to hitchhike up the road. I'll leave after duty on the Thursday, and to make sure I'm back in time for first parade and roll call on Tuesday morning, I'll catch the train back from Edinburgh on Monday evening, paying for the one-way ticket myself. Truth be told, I'm looking forward to hitching up the road. I've never forgotten how much I enjoyed it when I went AWOL from the RAF and hitched up to my Uncle Jim's.

It's just after five p.m. on the last Thursday in April, 1959. I step smartly out the camp's gates to start my journey to Seafield, West Lothian. I've no idea how long it'll take me, and I'm not in the least bothered. Dressed in greatcoat and beret, I'm carrying my emergency rations in my pocket – a bar of Cadbury's Dairy Milk and a Crunchie. I've got just over two pounds in cash. That's all I should need. I know my uniform is my ticket. Servicemen never wait long between lifts. Then there's also the 'feel-good' factor. I'm young, fit, and my sense of well-being gives me the feeling, the conviction, that all will be well. I'm Untouchable. King of the World. Now I know how my Uncle George felt before D-Day spoiled it all.

*   *   *

Just over an hour after leaving Chilwell, I step once more onto the Great North Road. I do love that name. As I take up a position at the roadside I feel a tingle of excitement as cars and lorries speed toward me. I wonder how many lifts it'll take to get me to my destination? How many folk will I meet briefly because they're good enough to stop, chat to for the duration of the lift, then never see again? Yet no matter how short the time we spend together, we've played a small part in each other's lives. Once again I wonder why I sometimes have thoughts like that. I can't be the only one. One thing's for certain, I won't be talking about it to them buggers in the billet. They'd take the piss for ever more.

As I travel through the evening and on into the night, I thumb only cars at first. Lorries are pretty slow, so I'll make better time if I concentrate on cars. After the pubs have shut the cars usually peter out sometime after eleven p.m. – unless you're lucky enough to get a sales rep on a business trip. Round about midnight it begins to be mostly lorries. Trunk drivers heading for the main towns and timing it to get there as the markets open.

By the early hours of the morning I've been travelling in a succession of lorries. Sometimes I feel as if time has stood still. Sitting in a warm cab, watching the road unfold hypnotically in the headlights, the Cat's-eyes seeming to open up to have a look at me. It becomes like a continuation of my journey of four years ago. Even the conversations are the same. Now and again I feel certain that if I look down I'll find I'm wearing RAF uniform instead of army. But now and again there are new things to talk about . . .

We're passing through the edge of a small village. 'See them two lorries parked on t'right?' the driver takes one hand off the wheel to point. They are parked in front of a small terrace.

'Aye.'

'There's two sisters live there. They do bed and breakfast for drivers. You can 'ave normal B and B, or, for a pound extra you can kip night with one of t'sisters!'

'Never!' I turn my head to have a last look as we rumble past. It's sometime after two a.m. I smile.

'Well, the two drivers should have had their leg ower by now.' We both laugh.

'Yeah, four or five nights a week you'll find two lorries parked there. Got to book in early, they tell me, or you'll miss your chance. Got a nice little business, they 'ave.'

'You ever tried them?'

'No. Thought about it, mind. Trouble is, I'd like to 'ave a look at them first. They reckon they're all right. In their late thirties, seemingly.'

As we trundle on, I fantasise a little about the two sisters. Probably be the ideal pair to introduce me to the longed-for delights of sex . . . 'There you are, missis, there's your extra pound in advance and, eh, will you "keep me right"? I've, eh, never been wi' a woman before . . . OOHYAH! Jeez! You've jist earned yerself another five bob there, hen!'

A couple of hours later I'm in another lorry and we pull off the road into the all-night cafe I'd stopped at back in '55. As we crunch over the cinder-covered car park, I wonder if the ladies of the night will be inside again, still plying their trade. Come to think of it, it's surprising how much nookie is available during the night on the Great North Road. As soon as we enter, I glance round and I'm quite disappointed to find there's no sign of them. Later, as the driver and I get stuck into egg and chips, I ask him if the girls are still doing business.

'Haven't seen them for a long time. The place has changed hands, you know. New owner's maybe chased 'em.'

Sometime after nine a.m., beginning to feel quite weary, I arrive in Seafield. As expected, Nancy's already left for work. Auld Sanny and Beenie are pleased to see me.

'By! Yer lookin' well. You've no' half put some wecht on.'

It's lovely to be sitting in this cosy wee kitchen again. Eventually, as expected, my long journey catches up with me, aided and abetted by the coal fire chuckling away in the grate. I can't keep my eyes open.

'Away and get yerself tae bed for a few hours,' Beenie begins clearing the table.

I smile, 'Aye, ah'm dog-tired.' I head off up stairs, get my toothbrush from my small pack and after a quick wash, climb into bed. 'Ahhhh!' Sheer luxury. I lie there in the light, airy bedroom. Daylight forces its way through pale yellow curtains. Jeez, it's nice to be back again. My thoughts go back to my journey. I really do love hitching. What time did I leave? About five p.m. Got here just gone nine. Sixteen hours. If I'd come by train that would've taken eight hours – and it would've seemed longer! Funny, that. The sun comes out from behind a cloud and forces its way through the thin curtains. The room's so light. I think I'll read for five minutes. Get me nice and tired again. Getting ready for bed has wakened me up. No matter how tired I am, or how late it is, I always like a wee read. Even if it's just a paragraph. I reach for the current book. A.J. Cronin's *The Citadel*. I'm pretty much through all his work. When I finish one, I just look at the list printed inside the cover, then pick up another one, in paperback, in a second-hand bookshop. Great characters, wonderful stories.

This bed is too comfortable! I've got used to my army one – firm. I start to get into the story, want to know what's going to happen next. The five minutes expands. Eventually tiredness asserts itself. Soon I'm reading the same bit over and over as my eyes begin to close for longer periods. I'll just finish this paragraph, then put it down . . .

Seven hours later I wake up, still in the same position. The book lies open on the eiderdown. The sound of Nancy coming home from work has woken me. It's time to get up!

*   *   *

Saturday night. We walk into the Bathgate Palais. I'm in uniform, I haven't bothered to bring my suit. I like being in uniform, my beret tucked under the left epaulette, the short battledress tunic unbuttoned. King of the World. I pressed my uniform before we came out – just like Uncle George would've. It's an added bonus to sometimes catch a girl looking at me.

It comes out of the blue. We're doing a smoochy dance, oblivious to all others on the floor. I have my eyes closed for long periods, we're hardly moving. Then Nancy speaks into my ear.

'When dae ye think we should set the date for getting married?'

I open my eyes, lean back a bit so's I can look at her. 'Do ye want tae get married while ah'm in the army?' That thought hadn't entered my head.

'Don't see why not.'

'Yeah, well, that's fine. Ah jist assumed you'd want tae wait 'til ah came out and had a job.'

'Och! That'll be too long to wait.'

On our return to Nancy's, about midnight, her mum and dad have gone to bed, so we have the mandatory heavy petting session on the sofa. Nancy, as ever, successfully fends me off from any advance on previous encounters. At breakfast next morning we tell her parents of our decision to set the date.

'Och well, youse are auld enough tae know yer ain minds,' says Beenie. I always have the feeling her mother thinks the seven-year age gap is too big. Auld Sanny is quite happy about it. When they're eventually informed, her older brother Alec and sisters Betty and Isobel are also pleased to hear our news. After a quick look at the calendar, and a short discussion, July the fourth is chosen. It's a while before I realise it's perhaps an ironic date to choose to be bound in matrimony – Independence Day!

Next evening, a Monday, I take the bus into Edinburgh and catch a train from Waverley Station back down south. After my short break I've finished up not having enough money for the train fare, so Nancy has had to sub me. I'd have been quite happy to hitch back, but I can't guarantee I'll arrive in time for first parade and roll call. Failure to be on it means you're instantly listed as AWOL. The British Army doesn't do 'late'.

As usual the billet is in its morning upheaval. Some guys are making up their bedpacks, others are in transit from the ablutions, a few are finishing dressing. The air is its usual shade of blue.

Butch Palmer kicks the bottom of Geordie Stokoe's bed. 'C'mon, gerr up! You won't 'ave time for brekkers.'

'Get fucked!' Stokoe turns on his side.

'Fuckin' charming!' Butch appeals to the rest of us.

Stokoe is noted for two things. His unashamed penchant for reading the *Dandy* and *Beano* – and his ability to fart at will. He sleeps in splendid isolation, with the bed-spaces either side of him unoccupied. As Butch pulls his jersey over his head, Stokoe lets go an enormous fart. Like a turtle, Butch's head is framed in the neck of his jersey. 'Dirty-arsed Geordie twatbag!'

Stan Deakin nods in the direction of Stokoe. In broad Scouse he says, 'Did you see 'is blankets flutter up about 3 inches inter the air when he let that one go?' There's a ripple of laughter. 'Do you think we should get a petition up to 'ave the foul-arsed git moved into a room of 'is own?'

'Fuckin' cells they should put 'im in,' says Titch.

'Can't put him in the cells 'less he's charged with summat,' Hinchie sits on his bed, brushing his boots.

'Spreading alarm an' despondency should cover it,' I suggest.

'Spreading crap and despondency, more like,' says Butch.

The subject of these malicious truths sits up in bed and looks around. Pale-faced and baggy-eyed, without a muscle in his body, this tall, gangly nineteen year old is one of the few who has escaped showing any improvement whatsoever during his first few months as a 'Soldier of the Queen'. 'Thoo lot are for ever gannin on aboot me. Thoose are just jealous 'cos ah'm gifted.'

Pete Smith, from Kent, puts on his posh, George Sanders, southern accent. 'Who was it said "A Geordie is a Scotsman with his brains kicked out and thrown over the border"? They appear to have got it absolutely right!'

'Oscar Wilde?' someone suggests.

'Ah'm gannin' for a piss,' says Stokoe.

'Could somone translate?' enquires Pete.

'Up yer pipe!' says Stokoe, giving him the 'V' sign.

'I say!' says Pete, 'Have a care!'

I sit on my bed and watch all this activity. 'Mo' Morris, a little Londoner, approaches Hinchie's bed-space to talk to him. Hinchie points dramatically at Mo's army-booted feet. 'STOP! Don't enter my bed-space.' Hinchcliffe is one of a number of guys who have two folded-up squares of old blanket permanently lying on the floor in their bed-space. They never, EVER, walk on the highly polished area at the side of their bed, in front of their locker. This space – three feet wide by five feet long – never feels the touch of bare or booted feet. Hinchie, along with his ilk, come walking into the billet and, on approaching their bed-space, step onto the ever present squares of blanket and slide about on them all the time. On leaving, they will glide to the edge of the sacrosanct area, step off the blanket squares and leave them 'parked', ready for use upon their return. They believe this means their bed-space is always immaculate and ready for the weekly inspection on Friday mornings. Most guys, including me, can't be bothered with such goings-on. We live in, and use, our bed-space all week. On Thursday evening, and last thing on Friday mornings, we polish it along with the rest of the billet to get ready for the C.O.'s weekly inspection.

At last Titch is ready. We can now go for breakfast. 'Well, Nancy and me have set the date.'

'What for?'

'Whit dae ye buggering think, for?'

'Oh!' he laughs. 'So, when's the big day, then?'

'July the fourth.'

'I suppose you'll 'ave to make arrangements this end?'

'Yeah,' I find lately I'm saying 'yeah' as often as 'aye'. 'Ah believe ah'll have tae ask the C.O. for permission to get married, then see the Padre about gettin' the banns read in the depot church, 'cause this is ma residence. And of course ah'll have tae get ma leave fixed up for the big day.'

As we speak, we collect our eating irons from our lockers then amble down the corridor side by side toward the mess. Already my few days' leave are a memory. I'm back in camp and, without thinking, routine is taking over. As a National Serviceman I'm not supposed to admit it, but I'm getting to like the army. It suits me.

The Queen of the Midlands

I liked the City of Nottingham on first sight. And second. Over the next twenty months or so, I grew to love it. Those twenty months would become some of the happiest times of my life. In the 1950s it's still a smallish city and, as yet, a start hasn't been made on modernising (spoiling) it. The Saturday nights spent in 'Notts' become the highlight of the week for my mates and me. Like all young men, after a few pints we feel the town belongs to us.

We've spent a lazy morning and afternoon hanging around the billet. As usual, most guys who live within striking distance have gone home for the weekend. There's nine left in the room. One of them is on guard tonight, two are courting local girls. Then there's our six. Titch, Butch, Hinchie, Pete, Stan and me. Butch and Hinchie could quite easily go home, but have soon realised they have more fun going into Notts on a Saturday night with their mates. It's usually sometime between five-thirty and six when we go into to our 'getting ready' routine. Leisurely baths or showers are taken. Faces shaved, hair Brylcreemed, trousers pressed and jackets brushed. Sometime before seven p.m. we gather at the stop nearest the depot and catch the bus into the city. We pile on, clamber upstairs, and sit near the back. We're all quite smartly dressed, but Hinchie always leaves us behind in the sartorial stakes.

Eventually we disembark from the bus in the town centre and stand for a moment, looking around with a proprietorial air. As

Chilwell, Summer 1960. Sunbathing by the barrack block. I'm sitting, extreme left. Hinchie, one of the Gang of Six, sits next to me. Note my trendy socks and plimsolls!

the army's aim is not to spoil us with too high a wage, the first topic of conversation is not birds, but where we can get half-pissed at minimum cost. It's just coming up for seven-thirty. Stan rubs his hands briskly together. 'Where we gonna go?'

'Ahs wants to get a couple o' pints of scrumpy down me 'fore ah dus anything,' Butch looks at the rest of us.

'Better head up to Yates, then,' says Hinchie.

We push open the grand double doors and enter the splendiferous establishment known as Yates's Wine Lodge. The Nottingham branch is the largest in the country, probably by far. I always get the feeling I'm entering a cowboy saloon. We stop for a moment just inside the premises. The vast, sawdust-covered wooden floor stretches out before us. I look around. It's a time machine. At one end of the balcony, in full evening dress, a 'Palm Court'-type sextet saw gently on their violins, accompanied by a pianist. Tables and chairs fill the remaining three sides of the balcony. Patrons, mostly couples, sit drinking while they look down, observing the hoi polloi gathered below. On one side of the large downstairs runs a long, long bar with a well-scrubbed top. A brass footrail runs the entire length of this bar. Here and there are strategically placed spittoons, also made of brass. High on the wall behind the bar hang various sized mirrors, some with etched reminders of whose premises we are on, others sporting the names of breweries both active and long gone. On a lengthy counter underneath the mirrors stand barrels of different sizes. Hand-painted onto their fat bodies, in black and white, are signs spelling out what they contain – 'Australian Dock', 'South African Port', 'Amontillado'. Customers stand in twos, threes or more at the roomy bar. Yet more folk sit on small casks which have been turned into seats, with slightly larger barrels serving as tables, spread out over the generous floor space. The staff, mostly men, wear long white aprons tied at the back. Now and again a customer tries – and usually fails – to hit a spittoon. The sawdust is changed regularly.

'Ah bet ye if somebody came back here for the first time in fifty years, they'd think they'd never been away.'

'They might find the price of a pint's gone up!' suggests Butch.

'What I'd like to know,' says Titch, 'is who's got the job of emptying them spittoons?'

'Aw man!' Butch puts his pint back on the bar. 'Thow's gonna put me off me scrumpy.'

'Who are you kidding?' says Pete, 'if they poured two pints of scrumpy into one of those spittoons you'd drink the bugger straight off.'

'Mmmm . . .' muses Butch, 'I 'spose it would give it a bit of body.'

I glance over to the doors just as a couple enter. 'Hey!' I say, lowering my voice, 'Do any of you know who that guy is who just came in?' They all look. There's a chorus of 'No's, except for Hinchie. 'I know 'is face, but can't put a name to it.'

'It's Wally Swift, the boxer. He's due to fight Brian Curvis soon for the British welterweight title. He's really good. Ah think he's world class. Works at the Raleigh Cycle Works in the town.'

'How do you know all this? You a pal of 'is?' enquires Stan.

'Naw yah daft bat. You've seen me with the Boxing News. I read it in there.'

Forty minutes later I've had two sweet stouts and two schooners of 'Australian Dock' red. A lovely glow suffuses my whole body. My feet will be tapping soon.

'So, where are we going, the Sherwood Rooms?' asks Titch. All heads turn toward me.

'Sorry boys. It's a PROPER dance I want, I'm for Colman's Dance Studio.'

'Colman's Old Boots Studio, more like,' says Butch.

'Look, you lot are only interested in trying to get your end away – which you never do – so you waste your time at the Sherwood Rooms wi' aw' these young lassies. I, as an engaged person AND as someone from Glasgow – "dancing city" as it is—'

Butch interrupts,

'From fookin' "stick the nut on you city" you mean!' There's general laughter, I try not to join in.

'That's a foul slur on the Second City of Empire, but what can you expect from someone from . . . where is it, again? Ah! Bilton near Rugby. Even on the largest of large-scale maps it's impossible to find, I believe.' I smile at Butch.

'Get fooked!'

'Get some in!' I respond. We all dissolve into laughter.

'Away, Doog. Ain't yah coming with us?' says Pete.

'Naw, honestly boys. The dancin's great at Colman's. Quickstep, foxtrot, tango. Ah really don't enjoy the Sherwood Rooms or the Palais. Don't do a thing for me.'

* * *

We exit the glorious premises and stand on the pavement for a moment. 'Right, ah'm going this way, lads.'

'See yah back at the billet,' says Titch.

'Don't forget,' Hinchie waves a finger at me, 'last bus is five to eleven.'

I look up at the sky. 'It's gonny be a good night. Ah'll probably stay 'til the last dance and just walk back tae the depot.'

'Huh! Better you than me. See yah later, Jock, Doog, Robert.' I smile as I set off. Never knew I had so many names.

I cross Slab Square – as the locals call the Old Market Square – and head up Clumber Street where Colman's is located. Right next to the close-like entrance where a flight of stairs lead up to the dance studios is the door to the Crystal Palace public house. Och, ah'll have a wee quick one before I go up. I push the ornate door, with its stained glass Art Noveau panel, and once more step back in time. The Crystal Palace is a late Victorian pub, with a long, narrow bar. There's almost as much room behind the bar as there is in front of it. Just as at Yates's Wine Lodge, on the wall facing me are some ornate mirrors with the names of brewers past and present. The beer pumps are originals from, as Butch once put it, 'time immortal'.

'A bottle of sweet stout, please.'

The glass and newly-opened bottle are placed in front of me. 'One and three, please.' I hold the bottle at an angle and fill the glass so as to leave a perfect 'head'. I take a sip, remembering to wipe off the moustache from my top lip. I look along the length of the bar. The majority of customers are between thirty and sixty. Most of them, like me, will be heading upstairs shortly. At twenty, it doesn't bother me that I'm not amongst my age group. This is the only place to be if you're interested in modern dancing. Anyway, truth be told, I've always found older women far more attractive than young girls. Give me Rita Hayworth, Rhonda Fleming or Shelley Winters any day. I finish my glass of stout in two swigs and I'm rewarded with a renewal of the boost that I love to feel. It's Dancing Time!

I climb the stairs, pay my half-crown, and enter the small, packed hall. Huh! Wish I'd arrived five minutes earlier. They're playing Tommy Dorsey's 'Sunny Side of the Street', one of my favourite numbers to quickstep to. Mrs Colman dances past and gives me a smile. Jeez! She sure is a good-lookin' woman. She's well into her forties, but SO attractive. Looks years younger than she is, great figure, terrific legs. She always reminds me of the Italian movie star Gina Lollobrigida. The Colmans were pro dancers for years. On retiring from competition they opened this as a dancing school, which it still is during the week. On Saturday nights it becomes this intimate dance hall. I love it. Not only can I have, as Ma would say, 'A good night at the dancin',' but up here my spotty face never bothers me. Mature, grown-up women are only interested in how well you can dance. Anyway, the lights are always low.

My dancing improves rapidly with my regular attendance at Colman's, and I especially come to love the quickstep. As my footwork gets better, it's great when I come across a partner who obviously likes her dancing. I'm now able to lead, and when we come to the corners of the floor I'm confident enough to spin her three or four times, throwing her out to arms length, then pulling her back to me, all in time to the music. It looks good, feels great, and I really enjoy it. Ma would be delighted to know that, at last, I'm getting as much pleasure out of 'the dancin'' as she did.

During my first summer at Chilwell, in 1959, I enjoy my dancing so much that nearly every Saturday night – providing it looks as if it won't rain – I'm so loath to leave Colman's to catch the last bus, and therefore miss some dancing time, I often stay 'til the end then walk the 5 miles back to the depot. As long as it's dry it doesn't bother me in the least. I set away at a good pace and, once

I leave the city centre behind, do my usual 'walk a hundred, trot a hundred'. I'm always back in the billet in less than an hour. As next morning is Sunday, I've still got plenty of kip time left. One summer night is especially memorable . . .

It's gone midnight, I'm stepping out and making good time. What a gorgeous summer day it has been. A real 'hot one'. The gang and I had our usual few drinks earlier until, as is now the routine, I'd bid them a fond farewell and headed for Colman's. I'd stayed until the last dance then, minutes after it finished, I set off to walk back to the depot. After a sizzler of a day it has turned into something we don't often get in England, or Scotland – a beautiful, balmy night. I'm young, 'fit as a butcher's dog', and enjoying my walk more than ever on such a night. There's a soft, warm breeze, and the heat from earlier in the day now seems to be oozing out of every stone and brick. By the time I reach Beeston, barely a mile from the depot, I've long ago taken off my jacket and carry it slung over my shoulder, one finger through the hanger loop. Even if it had been another two or three miles to Chilwell it wouldn't have bothered me, I was into such a good rhythm. Then it gets even better. All of a sudden the night air is filled with the scent of roses. A well known rose grower has a large nursery garden in Beeston. His beds cover a sizeable area and the entire premises are surrounded by a brick wall. It might be the heat of the night, or maybe it's the time of year, but these roses are ALL giving off their scent. His wall may stop folk getting in, but it can't stop the aroma of thousands of roses from escaping. By the time I'm walking past his premises it has become quite heady, intoxicating. As cars are few and far between at this time of night, whenever the road is quiet and I'm alone, I regularly stop and let it wash over me. It's a magical combination. A soft, balmy night. The pleasure of striding out, seemingly free of tiredness. Then, just when I think it doesn't get any better than this, I find I'm walking through the Garden of Eden!

* * *

It's nearly one a.m. when I enter the billet. Later than usual. All the lights are out. It's mostly our gang who are in residence, the others are all away home for the weekend. My lot probably returned forty minutes or so ago. They usually share a taxi. Butch switches on his bed light then leans up on one elbow. 'It's you, yah Scots twatbag, is it?'

'Ohhh man! Shut the fahk up! I was just dropping off, then.' Titch looks bleary-eyed at Butch. Butch pays no attention, he loves to blether when he's had a drink. He plumps his pillows, then leans back contentedly, arms folded in front of him. 'Did yow get yer leg over, then?'

I give an exaggerated sigh. 'I go for the DANCING, okay? It's you and the rest of them who go to the Sherwood Rooms and the Palais hoping to get your oats. Well, did you?'

'Did we fook!' We both laugh.

'Fahking 'ell!' says Titch in a tired voice, 'That's the second time I was nearly away.'

Butch and I try to keep the volume down. I undress in the overspill from Butch's bed light. I nip to the bog to clean my teeth and pay a last visit. When I return, Butch is still propped up in bed, his light still on.

'Didn't yow get away with one of the old boots, then?' he enquires.

'Why are you so fascinated with the fact that I like to dance with good-looking, mature women, while you like to sniff round vacuous stick insects?'

'What's vacoose?'

'Never mind.'

'Well, ahs thinks it's time for some kip,' says Butch. 'Goo' night, Doog. Goo' night, Titch.'

'Never mind fahkin' good night,' says Titch, 'I betcha I won't sleep a wink now. Good night, Robert. I ain't saying good night to that noisy git.'

'Oooooh, get her,' says Butch in a shrill voice, 'must be that time of the month!'

I laugh.

'Don't laugh at 'im. He'll carry on all bleeding night if you do,' warns Titch.

There is, perhaps, a minute's silence, then we hear Butch's basso profundo giggle from underneath his blankets. This sets the three of us off, totally helpless. It takes Titch three attempts to say, 'I'm gonna see the sar'nt major about getting a transfer out of this billet.'

'GOOD!' say Butch and I in unison. That's enough to touch us off again.

Eventually, sometime after two, we finally shut up and settle down for the night.

In the morning we all lie in bed until the last possible minute then, unwashed, throw on some clothes and hurry down to the mess, five minutes before they stop serving. On the way back, I catch the civvy newspaper man. He comes into the camp every morning in his van. As he sees me approach he selects a *Sunday Post* and holds it out. We exchange 'Good morning's. I head back to the billet, get undressed, and climb back into bed. The rest of our gang are already in their pits. Within half an hour all is silence as we make up for last night's lost sleep.

Independence Day

It's all very low key. I take a week's leave and apply for one of my few free railway warrants, which gets me a return ticket to Edinburgh. I arrive in Seafield with one week's pay and seven days' ration money. Around five pounds in total. A few nights at the Dorchester are definitely out. Nancy buys me a new suit for the wedding as my current one is past its best. The reception afterwards will be held in her parents' house.

On the morning of 4 July 1959, Nancy and I walk down the aisle in Blackburn Church and are joined in matrimony by the

July 4, 1959. On leave from the Army to marry Nancy.

Rev. Donald Stewart. And that's it. Still, we're both very happy to be married, after a courtship of three years, even if we do spend our first week as man and wife in the bedroom next door to her ma and da. For the first couple of nights I half expect her ma to come in at any minute and say, 'Stop that!' In spite of all that, it's a dream come true to at last find myself in bed with Nancy. There's plenty of kissing and cuddling before we finally go all the way. Silent loving is really difficult. Now I know why people traditionally go away on honeymoon. Even so, everything is as wonderful as I hoped it would be. It's also pleasing to know that, at last, I'm no longer a virgin.

For the rest of my week's leave, and our honeymoon, we don't stray very far. A day trip into Edinburgh on the bus is the highlight. Not having much money isn't really a problem, I'm used to that. Being in love, together – and now, married – is the main thing. We do all the touristy things in Edinburgh, especially the ones that don't cost much – visit the castle, stroll through the gardens, and window-shop on Prince's Street, giving our minds a treat by looking through the plate glass at what we'd buy if we had the money.

The week, of course, flies by. In no time at all I'm getting the bus into Waverley Station to catch the grimy overnight train for Nottingham. After what seems to be a more tiring journey than normal I eventually find myself yawning my way back into the billet. Jeez, last week already feels like it wasn't quite real. I brace myself for the reception I know I'll receive as soon as I set foot in the barrack room. As expected, the place is in its morning uproar, guys in various states of undress, some about to head for the mess, Stokoe ignoring all protests – claiming it's nature. Butch is the first one to spot me. 'Oy! Look who it is, lads!' He clenches his fist and moves his forearm back and forth like a piston. 'Bet you've been 'aving loads of rumpy-pumpy, Doog, eh?' He raises the expected laugh. 'None of your beeswax, fat git!'

'Ooooh! Thou didn't pick the wrong time of the month to get wed, did tha? 'Ave you had nowt?'

Titch is busy constructing his blanket-box. 'You had a good time, mate?'

'What was the most times in one night, Jock?' Stan looks at me expectantly.

'The secrets of the matrimonial bed are sacrosanct.'

'What's that?' says Butch. 'S'that some kind of dildo?'

'Ah'm tellin' you lot nowt!'

'Rotten bugger,' he replies.

I take my red plastic mug and irons from my locker and Titch and I head along the corridor toward the mess for breakfast. 'How's it feel to be married, then?'

'Huh! Not much different from being single. 'Specially when you're doing your two years.'

'Yeah. It'll be a handjob most of the time, just like the rest of us!'

I climb up on the big, diesel fork-lift and start the engine. Minutes later I drive into one of the many enormous warehouses and park, then go see the civvies working there. Let them know I'm here. This is where I've been allocated for the day. To be available to drive up and down the maze of aisles, locate whatever item is on the docket, then use my growing expertise with the fork-lift to retrieve it. Most bits and pieces are stored in four-foot-square metal pallets with wire-mesh sides. These are normally stacked six high. The three wheeled trucks have a small turning circle, which is a necessity for manoeuvering in the fairly narrow aisles. If something is required from, say, the third pallet up in a stack of six, I delicately remove the top three and put them to one side, then bring down the one in which the part is located. The civvies remove the item ordered. I now do it all in reverse. Put back the single pallet, then the other three on top again. A lot of my time is spent driving up and down myriad aisles, dwarfed by endless tall rows of pallets, that look like some mini-Manhattan. On a daily basis I locate and retrieve MT (motor transport) spares, large and small, and start them on their journey to army bases all over the world. It's a tried and true system and I enjoy being a part of it.

During my time at Chilwell I have just one serious mishap. While delicately inserting the forks of my truck into the topmost pallet of a stack one day, I inadvertently put them through too far. Unknown to me, the tips of my forks are just underneath the pallet behind the one I'm working on. As I lift the one I'm supposed to retrieve, the tips of my forks are lifting – and tipping forward – the unseen pallet behind. There's a tremendous crash as it falls 20 feet or so into the aisle. Luckily no one happens to be passing at the time. The loud noise is the sound of around 200 driving mirrors smashing! What mainly concerns me is, as they all smashed at the same time, is that covered by just one period of seven years bad luck? Or will it be 7 × 200? 1,400 years in total!

There are a large number of Asian and West Indian workers amongst the civvies employed at Chilwell. I find it quite interesting to work with them. I've had no experience of living near, or working with 'coloured people', as they're called in the fifties. The Asians are fairly quiet and seem to take a pride in showing you how efficient they are. The West Indians, mostly from Jamaica, have all emigrated to England since the end of the war. They are quite different from the Asians. They are always talking and laughing – a bit like National Servicemen! I like to listen to their rich West Indian argot which they use amongst themselves. Slowly but surely, I begin to tune in. The banter between the men and women is often full of sexual innuendo, and sometimes ends with the guys being given a playful slap and a telling-off.

I'm working with four or five Jamaicans. One of the guys says something salacious to the girls. As they laugh and giggle at what's been said, I catch their attention because I'm laughing too. There's a moment's silence, then they all go into shrieks of laughter, the girls covering their faces with their hands as they realise that the Scots soldier now knows what they're saying. And for how long has he known?

Dead-eye Dick Strikes Again

That's my first year behind me. The second is looked on as 'downhill'. This is when demob charts begin to appear, hung on the inside of locker doors. They're usually hand drawn on thick card. But not for Titch and me. Ours are much more elaborate. Titch works as assistant signwriter to Jack, a civvy employee. It's a real cushy number. Many seek – but seldom find – a cushy number. Titch has. Their office/headquarters/workshop/storeroom is a converted wartime air raid shelter located in the middle of the depot. It's down there, in his spare time (of which he has plenty), that Titch designs and creates two de luxe, hand-painted demob charts for him and me. They are long, rectangular pieces of plastic which show our remaining twelve months in descending order. The months are in various colours, and the lettering of each month is in a different style from the others. There is a 'slide' which we move slowly down the calendar toward that magic word: DEMOB. My chart ends in January 1961, Titch's in February. This fact I occasionally (daily) remind him of, with a merry, 'Get some in!'

The signwriter, Jack, is an interesting old guy. Coming up for sixty-five, he's a First World War veteran. In pride of place in their HQ hangs a framed print of a famous WW1 photo, which I already know from books and TV. It shows four tin-helmeted stretcher bearers struggling to carry a casualty as their putteed legs sink to the knees in the mud of the battlefield. With justifiable pride, Jack one day points to himself at a corner of the stretcher.

Dead-eye Dick Strikes Again

The shelter is a great little hide-out. Whenever I've got spare time between jobs I regularly make for this grassy mound, descend the stairs at the brick-built entrance, and open the door to their snug office-cum-storeroom. I'm immediately greeted by the aroma of turps, varnish and paint. Sometimes Jack and Titch join in; they're often in residence as a lot of their jobs can be done down here. As soon as they see it's me, the electric kettle is switched on. After a brew and one of Jack's tea biscuits, I make my exit, remount my sturdy steed and set off, once more, on my quest to confound the Queen's enemies.

Each summer during my two years I, along with twenty or so others, pack our kit and move 50 yards down the hill to the small barrack block which houses those who, for the next fortnight, will undergo a refresher course of infantry training, drill, PT and the odd 5-mile route march. There's also a couple of days on the range to sharpen, or restore, our skills with the Bren light machine gun and Lee Enfield ·303 rifle. Being 'depot soldiers', we're required to keep our infantry training up to a certain level. I look on it, as most do, as a break from the daily routine. It gives us plenty of exercise and gallons of fresh air, and at the end of the fortnight we feel ready and able to take on the might of the Soviet Union – or maybe the Isle of Man – should they turn nasty.

One of the great delights of these courses is the NCO who runs them. Sergeant Briggs, a Welshman who sounds as though he only left the Rhondda last week, is Wales's answer to Walter Mitty. The good sergeant, medal ribbons proudly displayed on his battledress jacket, is a great teller of tales and is surely descended from a long line of Welsh minstrels. There's nothing he likes better than to have a new batch of innocents to whom he can, yet again, modestly unfold the dramatic story of his major part in thwarting Hitler's plans for world domination. Whenever we finish a session of square bashing, or complete a route march, he always lets us fall out and loll about on the grass for a break.

While we are too exhausted to run away, he then seizes his chance to regale us with another ripping yarn from 'that last bit of bother with Germany'.

We stretch out in the sun, glad of a breather after a strenuous session of PT. Sergeant Briggs strides up and down in front of us. There's nothing to do but watch him. He suddenly halts, then turns to face us, legs apart, shoulders back to maximise every inch of his five foot four frame. The lilting Welsh accent begins to wash over us like molasses.

'1940 was the blackest year, lads,' he draws a breath in through pursed lips so that it seems he's whistling in reverse. He shakes his head, obviously saddened as he's forced to recall how desperate it all was. 'On our own we were. France had collapsed. Very unreliable the French, you know.' He shakes his head again – this is obviously very difficult for him. He looks up. 'Even worse than the Yanks!' He suddenly takes a few steps, turns, and comes back to the same spot. His eyes range amongst us as though trying to weigh up if we can take it. This is high drama. We give him our full attention. The fuller our attention, the longer we'll get to lie on the grassy bank. 'July and August were the worst, boys. RAF flying over'ead on patrol. Watching for . . .' he pauses, '. . . the Hun in the sun! That was the jargon of the time, lads. T'was on every pilot's lips.'

Titch and I know we daren't look at one another. Sergeant Briggs again sucks in air through his teeth. 'Effery night for a month we were on full AH-lert. "Condition Red" invasion imminent! German par-a-troopers expected to fall from the sky any minute. Rumour had it they'd be dressed as nuns! I didn't be-lieve that one, mind you. Ger-mans aren't that daft, boyo.'

A low moan comes from Stan Deakin who is slightly behind me. From the corner of my eye I watch as he leans over onto his elbow and tucks his head in out of sight to my rear. He then lies there quivering, further moans coming out of him continually.

'Every night for four weeks we slept, fully dressed, on TOP of our beds. Ne-fer 'ad them off once. At the foot of effery bed was a chair – carefully laid out – rifle, tin 'at, full ammo pouches and all our webbing. If the 'balloon went up' – that's more jargon of the time, bonny boys – we slid off the end of our beds, put our kit on, and even though we were one storey up – there was no time to use the stairs – we ran to the window opposite . . .' he pauses for effect, '. . . raised it, and leapt out!'

This is too much for Butch. He's the next one to succumb. I glance over at him. He's rolled over onto his stomach, is leaning up on his elbows and has his head bowed. There are tears in his eyes and he too is making strange, low sounds. I have to look away.

Our sergeant continues . . . 'On the grass below each window is an 'eap of sand to break our fall. Every second precious you see.'

There's a movement from Titch. He's suddenly taking a great interest in the grass between his legs. He runs his fingers through it. Perchance he's discovered a rare Alpine periwinkle? At the moment, however, I'm in no fit state to enquire.

At long last the bold sergeant finishes his tale. 'Right, c'mon grand lads, fall in.' As we rise and step onto the road to line up, Titch leans toward me. 'I thought I was gonna fahkin' die then!'

'Me tae! Ah don't know how he can't see the effect he has on folk.'

Butch falls in alongside us, still red in the face. He speaks out the corner of his mouth. 'Eeee, mate. That little Welsh bugger'll be the death o' me. Ah were lying at a bad angle, an' what with tryin' to keep me laugh in, the pain! Ah thought ah were gonna peg out!'

We gather outside the small barrack block. It's early morning, not long after breakfast. We all have our full webbing on. Sergeant Briggs goes round behind us, one at a time. He lifts our 'big packs' up with one hand, testing their weight. He finds a couple who've just stuffed theirs full of scrunched-up news-papers. 'Skiving buggers! I'll sort you lot out.' He goes over to a small, decorative cairn in the centre of the grassed area in front of the block. He selects four hefty stones from those making up this centrepiece, opens the straps of the miscreants' packs, and places two in each. 'There you are, lovely boys. You've now got the HEAVIEST loads to carry!'

It's a nice morning, so we're all in 'shirt-sleeve order', no ties.

'Atten-SHUN!' He stands in front of us in his usual, four-square stance. 'Is this your first route march?' There's a mixture of 'Yes Sar'nt's and 'No Sar'nt's.

'Right, I'm sure you all know by now it's a distance of 5 miles. Doesn't sound a lot. By the time you're 'alf done, you'll realise it is – 'specially when you're carrying about 30 pounds of kit.'

He looks around. 'Couple of you got a little bit extra! Idea of a route march is to get from A to B soon as possible – so it's NOT a walk. Okay? If you see mates beginning to flag, 'elp 'em. This is gonna sort out the wheat from the chaff. You'd better all be back 'ere in less than an hour – or I'll want to know the reason why. Corporal Eccleston and I will be with you all the way.'

We're just two miles into it. I'm surprised how knackered some guys are already, red in the face, sweat pouring off them. I guess all my walking/trotting to work in the mornings when I was with the Clyde Trust – and coming back from Notts on a Saturday night – is now paying dividends. The sergeant has us doing the 'march a hundred, trot a hundred', and I'm finding it no problem at all – the extra weight I'm carrying isn't bothering me so far. I blether away to Titch and I'm hardly out of breath. The sergeant and corporal continually exhort us to 'keep up the pace.' I am.

Somewhere between miles three and four, the sergeant decides to stop the 'trot a hundred'. Some guys are so tired they're unable to get their breath back during the 'march a hundred'. We're just marching now. Well, walking really. I and a few others are all for storming away and getting back to barracks early, but the NCOs won't let us. We've to stick together. One or two guys have taken to walking behind a mate, reaching out a hand under his large pack to support it. Taking the weight to help them out.

We're just passing the 4 miles. 'C'mon!' shouts Briggs, 'Let's get these spirits raised, bit of singing on the march. Less than a mile to go, boys.' He launches into the old favourite from two world wars – 'Tipperary'. It falters at first, but by the second chorus all but the terminally knackered have joined in. It's actually doing the trick! Crunching along a country road, thumbs hooked through shoulder straps, we are all – well, almost all – singing in unison. Heads are beginning to be held up again. As we finish, Corporal Eccleston obviously doesn't want to lose the momentum. 'Do you know this one?' he shouts. 'It's called "Yeah! Boo!"' There are sufficient 'Yes's for him to start it off.

'I'm gonna buy a pub!'

There's a collective, 'Hurrah! Yeahhh!'

'With only one bar!'

'BOOOO!'

'A hundred yards long!'

'YEAHHH!' By now, even those who've never heard it before have joined in.

'Only one barman!'

'BOOOO!'

'FIFTY BARMAIDS!' he bellows.

'HURRAHHH!'

So it goes on until we've run out of alternatives. Next, comes another old favourite – 'The Quartermaster's Stores'.

'There was beer, beer, that filled you full of cheer,'

'In the stores, in the stores,'

'There was beer, beer, that gave you diarrhoea!'

'In the quartermaster's stores.'

We do all the verses that we know, then we march on in silence, listening to the crunch of our boots. There must only be about half a mile or so to go. It's definitely raised the spirits, we're marching with a will again. I don't want us to lose it. I feel myself blush. 'What about that American marching song, Corporal, "Sound Off"?' I've watched so many American movies – as these guys will have – I'm sure we'll manage a few choruses. Whenever I've heard it sung in a picture I've always thought 'what a great marching song'.

'Start it off, then, Jock!' shouts Sergeant Briggs. Oh, shit, I didn't mean . . . Right, here goes:

'You had a good home and you left!'

'YOU'RE RIGHT!' thunders the squad. I feel my scalp tingle. Great! I do the next bit . . .

'Sound off!'

'ONE, TWO!'

'Sound off!'

'THREE, FOUR!'

Then together – 'ONE, TWO, THREE, FOUR. Sound off! SOUND OFF!'

My adrenaline is now flowing . . .

'I MET A GAL IN TENNESSEE,' I'm giving it big licks now.

'AND SHE WAS AWFUL NICE TO ME!' What a lot of guys must've went to the pictures!

'SOUND OFF!'

'ONE, TWO!' etc.

I then finish up with the last verse I know:

'YOUR MOTHER WAS THERE WHEN YOU LEFT,'

'YOU'RE RIGHT!'

'SOUND OFF!' . . .

Well, it may not be British, but it's a great marching song. 'Good Lad, Jock!' shouts the sergeant. I blush again. Anyway, it's done the trick. Our spirits have been revived for the last quarter mile, and a couple of minutes after 'Sound Off!' we come in sight of the depot – which raises them even more.

'C'mon now, bonny boys,' shouts Briggs, 'let's see you marching through those gates and into that depot s'if you've just been

Chilwell Depot, Summer 1960. Pity this isn't sharper. I'm on left. Look at that six-pack – before they were invented!

for a stroll – LEFT, LEFT, LEFT, RIGHT, LEFT! That's the way, my lads.' We march through the gates, shoulders back, arms swinging as though returning from the wars – which for some we are! We're halted in front of the training block.

'Well done, boys. DiiiisMISS!'

We clatter into the billet. Some collapse onto beds. Others strip off sweaty kit and make for baths and showers.

'That wasn't too bad, Titch.'

'No, could've been worse.'

Geordie Stokoe lies on his bed, near death. 'Ah divn't think ah've the strength left tae fart!'

It's during my second summer of infantry training that I have one of the few 'magic moments' in my life; the sort of thing I've only seen in movies. Like when Errol Flynn, as Robin Hood, is taking part in the archery contest. The winner will receive the favours of Maid Marian. Alas, all seems lost for Robin. It's down to the last two – and his opponent has just scored a bull's-eye! Well, that's it, isn't it? You can't beat a bull's-eye. It's all over. Then Robin comes forward (he's heavily disguised, no one recognises him except the Sheriff of Nottingham, evil Prince John – and the audience in the Blythswood), raises his bow, fires his LAST arrow – and splits his opponents arrow in two! Crikey Jings! Or there's that bit in *Sergeant York* (a real-life hero of World War One). Gary Cooper's playing him – who better? Whenever he's in a situation where he MUST NOT MISS, York just licks the tip of his thumb, rubs it on the front sight of his rifle – and another Hun bites the dust!

Whenever I see scenes like that in the movies I always get a tingle on the back of my neck, and my eyes smart with tears. Then one day I have the chance – ME! – to do it for real!

We're on the range, firing at 100 yards with the Bren light machine gun. A beautiful weapon. We all have five rounds, and it's set on 'single shot'. Sergeants Briggs and Cole are running things. 'Right, lads,' says Cole, 'five shots. We're looking for good grouping.' He looks at Briggs, then at us. 'Now, what we usually do to make it interesting, we all put a shilling in a kitty. That'll be twenty-two bob. Highest score takes all. Is that okay?' We all agree and chip in our shillings. As these two are the regular training sergeants, it means they're on the range on a weekly basis. We're only on the range, at most, half a dozen times in our entire two years. It's easy beer money for them. It's widely believed they split it between them.

There are four Brens, so four guys at a time get to fire. The few times I've been on the range I've always enjoyed it. I've always done well. Firing the Lee Enfield •303 rifle is spoiled somewhat because it has a kick like a mule. The Bren is a delight. It fires the same •303 round but it stands on small bipod legs and it has springs in the butt. These two take up almost all the fierce kick, which means you can relax and enjoy firing it. At last it's my turn. The two sergeants have already fired and, would you believe it, they are lying first and second! I get down on my belly, make myself comfortable, and nestle the butt into my shoulder. As I've been trained to do, I take a deep breath in, hold it, take aim, and put 'first pressure' on the trigger. I let half the breath out, hold what remains, finalise my aim on the target, then softly, so as not to disturb my aim, squeeeeze the trigger. CRACK! Shit! I've only got an outer. (There is 'bull', 'inner', 'outer' – then the rest of the target.) That's disappointing. I take the same careful aim the remaining four times. Result? I have a lovely close group of five – all outers. What should I do? I'm only a National Serviceman. But, I know I'm not *that* bad a shot. The close grouping of my rounds proves it. I roll onto my side, clear my throat. 'Eh, Sar'nt Briggs. This weapon's firing to the right.' Of course, I blush. He tries to hide a smile. Even one or two of the lads laugh. I hear one of my fellow squaddies say, 'Listen to Dead-eye Dick!' This makes the whole group laugh. I'm blushing all the way to my knees now. It's a flash guy called Geoff Fulleylove who's made the 'Dead-eye Dick' crack. Somehow this annoys me, makes me more determined. I stop blushing. 'If you look at the target, Sar'nt, I've got a good group – but all to the right.' He lifts his binoculars and looks down the range. 'Mmmmm, good grouping right enough. Here, give me a go, boyo.' He swaps places with me, reloads the weapon and takes five careful shots. He looks up at Sergeant Cole. 'He's right, it is a bit off. We'll give 'im another five.' He points to the Bren he'd fired. 'That one's definitely all right, use it, lad.' He's in the lead with three bulls, one inner and one outer.

Conscious that everyone's watching me, I get down behind the weapon. I can feel twenty-one pairs of eyes on me. Jeez, maybe I should have kept my gob shut. I'll look a right prat if I spray them all over the place. Into my mind comes Fulleylove and his 'Listen to Dead-eye Dick'. How many Fulleyloves have I met in my life? All at once my nerves vanish. I'm determined, yet relaxed. I know exactly what to do – the same as I did with my first five shots. This time the sights are correctly set. Five times I go through the routine again . . . Breathe in, aim, first pressure. Half the breath out, finalise aim, squeeeeze that trigger.

I fire my last round. I think I've done well. At least I know I won't have embarrassed myself, I'll probably have a high score. Sergeant Cole steps forward a few yards and lifts his binoculars. 'Fuck me!' he turns to Sergeant Briggs and says something. 'Good for 'im!' says Briggs. 'Go and get your target, boyo.'

I sprint down the range and run back with the target. All the lads crowd forward. I've got FOUR bulls and an outer. I feel the hair tingle on the back of my neck – but this time it's not for Errol Flynn or Gary Cooper. It's for me!

I hand the torn-off paper target to Sergeant Briggs. He and Cole look at it. 'Bloody good shooting, lad,' says Briggs. 'Well done, young 'un,' says Cole. Even though tonight's beer money has just been snatched away from him, I can tell he means it. 'Take off your beret,' says Cole. He pours the twenty-two shillings into it. Titch and my mates from our billet crowd round; I get a few slaps on the back. I look around the rest of the group and catch Fulleylove's eye. I give him a smile. 'Dead-eye Dick strikes again, Geoff, eh?'

What to Do?

There's no doubt about it, I really am getting to like the army. There is also no way I can let on to my mates. I'd never hear the end of it. Although we're for ever laughing and carrying on, enjoying the comradeship of being in the billet and working in the depot, they consider that that's in spite of being in the army. The penny hasn't dropped that it's because we're in the army! I know one thing. If I hadn't met Nancy, there would've been no problem – I'd quite happily have signed on by now. It would have been a lot better than returning to Glasgow, looking for digs and finding a job.

I regularly think back to my nine months in the RAF. How different it all is now. I said I'd make a go of the army. And I have. Maybe it's even more about proving it to myself than to 'them'.

As my first year melds into my second, the army puts me – and the others – on short courses and I take exams and begin to garner qualifications. I easily pass my Army Educational Exams which means, if I was a regular soldier, I would now be suitable for promotion up to the rank of Warrant Officer. Although I mostly drive a fork-lift I'm still a 'storeman technical'. Early in 1960 I pass the Trade Test exam which makes me a B2 Storeman Tech, and I now have a 'B' flash on my sleeve (a cloth badge with the letter 'B' surrounded by a laurel wreath). It also gives me a pay rise of sixpence a day – if I was a regular soldier it would be twice that. Later in the year I take the second part of the exam, pass, and I'm now B1. Another 3/6d a week. WOW!

* * *

313

During the summer we're all taken in batches to the range to have our skill – or lack of it – with the Lee Enfield ·303 rifle evaluated. A few weeks afterwards I'm delighted when I look on the notice board at the latest company orders and find I'm one of only seven who've been awarded their 'Marksman's Badge'. I'm really chuffed about that. I waste no time in calling in on the depot seamstress, a motherly woman around fifty years of age, to pay her sixpence and get her to sew the marksman's 'crossed rifles' onto the left cuff of my battledress jacket. Another 3/6d a week. Golly gee double WOW! Is there no end to it? There isn't . . .

It's early September, 1960. 'Private Douglas!'

'SAR'NT!' I put down my Penguin edition of *Lady Chatterley's Lover*. After the big court case and publicity over the publication of this long-banned novel – then the long wait until the civvy newspaper seller gets me one – I'm finding it boring. Dead boring. The perfect book to snuggle down with if you've got a touch of insomnia. I've spent a better night wi' appendicitis!

'Major Gunn wants to see you, lad.'

'Right, Sar'nt.'

'Ohyah! What yow been doing, Doog, if "Bang Bang" Gunn wants to see yah?' Butch raises his head from the pillow. It's lunchtime. Every bed is occupied by a sleeping or snoozing Soldier of the Queen.

'Buggered if ah know. Can't think of anything.' I get myself buttoned up, put on my beret and head for the battalion office. Jeez. No matter what job I have, I hate it when you're summoned to see the boss. 'Specially when you don't know what you've done!

The clerk looks up as I enter the large wooden hut. Like all good company clerks he's behind his desk, typewriter 'cocked', eating an apple, and reading *Tit Bits*.

'Hiyah! Major wants to see me.'

'Oh yeah. Private Douglas?'

'That's me.'

'Just knock the door, wait 'til he says "come in". '

I knock. 'COME IN!'

I open the door, step smartly into his office, shut the door, two paces forward, halt in front of his desk, come to attention and throw up a smart salute. 'Good afternoon, 404 Douglas, SAH!'

As he's sitting at his desk, not wearing a hat, protocol dictates the major doesn't return my salute. 'Thank you,' he says. 'Stand at ease.' I stand with my legs apart, hands clasped behind my back. He opens the file in front of him. Presumably mine. 'Now, yesss, you're due out beginning of January '61, just under four months from now. That right?'

'Yes, sir.'

'Well, I'm very pleased with all the reports I've read, and heard, about you. I want to promote you to lance corporal for your last few months. Will you accept that?'

This really is out of the blue. Not too many National Service-men are promoted. It hadn't even entered my head. I'd been pleased about getting my B1 and Marksman's Badge on my sleeve, makes you stick out a bit. But now to be promoted – offered a stripe. Jeez! 'Eh, yes, that would be really nice, sir.' 'Nice' hadn't been quite the word I was looking for. I couldn't think of anything else.

'Right, you can go to the seamstress and get her to sew your stripe up. It'll be on "Battalion Orders" in the morning. Well done, lad! Dismiss.'

'Thank you very much, sir.' I come to attention, throw a smart salute up, take a step back, right turn, and let myself out of the office. The clerk's absorbed in *Tit Bits*.

As I step out on my way back from the office, I'm quite excited. Jeez! Me, getting promoted! As I near the billet I begin to brace myself for the inevitable stick I'll get when I make my announce-ment. I decide attack will be the best form of defence.

I throw open the door and enter with much crashing of studded boots on floorboards. There's still about ten minutes to go before the bugler calls us to duty. The air is filled with assorted snores and 'zedds' floating up into the air.

'RIGHT! Listen up you lot!'

Numerous sleepy heads are raised. Stokoe turns and lets one go. Hinchie mistakes it for the bugler's last note and staggers off his bed. Titch, Butch and two or three others look at me through heavy eyelids. 'What's up with you, noisy Scotch twat?'

Might as well get it over with. 'You're now looking at your new lance corporal!'

'Get fucked!' seems to be the consensus.

'You 'aven't 'ave you?' Butch looks at me bleary-eyed. 'Hast thow fookin' sold out, Doog?'

Titch sits up. 'Have you taken promotion? Buggah me!'

'Scotch Git!' says Stan.

'What a conniving Scottish ratbag!' declares Pete. 'We've clasped an asp to our bosoms!'

'Grasped a what?' asks Butch.

'Who's got promoted?' enquires Hinchie, still not quite awake.

'Thank you for that storm of congratulations, PALS!' I say.

Hinchie has now joined us. 'What ya want to do that for?'

'Why not? When I hit my last three months it's worth another seven bob a week. Anyway, you're aw' just jealous!'

'Bullox!' seems to be the second consensus of the afternoon.

Two days later, newly blancoed stripe on my arm, feeling very self-conscious, I fall in fifteen or so guys from the billet preparatory to marching them down the depot to start work. This is my first time. It's all right for one or two guys to make their own way to work, but a squad has to be marched, it's too untidy if they just amble down. Right from the start Pete Smith begins playing silly buggers, being slower than everyone else when coming to attention or turning. As I set them off marching he continually goes out of step. There are one or two titters at his antics. I begin to get angry. What to do? 'SQUAAAD HALT!' Smithy deliberately bumps into the guy in front. I walk up to within a few feet of him, then speak loud enough for all to hear. 'Pete, you're taking liberties because we're mates. Nobody else is doing that. Just you. If you think I'll put up with it and won't put you on a charge, you're wrong! I have to march you all down the depot. Everybody accepts it – except you. I'm not going to be fucked around by a guy who's supposed to be a mate. I'm telling you in a reasonable manner. If you carry on acting like a stupid schoolboy, I'll put you on a charge. Get it? It's you or me.' As I walk to the rear of the squad to start marching them off, I hear Titch say, 'Cut it out, Pete.' Butch is next. 'Act your fookin' age, Smithy.' There's no more bother.

Next morning we're halfway down the depot when, horror of horrors, an officer appears! Captain Delap of the Women's Army Corps has rounded a corner. She could easily be mistaken for Margaret Rutherford; rotund, solid built, chin jutting out, even the purposeful walk is the same. I should order the squad to 'eyes right' while I salute her in passing. I haven't done that before. She's going to go by on the other side of the squad from me. I decide to turn a 'Nelsonian blind eye' to her. Are soldiers allowed to do that? We're just about past one another. I've got away with it. Then . . . 'Corporaaaal! Halt your squad!' Oh, shit! I feel my face go red. The 'Corporaaaal!' has been said in the same intonation as Sybil Thorndike's 'A haaandbag!' when she's Lady Bracknell. I halt the squad and go marching smartly back to her. It's now all about limiting the damage. I come to attention with such a crashing of boots that I hurt my foot, then I give her a matching salute which is so quivering it throws me off balance.

'Yes, Ma'am?' I can hear the faintest of titters from the squad. Bastards!

She points to the three pips on her epaulette with the tip of her baton. It's well known she sees red when not treated with the same respect as male officers. I already knew this. How stupid.

'Why did you not acknowledge me just then?'

For a second it crosses my mind – what if I offer to become her sex slave until I'm demobbed? I take another look at her. She's not ower braw! Never mind looking like Margaret Rutherford. More like Desperate Dan – with tits. I won't bother. Let's try the truth.

'I'm very sorry, Ma'am.' I try to keep my voice down, them ratbags in the squad will be straining their ears, hoping to hear a bit of grovelling. 'Eh, I just got promoted a couple of days ago and I'm, sort of, not very good at marching a squad, yet, Ma'am.' Her face softens. Beneath those brass buttons beats a mother's heart.

'Very well, Corporal. I trust it won't happen again?'

'It certainly won't, Ma'am.'

'Right, carry on.' I throw up another blistering salute – and hurt my foot again. She stomps off, honour restored. I limp back to my sniggering squad. Voices whisper from various parts.

'Oh, please Ma'am, don't take me stripe away, Ma'am.'

'If I comes up your quarters and gives you a good seeing-to will you let me 'orf, Ma'am?'

'C'mon, settle down.' I've difficulty keeping my face straight. Order is eventually restored and I march them down the depot without further incident.

The whole episode makes me realise that taking promotion isn't just a case of picking up another seven bob a week. I had to get a grip of Smithy yesterday. Today I realise even marching the squad down the depot is more than just, 'Fall in, quick march'. Other things are expected of me. Well, on the whole I think I managed quite well. Almost.

The following week we're marching down the depot when Captain 'Rutherford' hoves into view! I swallow hard. The moment of truth has arrived!

'Here's your mate coming,' says Titch, *sotto voce*.

What to Do?

I brace myself. It'll have to be done.

'SQUAD! SQUAD H'EYES RIGHTAH!' I call it perfectly, they're on the right foot, they take a single pace, then heads click to the right as one. At the same instant I turn my head to the right and throw up a textbook, vibrating salute. Tibby Brittain couldn't have done better!

'G'morning Ma'am!'

Gloves and baton clasped in her right hand, she touches the skip of her hat. 'Good morning, Corporal,' she trills. This is accompanied by a sweet smile.

We sail past her. I return the squad to 'eyes front' in case they walk into something. We march off into the distance.

'He's shagging her,' mutters Butch, 'I'm tellin' yer, he's shagging Miss Marple!'

Old Soldiers

We've decided Nancy will take a week's holiday and come down to Chilwell to see where I've been for the last eighteen months. First of all, I'll have to see if I can get digs for her near to the depot. I'll get permission to sleep out every night and come in every morning to report for duty. The question is, does anybody in the vicinity take in lodgers?

It's a lovely late September evening when I walk out the gate, turn right, then take the next right down Attenborough Lane. I'm wearing civvies. Halfway along a man is busy in his garden.

'Excuse me, I wonder if you can help me?' He comes over to the fence. I'm struck right away by his resemblance to Frank Johnston. Maybe that's a good omen. 'I'm stationed at the camp,' I nod in its general direction. 'I'd like to bring my wife down for a week's holiday, so I'm trying to find somebody local who'll put the two of us up for the seven days. It would be full board for my wife, but I'll be going into the depot every day to work, so I'll get my meals there. Do you think any of your neighbours might be interested?'

He looks thoughtfully at me. 'Welllll, just stay there a minute, I'll ask the missus. She may even be interested herself.' I watch him go back up the path, take his gardening shoes off, and enter the house. Jeez, am I going to be lucky right away? A few long minutes later they both come out and walk toward me. I give her a smile. She's a small, dark woman with a pleasant round face. I say, 'Hello.' She looks closely at me. I feel I've passed the test.

'It's just for a week, is it?'

'Yes. My wife's taking a week off work.' I always feel like I've just told a lie when I say 'my wife'. It just doesn't come natural.

'Oh, I think we could put you both up for the week. My husband says you'll be going into the camp every day to work.'

'Yeah, so I'll just get my meals in there. It'll be full board for my wife, if that's okay?'

'Yes, that'll be fine.'

'Great! Thanks very much. You're the first house I asked at. I fully expected to be trudging around for an hour or two knocking on doors.'

In their mid-forties, with a young son, Mr and Mrs Frank Dainty of 96 Attenborough Lane have solved my problem straight away.

'Corporal Douglas?'

'Yes, Sar'nt?'

'How'd you like to go on the POL (Petrol, Oil, Lubricants) duty roster? Means you won't do guard duty anymore. You have to be available – stay in camp – one evening and one night every second week. If any vehicle, or convoy, calls in for fuel while en route to another camp, someone has to be available to go down to the pumps, unlock, and fill them up.'

'Sounds good to me, Sar'nt. No more guards.'

The novelty of guard duty had worn off very quickly – like after the first one! That had been on a bitterly cold night at Blackdown, during my driver-training.

After a full day's work, nine or ten of us report to the guardroom wearing our best uniforms and greatcoats. It's around eight forty-five p.m. Once there, we are inspected by the Orderly Officer and Sergeant. There is always one man too many in the squad – for a reason. As an incentive for those about to go on guard to show up for that first parade as bulled-up as can be, the smartest soldier in the line-up is allowed to fall out and return to his billet – excused guard duty! He is known as the 'Stick Man'. The rest of us then spend all night in the guardroom, doing two hours on and four hours off. The two hours on are spent patrolling whatever part of the camp you're allocated to – armed with nothing more lethal than a pickaxe handle. This is known as being 'on picket'. During the four hours off you are inside the guardroom. You can have something to eat, have a rest, sleep even. But you can only take off your greatcoat and beret. Should the call come to 'TURN OUT THE GUARD!' you have to be ready in an instant to race outside and confront any interlopers.

In the guardroom are army beds with bare mattresses, and striped pillows without cases for us to lie on and read, doze, or sleep fitfully. As the night goes on I become increasingly hot and sticky. When it's time to go out for my two hours I almost welcome it. But not quite. I'm teamed up with a guy called Brian Archer. It's coming up for two a.m. when the sergeant shakes me. 'Right, Jock. It's your turn for picket.' Brian and I put on our greatcoats and berets and accompany the sergeant outside. Everything is covered by a heavy hoar frost. Minutes after leaving the steamed-up humidity of the guardroom, the freezing night claims us. I button my greatcoat up to the neck, put the collar up, and pull on my issue woollen gloves. I wish I had a scarf. The hot stickiness I brought out with me has rapidly cooled. I stamp my feet now and again and flail my arms as we follow the sergeant to relieve the guys we're replacing. We are to patrol the massive vehicle park. The fellows we take over from are chilled to the bone. They quickly hand us the staves and double off to the guardroom, glad to be finished.

'Right,' says the sergeant, 'keep your eyes peeled. And remember, the Orderly Officer hasn't been round yet for a visit. He can come anytime. Don't let him catch you skiving.'

'Okay, Sarge.'

He goes back to the guardroom and Brian and I are left to start our stint. We stand for a moment and survey the lines of vehicles.

The sound of the guardroom door closing echoes back to us. All at once there's a feeling of being alone in the silent, brittle night.

'This is gonny be a cauld one, Brian.'

'I'm bloody freezing already, Jock. Christ knows what like we'll be two hours from now.'

As we speak, our breath comes out in great clouds of condensation. The low temperature somehow seems to add to the silence, as though sounds are being frozen. Now and again comes a sharp crack as some panel or part of a vehicle succumbs to the intense cold and contracts even further. We walk down the middle of the park, our feet crunching on the heavy frost. It's so thick it looks more like a layer of snow. As we stride on I look at the array of Bedford and Commer lorries, Austin 'champ' jeeps, Landrovers and staff cars. All have a covering of frost which sparkles if they're near one of the overhead lights. With my gloved hand I hit the canvas canopy of a lorry. It doesn't move. Frozen solid. We walk to the far end of the vehicle park, away from the few lights, into the darkness. I look up. The sky is a mass of stars, just like it was the night I was hitchhiking.

'Look at them stars, Brian. Ain't that gorgeous?'

'Yeah. They seem brighter on a frosty night, don't they?'

'Aye.' We stand there, drinking it in, stamping our feet now and again to keep warm. 'I just read something recently, and this guy was saying "If the stars only came out once every hundred years, everybody on earth would stay up that night just to see the splendour of them." Yet because they're always there, we just take them for granted. That's true, ain't it?'

'Not half. Trouble is, on a night like this it's just too cold to hang about enjoying them.'

'Definitely!' I begin to run on the spot to generate some heat. Brian windmills his arms. We stand for a minute and look back up the park. The trees round the perimeter look all dressed for Christmas with their coating of sparkly white frost. It's March.

* * *

We walk on for a while. 'Are ye anywhere near the end o' that book, Brian? I noticed you getting stuck into it in the guard-room.'

'Just got the last half dozen pages or so. Should get it finished within half an hour of us going back in.'

'Great!' He's reading John Braine's *Room at the Top* and I'm 'two's up' on it. It got terrific reviews when it came out and I'm dying to read it. 'Did ye know they're making a film of it wi' Laurence Harvey and yon French actress, Simone Signoret?'

'Are they?'

'Yeah.'

At long last our interminable two hours are up and, teeth chattering, we return gratefully to the warm fug of the guard-room. As I enter I give an involuntary shiver. Five minutes later we're sitting down to pint mugs of tea, and cheese and onion sandwiches whose edges have curled another 20 degrees since we've been out. At last Brian closes the paperback and sits looking at the cover for a moment. The sort of look that shows he's enjoyed it and is now quite sad he's finished. 'Bloody good book, that.' He turns and tosses it over to me. I sit it on the table in front of me and while I finish my sandwich I occasionally look down at it, anticipating that moment when I'll open it and read the first paragraph.

With half a mug of tea still to drink, I rise from the table and go over to one of the bare beds. Propped up on two pillows, tea at my side, I sit back. 'Ahhhh!' Chapter One. I'll just read that, get a taste of it, then I'll get my head down for the best part of three hours – when you finish guard you still have to do a normal day's work in the depot. It's essential I get some shut-eye. Three hours later, as the long night comes to an end, I'm still wide awake, totally absorbed in the life and loves of Joe Lampton as he tries to find 'room at the top'. The story. The style in which it's written. The characters. They're all real. Although I've read many good novels, this one is different, modern – in the best sense of the word. It totally takes me over. Whenever I open its pages, I'm 'there'. I'm watching them going about their lives. When Joe abandons the woman he loves, just because there's 'room at the top'. I'm appalled. When she drinks too much to drown her sorrows, and dies in a car crash, I'm devastated. When I compare it with all the other good novels I've read, I consider it leaves them behind. Sets new standards.

My last guard before I go on the POL duty list, also proves to be memorable. It's at Chilwell. Not once, during all the guards I've done in the last eighteen months, have I ever been 'stick man' and got excused. When I'm rostered for this one I decide I'm going to make a major effort. This time it's going to be different . . .

I already have a smart, well-fitting greatcoat. I press it and put in two immaculate creases from each of the side pockets down to the hem. Butch bulls my boots until they look as if they are of black enamel. I brush my beret. Instead of having the issue 'staybright' badge, I borrow an old brass one from a guy and polish it until it gleams like gold. Minutes before leaving the billet to report for duty – and the crucial inspection – I stand in front of my mates.

'You'll fookin' walk it, Doog. You'll be back up here in twenty minutes,' says Butch.

'Dead cert, pal,' is Titch's considered opinion.

Stokoe puts the *Dandy* down for a moment. 'Nowt's a bother, Jock,' he says, then farts, 'and that proves it!'

As I line up with the night's prospects I weigh up the opposition. I'm quietly confident. A lad I know from another billet looks at me. 'Huh, you'll piss it, Jock.' On hearing this, another guy leans out to have a look. 'Cor, you'll get stick man no bother, Jock.'

I laugh. 'I hope you're right.'

'SQUAD! SQUAD AH-TEN-SHUN!' The Orderly Sergeant brings us to attention so's the Orderly Officer can inspect us. He moves along the line and takes a close look at everybody. He then comes back and stands in front of me, he's about to raise his baton. I feel a tingle of anticipation. It's Saturday night. Too late for me to go into town. But a lazy night lying about the quiet billet then going to sleep in my own bed. Better than a long, tiring night in the guardroom. The sergeant leans toward the officer's ear. 'Could I have a word with you, sir?'

We watch as he leads the officer a few yards away. Out of earshot.

'There's a fuckin' rabbit off, 'ere,' says one of the lads out of the corner of his mouth.

I watch as the sergeant talks to the officer, then directs his attention by pointing back toward us. The officer is also a National Serviceman, promoted under the 'Short Service Commission' rules. They usually tend to let themselves be guided by the more experienced senior NCOs. When they've finished talking, they approach us again. The officer has headed further along the line. He points his stick at a guy I don't know. 'This is stick man for tonight.'

'Right, fall out, lad,' says the sergeant, 'double away.' The guy right turns, salutes the officer, then makes himself scarce. I know something has gone on, but I can't figure out what. I look at the officer. He'd sounded a bit stilted, almost shamefaced as he'd made his selection. He now stands to one side, smacking his baton on the side of his leg as though impatient for the sergeant to dismiss us to our posts.

'SQUAD! To the guardhouse, FALL OUT!' We right turn and break ranks.

Somebody says, *sotto voce*, 'Jock should 'ave had that!'

'Too bloody true,' says another. The officer and sergeant are nearby, they must have heard that. They ignore it.

As we crowd into the guardroom I collar one of the 'voices off'. 'There was something went on there, John. It looked like ah was gonny get stick man 'til the sarge had a word wi' the officer.'

'Don't you know who Jackson is? The guy who got stick man.'

'Naw.'

'He's one of the star men in the battalion soccer team. They've got a game tomorrow. The sarge is one of the trainers. When he saw you were gonna get it he had a word in the officer's lug, didn't he! So you get shafted and Jackson gets a good night's kip.'

'Jeez-oh! Ah thought, at LAST ah'm gonny get stick man. Just ma poxy luck! Anyway, there's nae good complaining. Ah'd have nae chance against them two.'

''Fraid so, Jock. You know what the army's like with sport. You get handled with kid gloves if you represent the battalion at anything. Even fuckin' tiddly winks!'

For the rest of the night the sergeant never looks me in the eye once.

Enjoying Life

The locomotive draws into Nottingham station amidst great plumes of smoke and steam. Platform ticket in hand, I look along its length. Nancy's on that train!

At last it comes to a halt and the compartment doors all seem to be thrown open at once as a couple of hundred folk step down onto the platform and stream toward me. I stand on tiptoe, anxious for a first glimpse of her, then – THERE SHE IS! We kiss and hug, rather shyly, and I ply her with the statutory questions, as culled from books and movies.

'Did you have a good trip? Was it on time when it left Edinburgh? Have you had something to eat?'

'Ah would'nae mind a wee cup o'tea.'

'Right. Ah know a nice little cafe.' I take hold of her suitcase and lead her out into the town. I feel as proprietorial about Nottingham as I used to feel about Glasgow when she'd come through for the day. Once again she's in 'my city' and I want her to feel safe. Impress her because I know my way about and what I'm doing. I'm grown up, mature, reliable. She may be seven years older but I'm more experienced, wiser, because I'm a man. Her man.

After a mini-tour of the city centre we catch a bus to Chilwell. As we walk toward Attenborough Lane I point out the camp gates and what little can be seen of the depot.

Mr and Mrs Dainty make her very welcome and show us to what will be our bedroom for the week. It's all mildly embarrassing and stilted at first. Very British. By the time we've had the regulation cuppa and a blether, we all relax in each other's company – and that's how it stays for the week. The only problem that arises is the inability of the Daintys to crack Nancy's strong West Lothian accent. I'm well used to tempering mine to suit the company I'm in. Not Nancy. Even when folk say, 'pardon?' She seems incapable of speaking the Queen's English. They just get a repeat performance. I regularly have to translate. I tell them of the language difficulty between me and Jim Cleaver. One weekend afternoon there's only the two of us in our room. Jim ends up saying, 'Do you realise, we're both British – and we can't understand a blind word the other's saying!'

The week flies in. I rise in the morning just as Mr Dainty is about to leave for work. After a wash and shave – I don't half miss my morning shower – Nancy watches sleepily as I dress in my uniform. I feel so mature, adult, as I button up my battledress jacket with its stripe, B flash and crossed rifles. Once again I think back to Uncle George. How I'd watch his every move as he donned his Marine's uniform preparatory to going out on the town. I now know exactly how he felt. Young, fit, part of a 'man's world'. Immortal.

It's Friday evening. Our last night out. Nancy's taking the train back to Scotland tomorrow.

All the lads had turned up, on their best behaviour, when offered the chance to meet Nancy. I want to finish her week's holiday on a bit of a high.

The White Lion in Beeston is a busy pub with a fairly large concert room. After the phenomenon of rock'n'roll a few years ago, something called 'skiffle' has been the big thing this last wee while. Lonnie Donegan seems to be the main man. It has also done wonders for guitar sales. Tea chests, too, are in great demand as lads who can't afford a guitar make themselves a 'base' with tea chest, broom shank and strings, to accompany their mates. Usually, in a year or less, the enthusiasm of the guitar players wanes as they realise they haven't got the skill or dedication needed to master the instrument. One of our gang, Pete Smith, has. Every evening his guitar comes out of his locker and for thirty minutes or so we listen to him practising his chords then, for anything up to an hour, he'll play and sing – often songs he's written himself. For the last few months he has teamed up with a couple of guys from other billets; 'Geordie' Batey, who plays drums, and 'Doug' from Dagenham, who also plays guitar. After daily practice sessions, usually in the drying room – which has an echo – for the last few months they've been getting themselves bookings in local pubs and clubs, cashing in on the continuing popularity of the skiffle craze. The reason I've chosen the White Lion is because 'our' trio are appearing.

On the Friday evening we get to the pub early to ensure we get a good table, one that's big enough. By nine o'clock the beer is flowing, the air is blue with smoke and sometimes discordant music, as a few of the early 'turns' display more energy than talent. Pete, Doug and Geordie are the main attraction and live up to their billing as they give their all and draw great applause. Their last number is a terrific version of 'Apache', the Shadows hit, which they have to immediately repeat when the audience demand an encore! It's a very enjoyable finish to Nancy's short holiday.

In the depot I'm now spending less time on a fork-lift and more on learning about the receipt, accounting and distribution of petrol, oil and lubricants. One evening a fortnight I have to remain in camp on call, in case any vehicles drop in for fuel. I have to let the gatekeeper know where I am at any given time when I'm 'on' – in the billet, NAAFI, or Corporal's Club. They always know where I am during the night. In bed. Not once are my slumbers disturbed. Sure beats the hell out of guard duty!

The refuelling point is, quite simply, a little petrol station. A small brick-built kiosk with windows on all sides, and two pumps on either side. I spend a lot of time in there training to be, basically, a petrol pump attendant who can also do the accounting. During the day it's run by two elderly civilians, Perce and Arnold, who turn out to be great characters. As I get to know and like them, I increasingly spend time in the kiosk just chatting to them. They are always fun to be around and are quite oblivious to the fact that everybody in the depot, military and civilian, look on them as a double act. I soon realise I'm privileged to be able to drop in there any time I want because I'm on the staff of the POL section. They're always pleased to see me, especially if I drop in when they're in a huff with one another. The two of them are Nottingham men to their fingertips and speak in a rich vernacular which is not unpleasant, and which I can, mercifully, understand.

I come striding over to the kiosk, open the door, and step inside. Perce looks up.

''Ello, me duck.' He has the broadsheet *Daily Express* opened wide, covering the table. He is engaged in his lifelong quest to 'beat the bookie'. Arnold is filling in some paperwork on top of a small filing cabinet as he can't get on the table. He gives me a smile.

'All right, me ode?'

'Aye, fine, lads.'

Perce has already gone back to the racing section. Without looking up he says, 'Make tha'sen a cuppa.' As I wait for the kettle to boil I look at Perce. He must be pushing seventy. As usual he's wearing his worn blue pinstripe three-piece suit. The ensemble is topped by a brown check cloth cap that doesn't go with it. A cigarette droops from his lips. There are notices everywhere saying, DANGER! NO SMOKING. As ever, he has one eye shut against the spiralling smoke. This has now become such an ingrained habit that on the rare occasions he studies the paper without a cigarette, he still tends to close that eye. After I've made my tea, I usually stand and watch the ever-lengthening stalactite of ash gather on Perce's fag. No matter what he does – take a draw, clear his throat, write something down – it stays put. By the time three quarters of the cigarette has turned to ash I can hardly stand the tension. I'm now unable to take my eyes from it. It droops at an increased angle. Surely collapse is imminent? What happened to gravity? At last it falls off. In a silent avalanche it crashes down the slope of his waistcoat, breaks into a flurry of smaller bits, and leaves a trail all the way to his trousers. The dapper Arnold tuts. Perce doesn't even look, he knows what trajectory it will have taken. He gives three or four perfunctory brushes with his hand, rubbing more into waistcoat and trousers than off them. Slowly but surely, the blue pinstripe is turning to charcoal gray.

Arnold is also in his late sixties. He has a good head of white hair, is of stocky build, and usually wears a tidy brown wool sports jacket and cavalry twill trousers. Both have worked at the depot for years. Perce started some months before Arnold and is therefore, to Arnold's chagrin, 'in charge'. When I get to know him better I find that Arnold has a great sadness in his life. His only son died of cancer while an art student at university. One day he brings in a portfolio of his lad's work. All free-hand drawings, studies of hands, feet and torsos, they are beautifully executed in the classical style. After more than twenty years, Arnold's loss is still strong.

Perce laboriously writes his bet out. 'Will tha joost hang abaht for a few minutes whilst ah goes and puts this bet on, me duck?'

'Aye, nae bother, Perce.'

Enjoying Life

Arnold and I watch as he toddles off in his rolling, leaning forward gait, in search of the depot's illegal bookmaker.

'Silly old blighter!' says Arnold. 'Money that man's wasted on t'orses. Could've bought 'is own bleeding stables by now.'

I just laugh. They are great pals and work well together. But whenever one is absent, the other one always runs him down. They're like an old married couple at times.

GOT *Some In!*

I'm due for demob 7 January 1961, and all of a sudden it's looming. Yet at the same time I'm still attracted to the idea of signing on. Then the attraction increases.

'Major Gunn wants to see you, corporal.' Corporal Eccleston has found me talking to Perce and Arnold at the pumps.

'Right now?'

'Yeah.'

'Well, ah'd better away and see what old Bang Bang wants.'

'Oh it'll be nowt o' trouble,' says Perce. This causes the ash to fall off the end of his Capstan.

'Now how duss thee know?' asks Arnold, 'Thee's got nowt ter do whay it.'

'He's a good lad, our Jock. That's how ah knows. Ain't ya, me duck?'

'As far as a know, Perce.'

'There thee is. See! Ah told tha so.'

Arnold shakes his head, leans on the filing cabinet and looks out the window.

A few minutes later I'm entering the battalion office. It's very much *déjà vu*. Company clerk, desk, typewriter. But this time he's reading a book instead of *Tit Bits*. It's a Hank Jansen detective thriller. They're supposed to be 'risqué'. Huh! About as sexy as Keyhole Kate in the *Dandy*. Or was it the *Beano*? Jeez, I'm beginning to forget who appeared in what comic. Stokoe will know. He still gets them every week.

I wonder what the major wants? Probably just because I'm due out. Thank me for my service, something like that. I'll soon find out.

'Just knock and go in.'

I do. Then I throw up a smart salute. 'Good afternoon, sir. Lance Corporal Douglas.'

'Good afternoon. Just take a seat, Corporal.'

A seat? I didn't get a seat last time. Definitely must be the old, 'Thanks and goodbye'.

The major sits back, visibly relaxes. 'When are you due for discharge, son?'

'Seventh of January, sir.'

'How have you found the army?'

I smile. 'Well, I don't think National Servicemen are supposed to say this, sir, but I'm getting to quite enjoy it. In some ways, the way of life suits me.'

He opens what must be my file. He flicks through two or three pages, now and again stops to read. He closes it, sits back. 'Everybody who has had anything to do with you here at the depot – senior NCOs, civilian foremen – all give good reports on your ability, reliability, your enthusiasm,' he taps the file. 'These recommendations are as good as any I've read.'

I feel myself blush. 'Oh, well, I just enjoy my job, sir. And ah like the people ah work with.'

'Well, I'm going to make you an offer, Corporal. I don't need an answer right away.' He leans forward. 'IF you were to sign on as a regular, I guarantee you that you'll have your second stripe up by February! I'd like you to go away now and give that prospect some thought.'

'Right. Thank you very much, sir.' I stand up, come to attention, salute and go on my way. My head is buzzing with all sorts of thoughts. I make my way to Titch's paint store.

As I enter the former shelter, Titch and Old Jack are having – what a surprise! – mugs of milky instant coffee. The kettle is switched on again.

'I've just been to see old Bang Bang there. He sent for me.' The kettle has swiftly boiled, I begin making a brew. 'He says if I sign on ah'll have my second tape up by February.'

'You ain't gonna fall for that one, are yah?'

'Well, ah must be honest. It's tempting. If ah hadn't got married, I'd definitely sign on. Remember, ah was just staying in digs before ah got called-up.'

'Yeah, I know. But fuckin' hell, Robert. Signing on!' He screws up his face in distaste.

I look at Jack. 'Every National Serviceman feels obliged tae run down the army whenever he gets the opportunity. You're not supposed tae say a word in its favour.' I wink at Jack, then look at Titch. 'Well ah'm gonny say it . . . AH LIKE THE ARMY!'

'Yeeeuch!' is his considered reply.

As is the norm when the festive season arrives, all the English lads get leave for Christmas and the Jocks cover the guards and other essential duties. When they return on 27 December things are back to normal for a few days until, on the 30th, all the Jocks, as Butch puts it, 'head for Jockland'.

On Christmas morning around six-thirty a.m. all is quiet in our billet. There's only three or four of us in residence. There comes a clattering of boots, voices. Half the overhead lights are switched on and for a dreadful moment I think I'm back in basic training! I manage to raise my head. The Pride of Wales, Sergeant Briggs, accompanied by Sergeant McKay, plus a kitchen orderly carrying a tea urn have just come in. The two sergeants are wearing their No. 1 dress uniform!

'Merry Christmas, bonny boys!' says Briggs. 'Anyone for a drop of "gunfire"?' asks McKay. Putting two and two together I assume that gunfire, whatever it is, is in the urn. We get our pint mugs out of our lockers and I watch as Briggs takes hold of the urn and fills them all to the brim. It looks like tea. I raise mine to my lips. 'Mmmmm!' It smells good. I take a sip. 'Aw! Sarge, that's gorgeous. What is it?'

'Hot sweet tea – and a goodly measure of Navy Rum, boyo.'

'I don't remember getting woke up for this last Christmas morning. What's it all about?'

'It's a drink you get quite often in "the field" (active service), but in peacetime it's a tradition that some of the sergeants put on their number ones and come round the billets serving it to those who can't get home for Christmas. Dispensing a bit of good cheer, bonny boys.'

'Is it an old tradition, or new?'

'Oh, 'tis old. Don't know how old, mind you. But I reckon it'll go back to Victorian times.'

'Right, anybody want a top-up afore we go?' McKay looks around. We all say we're fine.

'All the best, then, lads. Let's go.'

In another clatter of boots the trio leave, switching off the main lights as they go. One or two of us switch on our bedlights. A sleepy quietness descends on the barrack room.

'This is bloody lovely,' says Stokoe, forgetting to break wind.

I prop my pillows against the wall and lean back. 'Merry Christmas, chaps.' We all wish each other the compliments of the season. Nancy will still be in bed, sound asleep. I don't think Auld Sanny will be round this morning with the gunfire. Jeez. This tea and dark rum is lush. I wonder why I never got it last year? Was I on guard? The thought comes into my mind. A fortnight from now I'll no longer be in the army. There's a click as somebody switches off their bedlight. Yeah, me too. I switch mine off, then snuggle down under the covers. I have a nice warm glow from head to toe. That was a nice surprise, seeing the sergeants coming into the billet on Christmas morning. I begin to doze off . . . once you've finished basic, the army's not bad at all.

I've been giving plenty of thought to the major's offer. I don't think I'll sign on. Nancy and I have been married nearly eighteen months now, and we've hardly spent any time together. No. If I wasn't married I'd sign on in a minute. But I fancy a bit of married life. Going to work, coming home to my wife, having my dinner, feet up watching telly. Even though we'll have to be staying with her ma and da for goodness knows how long, I still fancy being a civvy again. A married civvy.

On 27 December I visit the battalion office to fix up my New Year leave. I get a ninety-six-hour pass and I've got a few days leave to come from my leave allowance. And I've got a railway warrant to come. Great! I go on leave on 30 December – and don't come back until 4 January. Three days later I'll be off back home again – for good! As I'm talking to the clerk, the adjutant comes out of his office. He's been listening to our conversation.

'When are you due for discharge, Corporal?'

'Seventh January, sir.'

'And you're back off leave on the fourth?'

'Yes, sir.'

'That's a long trip to make for just three days, then to have to go all the way back up north again.' He turns to the clerk. 'Make out his discharge papers in advance and get him to sign them. When you leave on the thirtieth, hand all your kit in at the QM stores. Essentially, that'll be you discharged.'

'Jeez! That's very good of you. Thank you very much, sir.'

'It's just common sense.'

I go back to the billet and tell the lads. 'Right,' says Butch, 'We'd better get your demob party organised. Pronto!'

It's the evening of 29 December. I'm sitting in the White Lion at Beeston surrounded by Our Gang and trying to work out how it all came about so quickly. 'Do you realise, boys, I'm the first of us to go – and in just six weeks we'll ALL be back in civvy street.'

'Except for me,' says Hinchie, 'I've still got another two weeks after Butch goes. I'm the last.'

'Fookin' 'ell!' says Butch, 'Just imagine being in that billet without us, Hinch. We're all gone, nothing but sprogs left who 'ardly knows yah.' He raises his pint of scrumpy and looks around.

'Ah thinks thoo'll top thaself, Hinchie. It'll be the loneliness.'

'Piss off!' says Hinchcliffe. 'The peace and quiet will be lovely. Even Stokoe will be gone.'

'Ah'll grant yer, that's a foochin' blessing,' says Stan.

'Ah suppose, really, we should have asked him here tonight,' I say.

'WHAT!' says Stan. 'Yer joking. Yer can't ask a dirty-arsed git like that to come out in civilised company!'

Pete speaks up, 'Just think – some poor innocent will come into that billet and take over that bed,' he looks around, 'with THAT mattress. He'll lie there every night having these terrible dreams—'

Butch interrupts, 'And they'll always be the same – the same recurring nightmare – he's being chased and gets cornered down a lane, and shot wi' shit!' We begin to get the giggles. There now ensues a five-minute session in which we try to outdo each other with a plot for a horror story called 'The Case of the Haunted Mattress'! By the end of it we're sore laughing.

Eventually order is restored. After a few more drinks we move on to another level; the 'remember when?' section. The smoky, beery, companionable atmosphere – plus the three pints of Guinness I've had – are making me sentimental. Just look at them. Titch Gurney, Butch Palmer, Gordon Hinchcliffe, Pete Smith, Stan Deakin. We're all in our early twenties. We've been pals, good pals, for around twenty months. I nod and smile and only half-listen. What I'm doing is drinking in my last look at them. My mates. No, my ARMY mates. That's the difference. I've grown up listening to men, whether uncles or men I've worked with, telling tales about 'Me and my mate', 'Me and my 'oppo.' What is it about mates in the forces? It's got to be because you're together twenty-four hours a day. You work, eat, and sleep together, go out on the batter together. That's what does it. As a kid you play with your childhood pals, but at the end of the day you go home to your own house, your family. In the army, the guys in the billet, especially the ones you pal up with, they almost become your family. I look again at their faces; young, eager, shiny with perspiration because the pub's warm. After tomorrow I might never see these guys again. There's a good chance this will be the last time.

'Looking a bit pensive, Doug,' Hinchie's looking closely at me. He's as sharp as a tack, Hinchie. He'll have an idea what's going through my mind.

'So you're definitely not gonna sign on, then?' says Titch.

'Ah'll never speak to 'im again if he duss,' announces Butch, his chin jutting out.

I look at him. Got to get myself out of this maudlin mood. I point at Butch. 'That bugger is *definitely* Desperate Dan's secret love child. He's got the family chin!' Everybody laughs.

'Ah'll fookin' chin thoo in a minute, Scotch twatbag!' is Butch's response. 'Anyway,' he adds, 'Ah'll tell thuss why he's not signing on,' he points at me. 'He's been married to Nancy 'bout a year and a half, only slept with her about twenty times. That's why he's not signing on.' The chin juts out even further. 'Ooooh, ah'll bet he's on nest every night of week for a month when he gets 'ome. Poor lass, she'll be limping into work every morning.' We all laugh. Butch sees off his pint of scrumpy. 'Who's ont' bell?'

Pete puts on his ultra-posh southern accent. 'Really! I find this lascivious interest in the love life of one's fellows quite beyond the pale!'

'What the fuch's he on about?' says Stan.

For the last time I lie in the dark in an army billet and listen to the duty bugler play Last Post. I feel my eyes fill with tears. Then it comes to me. Can I trust myself to speak?

Late summer 1959. From the left: Pete Smith;
Gordon Hinchcliffe; Stan Deakin;
Butch Palmer; unknown; self; Titch Gurney.

'LADS! I'd like to say something.' Out of the darkness comes
solicitous voices. 'What, mate?'
'Yeah, Doog.'
'We're listening, pal.'
'GET SOME IN YAH BASTARDS!'

Civvy Street

As the train takes me north, back to Scotland, I've plenty to think about. When I left Glasgow, those two long years ago, I was a single man, nineteen coming on twenty, living in digs. I'll be twenty-two in a few weeks' time. I'm married, and we'll be staying with Nancy's parents – 'home' to her, but in a way, like digs to me. I now have to find a job. Not quite so easy in West Lothian, where unemployment is high. Even so, I feel quite confident that something will turn up. But what? I'm fit enough to take a labouring job if necessary, and know I have the brains to quickly learn and adapt if a semi-skilled position comes up. I also have my fork-lift truck licence. I sneak another look at the reference I've been given in my army discharge book.

'L/cpl Douglas has been employed in the transport section of a Central Ordnance Depot. He has dealt with the receipt, issue and accounting of POL. He works hard and has carried out his duties efficiently and with the minimum of supervision. Is not afraid to accept responsibility and should develop into a good supervisor.' My 'Military Conduct' is given as 'Very Good'. There's no mention of my marksman's badge. I suppose there isn't much call for snipers in civvy street. On the whole I'm not a bad prospect for a potential employer. I learn quickly, I'm conscientious. I think the army's comments will stand me in good stead – if I get as far as an interview.

As usual, I spend the next six hours on the main line express to Edinburgh, reading, thinking and dozing. The train always has a soporific effect on me. The gentle swaying and clickety-clack of wheels regularly has me nodding off. In between times I think about the future. It's as if this long journey is a transition. I came aboard the train at Nottingham as a soldier. I'll step off it in Edinburgh as a civilian. During the journey I'll have to come to terms with that. When I set foot on that platform in Waverley station I hope to be tuned in.

My thoughts aren't all about the future. Now and again I wonder if I should have taken the major up on his offer. I suppose it was quite flattering; I'd obviously been seen as a likely lad. It certainly would've been grand. Just turned twenty-three and a full corporal. How long would it have taken me to get my third stripe? We'll never know. I somehow feel that if I'd signed on for another three years, or even five, there would've been times I'd have felt trapped. Just like I had in the Boys' Service. If you get fed up with a job, you can pack it in. Not in the army. Once you've signed on you have to do your time.

As I watch the apparently inexhaustable line of telegraph poles by the track whizz by, my thoughts turn to my mates. They're seeming further and further away. In my mind's eye I can picture what's going on at Chilwell right at this moment . . . the burly figure of Butch will be sitting astride his fork-lift as he chats away to the civvies he's working with today. Now and again that big booming laugh will ring out. I look at my watch. Titch will be down the shelter with Jack. Probably on their third cup of Nescafé. Titch and I are really good mates. For twenty months we had adjoining bed-spaces. We went into fits of laughter at the stupidest things. Like the time I tried to describe this corporal who'd come looking for him.

'It was Lance Corporal Hutchinson, you know him.'

He shakes his head. 'Don't know 'im by name. Whass he like, then?'

'Yes you do. He's very fair. Wears rimless glasses. Real fusspot, always fiddling on, things have to be just right.'

'Ohhhh! You mean MARY Hutchinson!' For the next ten minutes we were helpless.

Yeah, I'm going to miss them all. Pete Smith, who says he's determined to make it as a singer. Gordon Hinchcliffe, Stan Deakin. But especially Titch and Butch. I've written down Titch's address in Benson, Oxfordshire and Butch's at Bilton, near Rugby. We've promised we'll keep in touch. Just a few weeks and they'll be out, too.

I take to staring out the window again. This is it, kid. You've done your two years. I'd promised myself I'd give the army 'a good go'. There's no doubt about it, I kept that promise. I now feel I've made up for that wasted nine months in the RAF.

I get into Seafield shortly after Nancy arrives home from the factory. It's 30 December 1960. Everybody gets a kiss – except Auld Sanny. We all sit round the kitchen table with its pale green Formica top. The bright overhead light shines down. The fire in the small grate is still chuckling away to itself. It seems no time since I was sitting here thinking. 'I'll be away to the army next week'. Now here I am, it's over. Not only that, I'm married to Nancy now. And I'm going to be living here. Auld Sanny's in great form. 'Yah bugger! We've hud peace'n' quiet here fur the last twa years, except when ye wiz oan leave, could ye no' huv taken the Major's offer and signed oan?' He goes into kinks at his own joke.

'Eh, poor laddie. He's no' oot the army five meenits.' Beenie busies herself putting the last touches to the dinner.

'Never mind, Ma,' I say, 'ah've got some more bad news for him. Ah don't have tae go back tae camp after the New Year for ma last few days. They've given me ma discharge. Ah'm oot for good!'

'Oh, that's great!' says Nancy. 'We can celebrate Ne'erday knowing you're finished wi' the army.'

Sanny shakes his head in mock sorrow. 'Well, ah micht as well go tae ma bed before the bells the morra nicht.' He gives me a playful poke in the ribs. 'Mind, the morra is just the thirty-first – you've time tae go oot and start lookin' for a job before the businesses shut doon for the holidays!'

'Huv ye ever heard the like,' says Ma, 'Is that no' the awfiest man?'

'Whit?' says Sanny, trying not to laugh. 'He need'ny think ah'm gonny be keepin' him.'

'Ye could'nae keep pigeons!' says Nancy.

'Oh, well. Tae think ah was gonny take him up tae the Seafield Inn for a wee brandy or two tae celebrate ma demob. Ah don't suppose he'll want tae go wi'—'

He interrupts me. 'Wiz ye gonny gie me a wee treat, son? That wid be nice.' he strokes my shoulder.

'Is that no' a twa-faced auld devil,' says Beenie. We all kill ourselves laughing.

Once again, just for a second, it's almost *déjà vu* as I recall sitting here for what was the last time before I went into the army.

It's all behind me now. It's done. I'm home for good.

Getting a Start

After a year and a half Nancy and I can now start living as a married couple. Full-time. Up until now, the longest spell we've been together is when I've taken a week's leave. When we married, a year past July, Nancy put our names down for a council house – but only in Seafield. We don't want one anywhere else. God knows how long that'll take. Could be three or four years. Longer.

The first thing on the agenda is a job. There's the pit and the railway. There's only vacancies on the railway now and again. Plenty of jobs going in the pits, but Nancy would rather I try for something else.

On the first Friday in January, the weekly *West Lothian Courier* comes through the door. I immediately turn to the 'Situations Vacant'. 'Here's a job might suit me!'

Beenie is pottering round the house as usual. 'Whit's that?'

'The Gas Board in Bathgate has a vacancy for a meter reader collector. Nine 'til five Monday tae Friday, nine 'til twelve on Saturdays. That would be a good, steady job.'

'Oh, aye. Jobs like that dinnae come up very often.'

I rise from the chair. 'Aye, it'll be superannuated, too. I'll get a letter written off right now.'

'There'll be plenty of folk after that,' says Beenie.

Ten days later, wearing my best (only) suit and carrying my army discharge certificate with its good reference, I present myself at the small Scottish Gas Board office and depot in Waverley Street, Bathgate. There are already seven or eight men, of various ages, waiting to be interviewed. There's a doctor's waiting room atmosphere as we all sit in silence. The occasional cough shatters it. There's only one post. We know we're all in competition for it. The odd stilted conversation is started but soon peters out, probably because everybody is listening. At last my name is called.

A thin little woman with glasses gives me a smile, then leads me through a large room and shows me into a small office, shutting the door behind me. A short, stocky man with white hair half rises. 'I'm Mr Doull, I'm the depot manager. He points to a man beside him. 'This Is Mr McNeice, the area manager.' We both say 'hello'. I thought names like 'McNeice' only issued from the pen of A.J. Cronin. His Scottish 'doctor sagas' were full of Dr McFinstries and Mrs McNestrys and such like. Mr McNeice is plump, well groomed. I'd imagine he enjoys his position. Then again, why shouldn't he? He hands me a clipboard. So, they've followed me from the army, have they? 'There are a few calculations to be made on that sheet of paper. Would you do them, please.' Mr Doull gives me a brand new pencil with 'Scottish Gas Board' printed along its side. The sums are simple. 'The reading on a meter three months ago was 19338. The reading today is 19642. How many units have been used? If the price of a unit is 2d, and the Standing Charge for the quarter is £1.2/6d, what is the total bill?' There are a few along these lines. Mercifully I've always been good at arithmetic. I work them out in minutes – and double-check them. I hand the clipboard back to Mr McNeice. Thank God there wasn't any algebra. It would have been a short interview. Thanks to Mr Forshaw, I and quite a few of my classmates at secondary school never even got past 'first principles' of algebra. It will always be a mystery to me. I sometimes wonder what the point of it is. Who uses it? Research chemists or somebody?

'I believe you're just out of the army, Mr Douglas.'

'Yes, sir.'

'What did you think of it?'

I laugh. 'Well, it seems to go against the grain for a National Serviceman to say this. I quite enjoyed it.'

'Fine. I think that's about it, Mr Douglas. You'll hear from us in about ten days, one way or the other. Is there anything you'd like to ask?'

'No, thank you. The interview's been pretty straightforward. I'm obviously just going to hope I'm successful.'

'Thank you very much, Mr Douglas.'

'Thank you. Bye.'

During the next week I pay another visit to Bathgate. As my ration money and pay ran out I've signed on at the labour exchange. I have a look at the board to see what jobs are available if I don't get the Gas Board one. The words 'crap' and 'underpaid' come to mind. I sure hope something better comes along. Anyway, if push comes to shove I'll just have to go back to the pit. I won't really mind. The money's good. I'm old enough to work on the face now.

Just over a week after my interview the long white envelope with 'Scottish Gas Board' on it lands on the hall floor. Nancy's already left for work. Ma hands it to me. I use my table knife to slit it open – then pause. 'Well, here goes, Ma.' She watches as I slip it out the envelope and unfold it. My eyes race over the first paragraph . . .

Dear Sir,

With reference to your application and subsequent interview, I now have much pleasure in offering you the above appointment, at a commencing salary of £530 per annum . . .

'Ah've got it, Ma!' I feel excited, pleased, relieved, all at once.

'Oh! That's grand. That's you got a good, steady job. Nancy will be fair pleased.'

I try to calm myself so's I can read, and make sense, of the rest of the letter. 'I start next Monday at the Bathgate Depot.'

'Ah'll put the kettle on. There's the baker's van jist pulled up. We'll have a cup of tea and a cake tae celebrate.'

On Monday 23 January 1961, I catch the workers' bus into Bathgate and present myself, once more, at the little yard which is the Gas Board's depot in Waverley Street. As I enter the stone-built cottage that is the office, I can hear laughter and voices. Behind the counter in the big room a few men are sitting at a table. Most of them are indulging in that perennial/traditional Scottish custom – the post mortem of Saturday's football. Sometimes this happens twice a week if 'the boys' have had a game on the Wednesday night. I got used to it when I'd worked for the Clyde Trust.

The only one I recognise amongst the half-dozen men is John Doull. Originally from Dalbeattie in south-west Scotland, John is a bachelor with a liking for good whisky – as his ruddy complexion testifies. John, nominally, runs the office. He stands listening to the banter from the men at the table. Flitting about in the background is the one who really runs the office, Jessie Gardener, the woman who'd ushered me in for my interview. If central casting had Jessie on their files she'd almost certainly be listed thus: TYPE: Middle-aged spinster. Thin. Wears spectacles. They probably wouldn't have been interested in: lives with ageing parents, is a bundle of energy, deadly efficient, and belying her staid looks, good-natured and full of fun.

Jessie spots me and comes over to the counter. As she does so, John also sees me.

'Lads! Lads! Bit of order, please.' The hubbub lessens. 'Eh, this is oor new start, eh, Robert Douglas.' I do my initial blush. Lately I find I don't blush as much as I used to. Almost certainly because my acne isn't quite as virulent as it was. The men at the table say 'Hello' then get back to dissecting Saturday's football. Jessie gives me a big smile as John introduces her properly. She lifts the flap to allow me past the counter, then sticks her hand out. 'Hello, so you're joining us, are you?' We shake. Probably in her late forties, just over five feet tall, her dark hair set in an almost thirties style, Jessie wears a bright floral buttoned-up smock. She pushes her horn-rimmed specs back up on her nose with one finger. 'Och, ah'm sure you'll soon fit in. It's time we had some young blood.'

John smiles. He points at Jessie. 'Eh, this is my eh, right-hand woman.' For the first time since I met him at my interview I notice he has a slight stammer. Somehow it adds to what he says. Especially if he's trying to be funny, it makes it even funnier – just like Patrick Campbell on TV with his affected stammer. A tall, red-headed man rises from the table and comes over.

'Hello, ah'm Robert Meek.' He offers his hand. 'Never mind this auld reprobate here' – he puts a hand on John's shoulder – 'saying "Jessie's ma right-hand woman" – she's his right-AND left-hand woman. Place wid fall tae bits if it was'nae for Jessie. Widn't it, hen?'

'Och away wi' ye!' says Jessie. She goes back to her desk and filing cabinets.

John looks around, bewildered, in the way Jack Benny the American comedian would. 'Eh, here, if ye don't mind – ah resemble, eh, resent that!'

'C'mon, ah'll introduce ye tae this bunch o' hooligans ower here. Aw' we ever get, especially oan a Monday, is fitba, fitba, fitba.' Robert Meek ushers me over to the table. 'Are ye a fan?'

'Can't stand the bloody game,' I say, with a smile.

He laughs out loud. 'Good man, yerself! Ah've only a passing interest in it, but some o' them here eat, sleep and drink it. Best of order, lads, best of order! This is, as ye've heard, Robert Douglas.' He points at them in turn. 'This is Charlie, Harry, Frank and Peter.' They all say 'Hello' again then get back to the business of the day. 'Where was ah?' Peter pauses for a second. 'Aye, ah'm no' kidding, talk aboot luck. We hud ten shots at goal, only scored wance. They hud three shots at goal – put every wan o' them away! We ootplayed them, shut them oot, they only get three shots and they win the bloody game. Talk aboot luck!' He looks at me.

'Are ye a fitba fan, Robert?'

''Fraid not. Dis'nae interest me.'

'Zat no' terrible? Dis'nae like fitba.' The conversation goes on for a few more minutes. When he talks about football, especially 'his' Rangers, Peter is voluble.

'Right, lads!' John Doull looks pointedly at his watch. 'Time youse, eh, were getting oot and, eh, aboot.' The meter reader/collectors – I bring the number up to six – rise and start getting customers' cards, receipts, carbon paper, cash sheets, money bags, and their Gladstone Bags together. In the background Jessie's already been hard at it for the last half-hour, arranging for repair men to call, making appointments for 'special readings' and fielding phone calls for any of the hundred-and-one problems, requests or faults that will come in today. Already I'm beginning to get a feel for the place. John, Jessie, and Robert Meek have made me feel welcome. The rest of them are football fans – it'll probably be tomorrow before they notice there's a new man. I soon come to realise how highly regarded John and Jessie are by the staff. At first glance I like the look of the small team I'll be working with. There are also a few engineers and fitters at the depot, located in another building in the yard, but our paths only cross now and again.

'Eh, Robert, ah'm going to put ye with Harry for the two or three weeks that you'll, eh, need tae learn aboot the slot meters.' Harry comes over and shakes hands. In his late forties, Harry Dougan is a Bathgate man and, like John, a lifelong bachelor. He proves to be a quiet, non-swearing, devout Catholic who teaches me well. He has a vague likeness – in manner and looks – to the actor Alastair Sim. He is looked on as being rather dour. If anyone has a blue joke to tell, they always wait until Harry's out the road.

While he trains me, I'm not issued with any of the kit that

readers/collectors need. I just use Harry's gear when, after a few days, I tentatively start emptying and working out the bills on the slot meters. I pick it up quickly and less than a fortnight later Harry announces that I'm ready to go it alone. Being with Harry every day lets me discover he's not quite as dour as folk think. He has a pawky sense of humour, though it's sometimes hard to find.

A few days after I start, John Doull boosts my ego. 'Do you know, eh, how many applicants there were for that job, eh, Robert?'

'No, I never heard.'

'Eh, ninety-two.'

'Jeez! Was there?'

Well, I might not be 'one in a hundred', but that's pretty near.

It's All Happening

There isn't just a new job to celebrate. As we'd brought in the New Year, 1961, Nancy told me she might be pregnant. By the end of January it's definite. Time to tell her parents. They're as delighted as we are, even though it's many a year since early-morning feeds and a washing line full of nappies was the order of the day at Cousland Crescent. Nancy's sister, Betty, who lives at the next house down the hill, already has a daughter, Sandra.

As the new year ambles along and I settle into my job, discussions are held. Nancy will carry on working as late as she can at Manclarks. As head supervisor the job isn't physically demanding, so hopefully there shouldn't be a problem. After the baby's born she'll return to work; her mother's quite happy to look after the bairn.

Nancy attends the antenatal clinic for all the tests and we're soon given a date. The middle of August. Jeez, I'm going to be a daddy! I write to my father to let him know he's about to become a grandfather. He says he's pleased. I, of course, have to tell my workmates and am subject to all the usual kidding on and congratulations that such an announcement brings.

'How did that happen?' Peter looks at me as we sit round the table with our morning tea.

'Huv you been daeing dirty things tae that lassie?' asks Frank.

'Who? Me? Never laid a glove oan her.' In the background, Jessie giggles away to herself.

Robert Meek looks at John Doull. 'Here, John. If there's any overtime going make sure this lad's first oan the list. Fatherhood dis'nae come cheap, he'll be needing aw' the money he can get.'

Nancy and I decide we'll make the best of what time we have left before she starts showing. As we both love dancing we start having quite a few Saturday nights at the Bathgate Palais, only calling a halt when she can't get into her dresses and skirts anymore. From then on, it's nights at the pictures.

I'm quite excited at the thought of becoming a father. I feel a great tenderness toward Nancy. She's pregnant. She has my baby, our child, inside her. August seems a long way away. I wish it was here. What will it be? I really have no preference. A wee boy would be great – so would a wee lassie. If it were possible for me to make a choice right now, I couldn't. I'll very happily take what comes. There's one thing for certain – I'll be a better father than mine ever was.

As winter lets go and becomes spring, Nancy is most certainly pregnant. Summer takes over and June seems to last for ever. At last it's July. I can now say, 'We're expecting our first baby. Next month!'

Four Quarters

The reading of meters is not a problem. We're in and out the premises fairly quickly. Slots take a lot longer. We have to empty the meter, count the money, work out the bill, then take the sum required to cover it. What's left over, known as the rebate, goes to the customer. In 1961 gas is fairly cheap. Many of our customers, especially pensioners, still have 'penny in the slot' meters and insert about three pounds or so in a quarter. Families with one or two kids have mostly 'shilling' (five pence) meters fitted, and might put in eight or nine pounds during the winter quarter. The company has recently started installing 'two bob' (ten pence) meters into the homes of really heavy users. We can take as much as twenty pounds out of one of them in the winter!

With the amount of coins we collect – especially the large, heavy pennies – Charlie comes round twice during the morning, and once in the afternoon, to empty our Gladstone bags into the safe in the back of the van. As we empty our meters, we 'bag' the money in the appropriate bank money bags so as it's all ready for him.

As I kid I used to be fascinated watching shop assistants cashing up near the end of the day. Emptying an avalanche of coins onto the counter and, fingers flying, counting and stacking them prior to putting them into different coloured strong paper bags with '£1: IN PENNIES' or '£5: IN SHILLINGS' on them. Now it's my turn.

With a satisfying swishhhhh, seven or eight pounds in shillings spills out and covers half the kitchen table. The customers' kids go, 'Wowww!' as this cornucopia, like pirates' treasure, flows then quickly halts. They watch as I get to work, whisking the coins unerringly, two at a time, into my palm then onto the table in stacks. I glance at their wide eyes – which never once leave the coins – and see myself not so long ago, watching the girls in Andrew Cochrane's the grocer on Maryhill Road as they cashed up on the marble-topped counter.

I love going into the depot in the morning. Most of the guys come in early for a cuppa before we go out. John sorts out the day's work, a mixture of meter reading and slots. He gives it to Charlie who then dishes it out to us. Peter Halliday, the Rangers fan, is usually the first voice to be heard as you approach the door. It's usually football. If it's not football it's politics; Peter is somewhere to the right of Genghis Khan. Stockily built, balding, speaking quickly as well as loudly, Peter usually holds the floor. If he isn't holding forth about his usual two topics he'll be having a moan. Frank is thin, like a whippet, and wears his cloth bunnet indoors and out. He could be mistaken for a retired jockey. He speaks even faster than Peter – but with the volume turned down. Charlie Fleming is plump, rosy-cheeked, wears horn-rimmed specs, and is quietly spoken. Harry Dougan, as described, is also fairly quiet. Robert Meek is the life and soul of the team. He loves company, conversation, and laughing. He sees the best in everybody, though he's not averse to a little bit of gossip – especially if he's the first with the news, and can melodramatically enlighten the rest of us. With the exception of John Doull, they're all in their forties. At twenty-two I'm very much the junior. Although she looks, and most certainly is, a prim little spinster, Wee Jessie is full of life and fun. It's obvious she likes being the only woman amongst so many men and loves to be included in the banter. Because we all know our jobs and are good at them, everything runs at a leisurely pace. It's a good place to work.

We're ready to head out for the day's calls. The six of us pile into the 1950s Ford 'ten hundredweight' green van with its black mudguards. It's the same routine every morning. Charlie drives. Harry, as next senior, has the front passenger seat. The remaining four of us sit in the back on low wooden benches, facing one another. Off we go to Armadale or Fauldhouse, West Calder or Whitburn, or any one of the small mining villages dotted around West Lothian. If we're working less than 3 miles from Bathgate, Charlie picks us up at lunchtime and brings us into the depot for our piece. If we're more than 3 miles away we're given a meal allowance of five shillings (twenty-five pence). Charlie then picks us up and takes us to any one of a number of cafés or cheap restaurants or, if we're in the vicinity, a nearby temperance hotel. There we'll have the 'Businessman's Lunch'. As a counter to the drunkeness of Victorian Britain, the temperance movement came into being. Strongly connected with the church, the idea was to show people, mostly the poor, the error of their ways. Later someone had the idea of setting up temperance hotels. Exactly the same as any other hotel, except no liquor is sold, or tolerated, on the premises.

I like the rather formal temperance hotels, with their air of faded gentility. Feeling somehow as if I'm on a day trip, I sit with the rest of the squad in the old-fashioned dining room. The conversation round the damask covered table with its silver-plated cutlery is always subdued. Gliding into the room come two black and white clad silver service waitresses, of indeterminate age, complete with lace 'fripperies' on their heads. It's all very 1930s – maybe earlier. When we've finished our three-course meal, Charlie pays for it from the expenses John gave him that morning. It's all very civilised.

Once I'm fully trained and working on my own, I soon find there are a couple of lucrative extras to the job. A large number of 'heavy users' amongst the slot customers often give you a two- or three-shilling tip when they've had a rebate of three or four pounds. Many more ask you to set their meter higher than the official setting. This means they're putting in more money than necessary – but get it back as a big rebate when the meter's emptied. Because the extra money means there's all the more to count, most will say, 'Here's a few bob for your trouble.' This can be as much as five shillings if they have a lot back. Another tip, once more as compensation for extra work incurred, is from folk who insert sixpences into their meter to save them up. The sixpence coin is too small to register, it just falls into the money box. Once the coin is in the meter they can't get at it until the collector calls. Technically they shouldn't be putting these 'foreign objects' into the meter. We turn a blind eye to them using it as a savings bank. When we empty it we have to flick these sixpences to one side so's we can count the shillings or two bobs. Once more, for causing us some trouble, most of them will give us two or three shillings as a thank you. By the end of the week, we nearly all go home with up to three pounds in tips to supplement the nine pounds plus we get in wages. A welcome, tax-free bonus!

Both Doing Well

'Aye, that's her started her labour!' Nancy's ma is cool, calm and quite relaxed. Well, she's had four of her own so she should know what she's talking about. Nancy also seems quite calm. Probably because her mother's with her. Jeez-oh, wish I was as laid back as them. I tell myself everything will be all right. She's had a trouble-free pregnancy. Because it's her first, she'll be going into the maternity ward at Bangour Hospital.

'So is it time tae ring for the ambulance?' I look anxiously at Ma.

She tuts. 'Plenty time. This is jist the very first stages. Don't get yourself aw' worried. We'll have her intae the hospital well before her time.'

I try and talk to Nancy as if everything's normal. Trouble is, now and again she'll give a little wince as another contraction comes along. It's been great fun these last couple of months as the baby's movements, then kicks, get stronger and stronger. All the usual jokes like, 'With a kick like that it's got to be a boy,' have been trotted out. Then, of course, there's the old wives tales . . . 'Oh, if your bump is high, then it's a boy. If it's low, it's a girl.' Or is it the other way about? I can never remember. Anyway, we'll soon find out.

At last it's time for the ambulance to be sent for. Sandy Lang, the much respected local GP, has popped in. After examining Nancy he's suggested it's now time she was away to Bangour. Things are moving. In more ways than one!

*   *   *

Now she's in the maternity ward I feel a lot better about things. I can pace up and down the corridor, or sit *not* reading the magazine I'm holding. A couple of hours after admission, the nurse who received Nancy into the ward comes out of a door and heads toward us, smiling.

'Everything's gone as expected. Mrs Douglas has just given birth to a boy. They're both doing well.' I can feel tears well up in my eyes. I manage to say, 'Oh, good.'

'That's grand,' says Ma, 'will we be able tae see her for a couple of minutes before we go?'

'Yes. She's a bit tired, but I think she'll manage a few minutes. And before you leave you can see young Master Douglas through the glass.'

Nancy's lying back on her pillows, resting – tired, but definitely well. I give her a kiss.

'How was it?'

'Och, no' sae bad. I'm jist looking forward tae a nice sleep now.' I sit on the chair by the bed and hold her hand. Her ma gives her a kiss and they chat about things in general. 'Ah would think you'll be oot in a couple o' days. They don't keep ye in for long nooadays when there's nae complications.'

The nurse comes in and suggests Mrs Douglas should be allowed to rest now.

'Right, ah'll come up the morra night after work,' I say. I bend down and give her another kiss.

'Thanks for a son.'

'That's all right,' she says.

On the way out we stop to look in the window where all the cots are. Another nurse is on duty there. 'Baby Douglas, please,' says Ma. The nurse goes to a cot and fetches a little bundle over. She holds him up to the glass. As expected, he has a wee red scrunched-up face. Looks a bit pissed off. Was probably quite happy where he was before all this upheaval. As

we walk out into the large grounds, it comes into my mind.
'What's the date, Ma?'

'The sixteenth.'

'Right! I must remember, 16 August 1961. That's when he was
born. I'm awful at dates!'

On the way home, in between talking to Ma, all sorts of thoughts
are going through my mind. Well, you're a father now. That's
another milestone. It'll be great in a few months when he is
taking notice and knows who folk are. Those close to him. Then,
when he's older, toddling, I can romp with him on the floor. I
really think I'll enjoy being a father. Jeez. That would've been my
ma a granny. She'd have loved that. I work it out, she'd be just
forty-three if she was still living. Hey! We need a name. A few
ideas have been tossed about during the last few months. Well,
one will have to be chosen now.

I walk into the ward. 'Just for you.' I hand her a bunch of
flowers.

'I should be out tomorrow.'

'Great! How's he been today?'

'He's a hungry wee bugger!'

I laugh. 'Are you breastfeeding him?' I still feel a little
embarrassed even though it's Nancy.

'Aye. There's nae problems, the nurse says he's getting plenty.'

'Any thoughts yet aboot a name?'

She smiles. 'Ah've been lying here aw' day thinking aboot it.
I'd like tae call him "Scott." '

'Yeah, ah like that. But ah wouldn't mind Robert for a middle
name. There's always been a Robert going way back. Me, my
faither, my grandfaither. How about that?'

'Aye. Ah like the sound o' that, Scott Robert Douglas. Shall we
settle on that?'

'Yeah. Definitely.'

*   *   *

Next day, held firmly in his mother's arms, Scott Robert Douglas arrives safe and sound at his grandparents' house in Seafield, West Lothian.

And then we were three.

Committed to Prison

Life has settled into a routine. A dull routine. Oh, not with Nancy and Scott. Nancy and I both go to work, we contribute to the household expenses and Nancy, always a good saver, is putting money by for the future. That's what the trouble is – the future. What sort of future is ahead of us? At best, dull. I enjoy my job, get on well with the guys I work with. But something's missing. Since I came out the army nearly ten months ago this feeling, this dissatisfaction, has slowly grown. I think the fact I've just become a father has been the cause of much of it. I already feel I'm into a rut. I want better things for my wife and child – and me. Yet how can I achieve them? I don't have a trade. We don't have a house. I know I have a brain, but I'm not educated. Haven't got an O level to my name. I want a better life, a more interesting life. I especially want the things that only money can buy; material things.

I often think about all the years, as I grew up, that I was continually called 'stupid' by my father. 'C'mere stupid', 'Whit ur you daeing, stupid'. I was about thirteen or fourteen before I realised I wasn't stupid. As I entered my teens I began to take an interest in things that, to my pals, were really dull – Greek mythology, the embryo space technology which had begun to develop after the war as the USA put captured German rocket scientists to work with unlimited funds. My voracious reading of just about anything, fact or fiction. My ability to look after myself from sixteen onwards after Ma died. Then my two years in the army. I'd really begun to blossom. I found out I was better read than most of my contemporaries, thought more about life. Could hold my own in company even though I wasn't educated beyond the age of fifteen. I suppose that isn't strictly true. I wasn't schooled beyond the age of fifteen, but I've continued, in many ways, to self-educate myself. Mostly by reading or watching documentaries on TV. I retain things, facts and figures. No, I know I'm not stupid. In fact I now know that I'm of above average intelligence, for all the good it'll do me! You need certificates, qualifications, to prove you're intelligent. I don't think prospective employers will just take my word for it. But what can I do? I want to better things for me, Nancy and Scott. Until I think of something, I'll just have to plod away for the Gas Board – and be thankful for small mercies. There are worse jobs.

As well as my Friday nights at The Croon with my friend from work Robert Meek, I often have a night at Blackburn's other pub, The Turf. This is where my Uncle Jim likes to go for a pint. The Turf is also an old-fashioned pub, standing on a corner at Blackburn Cross. It still sports most of its fixtures and fittings from the thirties or earlier; dark, varnished wood, the gleam of brass, and a mixture of etched and stained glass here and there. There's a little snug-cum-alcove just to the right when you come in. That's where Jim and his pal from the pit, George McAdam, like to sit and blether, well away from the noisy football aficionados. Maybe once a month I'll arrange to meet him there. I always like to be in Jim's company, not just for himself, but because he's Ma's brother. Ma's middle brother has also come to live in Blackburn. Bill lives round in Yule Terrace with his wife, my Aunty Annie. He doesn't come out for a drink, Bill. When I want to see him I go round to the house. Yet Bill has a goonish, surreal sense of humour. He is also a voracious reader. He's quiet, maybe a bit introverted, but always opens up in my company.

*　　*　　*

Sometime during the evening, in The Turf, I usually swing the conversation round to when Jim and Ma were children back in the twenties and living in Sandyford Street in Kelvinhaugh.

'I'd imagine now and again, when youse were kids, youse were often a bit hard up, Jim?'

'Oh, God, aye. The auld man wiz often oot o' work. He had a trade, mind. He was a journeyman brass finisher. Worked for long spells at the Saracen Foundry, then he'd get paid off when the orders ran oot.'

'Was he much o' a one for the drink?'

Jim shakes his head. 'Naw, ah don't remember him as being much of a drinker. It wiz the gamblin'. He wiz a bugger for the horses. There used tae be some right rows between the two of them.' He sits silent. Remembering. Takes a sip of beer. 'Though mind, we were lucky in a wye. Oor mother could alwiz make a few bob wi' her being a Spey Wife (fortune teller). There wid regularly be a knock at the door and it wid be somebody wanting their cup read.'

I interrupt him. 'She must have taught my Ma how tae read them. Ah remember quite often some of her pals would be in for a cuppa and they'd say, "Gonny give me a reading, Netty?" and Ma would say, "Och, ah canny be bothered, ah hav'nae done it for ages." And they'd keep coaxing her and eventually she'd say, "Oh, aw'right. Swill the dregs roond inside the cup then turn it upside doon in the saucer, then hand the cup tae me." Ah used tae come ower beside her and look inside it as she read it, trying tae see the things she was saying she could see. Ah never knew she'd learned it from her mother.'

'Oh, aye. She wiz good, well known. They used tae come fae all ower the city tae get their cups read – nae matter how hard up we were, she always had a packet o' tea in the hoose in case anybody called. That wiz her stock in trade, dry tea. Aye, there wiz plenty came tae get a reading fae auld Maud. And of course when she'd finish, they'd have tae cross her palm wi' silver – otherwise anything good she'd told them might no' come true!

Even if she only got a tanner (sixpence), it wiz always a help if she wiz short o' money.'

'Ah'll tell ye another thing ah remember, Jim. Ah mind ma Ma telling me she had tae read the paper tae her mother. She could'nae read or write.'

'Aye, that's right. She had'nae been tae the school. She had aw' her buttons, mind. She wiz bright enough – she could tally money nae bother – but she just had'nae been educated.'

Eventually the landlord calls time. Just after ten p.m. Jim, George and I say our goodbyes on the pavement in front of the pub. 'Right, ah'll come doon again in another couple of weeks, Jim. Tell Jenny ah'm asking for her.'

'Right ye are, son. Are ye no' waiting for the Seafield bus?'

'Naw, by the time it comes ah'll very near be hame.'

I set off to walk the 2 miles or so on the uphill brae to Seafield. When I'm at Blackburn on a Friday or Saturday night, whenever I leave The Turf or The Croon I'm always pleased if it's dry. Striding out with a good, brisk pace gets me home in around thirty minutes. Sometimes, on a cold starry night, I'll revert to my old army routine – trot a hundred, march a hundred. I love it. If I was offered a free ride on a dry night I'd refuse it. I enjoy my walk home. Keeps me fit.

As 1961 becomes 1962 I again begin to feel unsettled, and can't seem to shake it off. It's now a year since I left the army. I've got my job off to a T and easily get my day's work done well before finishing time. I'm very much part of the team, yet sometimes as I sit at the table in the morning as we drink our tea, I look at my workmates. I'm twenty years or more younger than them. That's a big age gap. It's a good steady job if you're an old married man, but I'm a young married man. If I stay on here, maybe in about twenty years I'll get John Doull's job. It's forty-two years until I hit sixty-five, retiring age! I can't stay in this job for all that time. There's no sign of us getting a house in Seafield in the near future, or the far future. It's okay living with Nancy's folks in the short term, but what if it turns into years? Yet what can I do? No qualifications, no trade. I somehow feel I'm meant for better things. Huh, doesn't everybody? Surely it's not going to be working at the Gas Board, living in a council house, anything we want has to be bought on hire purchase. I don't even have a car and probably won't ever have one – can't bloody drive anyway! A life of hard graft for little reward looms, just as it does for everyone on the estate here in Seafield. Just as it does for everybody on every estate in the bloody land!

It all seems to happen at once. I'm sitting reading the *Sunday Express* and an advert catches my eye. 'PRISON OFFICERS REQUIRED FOR ENGLAND AND WALES SERVICE.' I read it a couple of times. Could this maybe be the job to get me out of the rut? And it would get me back down to England. The starting wage is more than half as much again as I'm getting now – over sixteen pounds a week. Regular overtime available. AND living quarters provided, or rent allowance in lieu. A more interesting job, more money, a place of our own. Down in England again. What I'd seen of England during my two years I'd really liked. Might try and get back to the Midlands. But will Nancy be interested?

'NANCY! Come and see this.' I watch her face as she reads the ad. 'What dae ye think? Would ye fancy living doon in England?'

'Oh, aye. Ah would'nae mind. Be a chance tae get oot o' Seafield. Ah don't fancy being stuck here for the rest o' ma life.'

'And ye don't mind going doon there wi' a young bairn?'

'No, not at all.'

'Okay. Ah'll write away for the application form.'

After receiving, completing and returning that form, two weeks later I'm heading into Saughton Prison, Edinburgh, for a medical. There, I'm subjected to a head to toe examination.

'How long will it be before I hear from them, doctor?'

'I'm afraid I couldn't tell you. The Scottish and English prison services are quite separate. Scotland has its own Home Department and runs its own prisons. We just give you a medical on their behalf. All communications in future will be from London.

There's a wait, maybe ten days. I come home from work and a long, brown envelope is lying on the sideboard. Nancy's not in yet, but I can't contain my curiosity. I tear it open. I've been accepted as a 'prison officer under training' and I'm to report to the nearest English prison for one month's preliminary training. Normally this would be Durham. However, Durham has its full quota of trainees, so I'm to report to Preston Prison on 2 March 1962. If accommodation isn't available in bachelor quarters for the duration of my stay, lodgings will be found locally and an allowance paid. The letter ends, 'Please find an enclosed railway warrant and a postal order for ten shillings as travelling subsistence.' That's gone up! The army only gave me four shillings.

So that was how, once more, I came down to England. At the time of writing, that was forty-five years ago! Now in my late sixties, reaching back into all these memories, recalling my feelings and reasons for joining the prison service has been a journey I haven't taken before. I distinctly recall wondering if I could hack it as a prison officer. I did. For the next fifteen years. For most of the sixties and seventies I came across, and handled, some of the most notorious 'heavies' of the era. Mail train robbers, a Russian spy, London gangsters – mostly in Durham Prison's top security E Wing. For six weeks during November and December 1963 I sat in the death cell at Bristol Prison with one of the last half-dozen men to be hanged for murder. Just nine months later, the last executions took place. On an everyday basis during those fifteen years I'd rub shoulders with more murderers than you could shake a stick at, including Ian Brady.

But all that was ahead of me as once more I travelled south of the border. The next fifteen years could certainly be described as 'never a dull moment'! And then some.